Talking, listening, and learning

The development of children's language

Acknowledgements

We are grateful to author's agents for permission to reprint the poem 'Timothy Winters' by Charles Causley from *Collected Poems*, published by Macmillan Publishers Ltd.

Talking, listening, and learning

The development of children's language

Janet Ede
Senior Lecturer in English, Matlock College
of Education and Warden of the Language and
Reading Centre run jointly by Matlock College
of Education and Derbyshire Local Education
Authority
Jack Williamson
Head of the Faculty of Humanities and Tutor with
responsibility for In-Service Education at Eaton
Hall College of Education

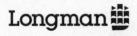

LONGMAN GROUP LIMITED
London
Associated companies, branches and representatives throughout the
world

First published 1980

ISBN 0 582 36308 X cased
     0 582 36309 8 paper

Printed in Great Britain
by Spottiswoode Ballantyne Ltd.,
Colchester and London

The cassette

Because transcripts alone cannot do full justice to a conversation, there is a cassette available to accompany this book, containing extracts from many of the tapes on which the transcripts are based. These extracts are indicated on the transcripts as follows ▮▮

Authors' acknowledgements

We should like to thank the many people who have made it possible in their various ways for us to write this book. Our interest in children's language was sparked off in the case of Janet Ede by working with Douglas Barnes of Leeds University, and in the case of Jack Williamson by attending a course of linguistics lectures given by Margaret Berry at Nottingham University and subsequently by the ideas of M. A. K. Halliday. The recordings and transcripts were made in the first instance out of personal interest and as a means of introducing college of education students to the study of children's language. It was only after they had been tried out with groups of students and teachers in different parts of the country that we decided, largely at the suggestion of Ian Forsyth of the ILEA Centre for Language and Reading, to make them available to a wider audience.

We are grateful to Ian Forsyth, therefore, and to the many students and teachers who have helped us to see the material through new eyes, not least to the teacher groups at Alfreton Hall Teachers' Centre and to our fellow members of the English In-Service Advisory Committee at Nottingham University. We should particularly like to thank all the adults who made it possible to produce the recordings in the first place: Mrs Christine Byron, Mr and Mrs Brett, Mrs Hilary Owen, Mrs Annette Parkin and Mr Peter Godfrey.

It is no small matter for parents and teachers to have their privacy thus invaded, and we appreciate their cooperation and forbearance. Most of all, of course, we should like to thank the children whose names and language appear in the following pages: Helen, Ralph, Matthew and Daniel; Michael, Elaine, Stuart, Judith, Julie, Mark and Andrew. It has been a pleasure to listen to their talk, and the learning has all been on our side.

Contents

Note: words in **bold** type in the text are explained in the Glossary (p. 286).

1 General introduction

Talking to the headmistress of a primary school recently, I was surprised to hear her say of a reception class: 'Of course they've got no language when they come to us.' Five minutes earlier I had been in the classroom, trying to talk to the students above the chatter which accompanied every activity, whether it was play in the Wendy House, in the water corner, during the sorting and counting of shapes, or just the intensely whispered conversation of two small girls dressing dolls. To say that they had *no* language was obviously untrue. They were already using language to maintain social bonds, to express their ideas, and to direct others. What was remarkable in that classroom was the language that they had already developed. All children, except perhaps the special cases of the deaf or retarded, do come to school able to use language, which, though it may not be recognised as such by the teacher in the school situation, is adequate for them in their home setting where it enables them to participate in the activities of the family, to communicate with adults and siblings. However, we have to recognise that school may make other demands on children's language skills, and that language for learning, which is the subject of one of the chapters of this book, involves skills such as asking questions, which may have to be fostered in some children whose home backgrounds have not given them the opportunity to use language for this purpose.

It is likely that any child entering school is already a skilled language user in situations with which he is familiar, but this command of language may be inadequate in the unfamiliar setting of school with an extended peer group and new adults, and when he is faced with learning the bewildering new skills of reading and writing. It is vital, however, that the teacher assesses honestly what the child brings to school, and builds upon that language. As Jimmy Britton says 'There are plenty of teachers who, as far as language is concerned, attempt something of a fresh start. A "fresh-start policy", although they do not realise it, will inevitably tend to cut off a child's principal means of entry into the new worlds that schools and teachers can offer.'[1] It seems a paradox that as educators we can hold two quite contradictory views. On the one hand we regard the child entering school as a blank upon which we stamp the impress of our education, and on the other hand we argue that the child has already learnt a great deal which now proves inadequate. Neither of these assumptions reflects the actual situation and both lead to misconceptions about the role of the teacher. As Eric Ashworth comments, 'In Britain, the real danger is not of a frontal attack on the child and what he is, but of ignoring what he is and consequently undervaluing him. Teachers who are enlightened enough to accept a child's art, or his ability to move as he expresses himself, and who are therefore well on the way to valuing the child, and the child's own sort of integrity, may nevertheless find it difficult to accept his language, even though, as I shall argue later, his language is deeply involved in the child's most creative efforts.'[2] This view is emphasised in the first chapter of the Bullock report, which makes a plea for all teachers, not only those teaching English, 'to learn more about the nature of children's language development, its application to their particular subject, and their own role in the process.'[3]

A great deal of work needs to be done to dispel the myths about initial language learning that persist in some areas since they can do such damage to children who come into contact with them. Language is a characteristically human activity through which we realise our human potential and it is therefore a matter of interest and importance to a wide range of people, but it must be a matter of urgency for those concerned with growing children, many of them teachers of both native and immigrant children. The evidence which the National Association for the Teaching of English presented to the Bullock committee defines five areas of importance to the teacher:

1 insight into the creation of language
2 the relation of language to thinking and feeling
3 the role of language in society
4 the nature of linguistic deprivation
5 the role of language across the curriculum.

Parents, too, are showing an increasing interest in language learning, and some parent–teacher associations are organising activities which will promote parents' understanding of their children's development in this area. The Workers' Educational Association in some areas is running courses on children's language development for parents as well as play-group leaders and nursery-course

3

trainees. Norwich is tackling the problem at the pre-school level through the use of home visitors who help and advise parents on language development, and no doubt a wider range of parents could be involved through local health clinics and community schools. There seems to be some awareness of the need to educate future parents in that some schools in their RSLA programmes include a section on children's language development in the Preparation for Parenthood courses. In writing this book we have attempted to bear in mind the needs of these different groups of readers, and have divided the material into two main sections, the first being concerned with initial language development, and the second with language in the classroom.

As many people do not have easy access to young children growing up or working in the classroom, we have collected tapes of young children talking, which, together with the accompanying transcripts, give examples of children using language in a variety of situations. The first tapes in the book are of Helen, her brother Ralph, and Matthew, and through them we trace the development of language from birth to the pre-school period. It is possible only to give samples which illustrate this complex process, and the ideal study would show the almost daily increase of the child's command of language. Consideration must also be given to the fact that children do not progress at identical rates, although it is likely that the stages in the developmental process follow the same sequential pattern. However, it is hoped that this collection will be sufficiently stimulating to encourage you to make your own tapes. The tapes in the book show the development of Helen, Ralph and Matthew's language in a variety of situations which are part of any child's day, such as preparing for a shopping expedition, playing at tea parties, using Lego building bricks, and walking in the park. They also show the part played by adults in encouraging the child to use language. The view that language is learned solely by imitation is now seen to be inadequate because so many of the child's utterances cannot be accounted for by imitation alone. Children are active agents in creating meanings for themselves out of the sounds and situations around them, developing an awareness of the systematic patterns of their native language, and using the information to make their own meanings. The child's language can no longer be seen as an imperfect imitation of adult language, but must be viewed as a system in its own terms. The tapes emphasise how rapidly early development is consolidated as the child learns by listening and talking and being listened and spoken to. In the interchange between her and the adults around her, Helen is learning far more than just language; she is absorbing the attitudes and meanings embodied in the language used by the adults, so that they are shaping her own ability to mean and understand. Helen learns, for example, that play is a cooperative effort in which she is consulted: 'Shall we build a farm . . . a Lego farm?' The tapes make it abundantly clear that the child *does* come to school using language and any teacher who ignores this, however inadequate the language may seem, is in danger of ignoring the child. In the second part of the book we concentrate on children talking in the classroom both with and without the teacher. Elaine and Stuart explore a tank of snails, Michael talks to his teacher about the new experience of school, Judith, Julie, Mark and Andrew talk as a group about growing up and their reactions towards the move to secondary education.

In many primary schools the main emphasis soon changes from spoken language to a concentration on reading and writing. Despite much of the work which has been done on spoken language in schools, or 'oracy' as Wilkinson defines it, there have been few radical changes in many school communities.[4] This may be for a number of reasons. It is not possible for teachers to change their attitudes to spoken language without a more thorough understanding of the way in which language works. An understanding of the differing nature of spoken and written language is necessary for any evaluation of the individual or group utterance. Spoken language does not lend itself easily to evaluation, and while it could be unnecessary and even damaging to mark oral work, the doubts of teachers about the value of something apparently ephemeral are understandable. An emphasis on the importance of talk on the part of teachers and pupils could lead to the praise of 'mere garrulity' in the classroom, without any clear idea of what pupils have gained, or what the teacher's contribution might be in the learning process. In the second part of the book we have attempted to provide the teacher with a collection of material on which he can sharpen his awareness of the nature of spoken language, and the knowledge both to create working situations in which pupils can learn to talk, and to assess that talk.

References

[1] Britton, J. (1973) in N. Bagnall (ed.) *New Movements in the Study and Teaching of English* Temple Smith, p. 19

[2] Ashworth, E. (1973) *Language in the Junior School* Arnold, p.29

[3] Bullock, A. (1975) *A Language for Life* Report of the Committee of Enquiry appointed by the Secretary of State for Education and Science, HMSO

[4] Wilkinson, A. (1965) *Spoken English* University of Birmingham Press

PART ONE
Born talkers

2 Introduction to part one

In part one there are three chapters that serve as introduction to the material in part two and part three. Since we are concerned with children talking, it is important to stress certain aspects of spoken language and some of the problems of transcribing it: this is the subject of chapter 3. In chapter 4, some of the relationships between language and learning are discussed. This is central to a book which shows children learning to talk in the first set of transcripts and talking to learn in the second. Chapter 5 is more relevant to part two: a general view of the study of language acquisition, intended to enable readers to put our transcripts and commentaries into some kind of perspective, and to enable readers to pursue the subject further.

3 Spoken language and transcription

1 Spoken and written language

Having acknowledged the importance of the study of children's spoken language, one has then to decide how best to carry this out. Because of the rapidity of speech it is difficult to work in depth on a stretch of spoken language without a permanent written record – a transcript.

Transcription serves to focus attention on a number of features of spoken language which normally we may be unaware of. We are unused to considering the form of spoken language, because generally for speaker and listener the emphasis is on content, what is being said, rather than how it is conveyed. It is only on special occasions that we are concerned with the 'how', rather than the 'what'. Sometimes letters in women's magazines request help about the forms of address to be used to visiting Royalty, and these reveal a sudden awareness of the importance of the right form. Is it to be 'Ma'am', 'Your Majesty', or 'Your Royal Highness'? Normally our familiarity with a wide range of people and situations enables us to forget the question of form; we know not only what to say but how to say it from previous experience. The education system tends to make us aware of the question of form much more in written than in spoken language. We have all in our time, for instance, grappled with tricky exercises in punctuation, using colons and semicolons.

It is easy initially, therefore, to bring to the study of spoken language preconceptions based on our experiences of written language. Almost the first thing students say after listening to themselves for the first time on tape is that they don't finish sentences, and that their words trail off into the air uncompleted, and this comment generally carries with it implications that speech is therefore inferior to writing. Speech and writing are different manifestations of an underlying and abstract language form: speech uses patterned sound waves moving through the air between speaker and listener to convey meanings, and writing a system of marks on paper interpreted by the reader. Although our education system emphasises the importance of skill in writing, it is likely that, in terms of historical development, speech preceded writing by many thousands of years. (In *The Inheritors*, William Golding (1955) gives an imaginative reconstruction of the emergence of speech in a primitive society.) Neither spoken nor written language should be seen as inherently superior, and in educational terms particularly, we need to bear in mind the circumstances and purposes for which each is appropriate, so that due attention can be given to teaching the skills in each area.

For readers unfamiliar with listening to spoken language on tape and methods of transcription, work on a selected passage from the tape would be helpful at this point. Extract 15 forms a useful starting point. Try to produce a written version from which you can reconstruct the spoken language of the tape for detailed study. If it is possible to listen to the tape as a group, this will make the reconstruction and comparison of transcripts easier. It is surprising how an individual listener will notice aspects missed by another listener. From a set of individual transcripts a final composite version can be made. The discussion which is inevitably part of the process enables the listeners to check doubtful passages and arrive at the best methods of notation. Before you make any attempt at transcription, listen to the extract in its entirety, to familiarise yourself with the speakers and subject matter, and then replay it, small sections at a time. The extract suggested for transcription is part of a discussion between two $6\frac{1}{2}$-year-olds, Elaine and Stuart, who are looking at a glass-sided tank of snails in the classroom, using a magnifying glass (see chapter 17). Initially the teacher was present with a visitor, and, while talking about school matters, they threw out some questions to the children about the appearance of the snails and the number of eyes they possessed.

Some of the outstanding features of Elaine and Stuart's conversation are given below, but the attentive listener will no doubt be able to add to this list. The entire tape is transcribed on pp. 220–33.

1 The lack of sentences as we recognise these in written language.
  ELAINE I'm having a job . . . it won't . . . It's a bit sticky.

For easy reading in written language, we leave spaces between words which suggest pauses. But in reality speech is a continuous stream of sound, broken by pauses, which does not altogether correspond to written sentences. However, because of the significant placing of pauses, and intonation patterns, we rarely have any difficulty in understanding the meaning of what is being said.

2 The 'untidy' nature of speech – a number of people may be speaking at the same time, and speakers appearing to interrupt each other rudely or completing each other's sentences.
  ELAINE I think it's because
  STUART It's leaving wet behind i'n't it?

3 The repetition of words and phrases, which is often greater than that found in representations of dialogue in plays and novels.
  ELAINE Eh, shall I pick one, shall I try and get one off? Shall I? Eh, shall I touch this, shall I touch it in here?

4 Hesitations as speakers appear to grope for words, and often fill the resulting pauses with sounds such as 'er' and 'em'.

5 Contractions of the standard written forms which may be dialectal, or the result of rhythm and stress in the flow of speech.
  gonna (going to): dialectal
  'N'you (thank you): a result of rhythm and stress

6 References such as 'it' which, in written terms may be ambiguous in meaning, but which in spoken language refer to features of the situation, and are quite explicit in context.
  STUART It's leaving wet behind, isn't it?
  ELAINE I know, but it's beginning to dry up there . . .

The 'it' in Stuart's case refers to the snail, and in Elaine's comment to the wet trail left behind by the snail. Given that both things are present to Elaine and Stuart, they have no need to be explicit about what 'it' is in each instance. If this episode were being recounted in written terms, then it would be necessary to make the references to the snail and the slime quite explicit.

7 The overall impression of excitement in the voices of Elaine and Stuart at the discoveries they are making, conveyed by the intonation of their voices. This is difficult to represent in writing except by the occasional rather tame comment such as 'said excitedly' or 'shrieked'.

The important thing about their language is that, given the background knowledge of the school situation and the presence of the snails, what Elaine and Stuart say makes sense to us as we listen, and clearly makes sense to them. This dialogue between Elaine and Stuart does not present a special case, and practically any spoken language will show some, or all, of the features listed here, as a few minutes' taping will show.

2 Spoken language and its appropriateness for different purposes

Although we have used the term 'spoken language' as a matter of convenience, it is a simplification in that it suggests we are speaking one kind of language, for one purpose, when in fact there are as many spoken as written varieties of language. The British obsession with the weather is a joke among foreigners, but a number of examples of spoken language, each concerned with the subject of weather, provide a good idea of the range of spoken language used.

The first example might take place between friendly neighbours meeting briefly in the garden as they concern themselves with household jobs.

SPEAKER 1 Lovely

SPEAKER 2 Marvellous, isn't it?

This message supplies the minimum information about the weather. Both speakers are already aware of the fine day, and certainly don't need to be told about it. The aim of the utterance is to establish a social relationship, a form of greeting by which each neighbour can acknowledge the presence of the other, without engaging in a lengthy conversation. The anthropologist, Malinowski, referred to this use of language through which we maintain social relationships as **phatic communion.*** In English many greetings are of this nature. 'How are you?' usually receives a brief answer such as 'Fine', and is rarely taken as a genuine request for information about our exact state of health.

This second example is from a weather forecast preceding the evening news on television.

As this low pressure moves south it will fill up and allow this

* Words in bold type are explained in the Glossary (p. 286).

high pressure to come towards us with the promise of a reasonable day, but as we look into the beginning of next week these further fronts will bring rain to many of us.

The main emphasis of the speaker here is to present the audience with a maximum of information within a brief period of time. To do this he assumes a certain knowledge and interest on the part of his audience and uses technical terms such as 'low pressure', without explaining them in detail. He is not primarily concerned with establishing a relationship with his audience, but he does contact them with his use of the word 'us', by identifying with them as sufferers from the whims of the weather. An interesting point to note is the way his language refers to features on the charts such as 'this low pressure', 'these further fronts'. The forecaster makes clear which he means by pointing to the chart, but in writing the references are ambiguous since 'this' and 'these' might refer to any of such features.

These exchanges are clearly not interchangeable. The weatherman's forecast would not be appropriate between the neighbours, just as the greetings of the neighbours would not be a suitable replacement for the weather forecast. Each example of speech serves purposes for its speakers, is appropriate to its function, and has been chosen by the speakers to affect the listener in a particular way.

3 Varieties of spoken language

There are two major factors which govern the type or **register** of spoken language we consider to be appropriate in any given situation. One is the person or people we are speaking to, and the other is the subject matter of our conversation. A number of technical terms are used to describe the kinds of language used for specific purposes, but we shall use here Wilkinson's terminology as it is described in *The Foundations of Language*.[1] He describes a communications model in which the language used is affected by the two factors already mentioned with the addition of two further influences.

 a the person speaking – the addressor
 b the person spoken to – the addressee
 c the subject matter of the conversation
 d the context – the situation in which the language takes place.

When the speaker is chiefly preoccupied with the subject matter of the conversation, and any specialist terminology is used as a result of this, we speak of the **addressor/subject register**. An example of this is the following sentence from a discussion of the Transatlantic Yacht Race: 'Well, should she keel over in heavy seas the life raft is equipped for survival and I should be able to avoid severe exposure.' Most of us would recognise here a subject register concerned with the sea and boats. This register consists of specific lexical items such as 'life raft', collocations such as 'severe exposure', and special verb constructions such as 'keel over'.

When the speaker is principally concerned with the listener, the **addressor/addressee register** is used. An example of this, continuing the nautical description, might be the terms of address used on board ship, such as 'skipper', 'captain', 'mate', 'sparks', which indicate different relationships between the speakers, resulting in varying degrees of formality in their terms of address to each other. (Alternatively, the degree of formality is sometimes referred to as the **style**, and the word 'register' reserved for the use of specialist terms, by people of shared occupations for example.) The two influences of audience and subject matter are not mutually exclusive in any stretch of spoken language, and sometimes both factors may be confusingly intertwined.

A good example of this comes from a talk given by a butcher to a group of housewives in which he said 'Now take the belly pork ... er ... tummy pork, we don't want to upset anyone, do we?' Here his use of the specialist term 'belly', quite acceptable in butchery, conflicted with his view that the word 'belly' is considered rather vulgar in some circles, and might not be 'nice' used in front of women. It can be seen from this that social judgements also play a part in our choice of language.

The issue of addressor/subject register is not merely an academic one and has particular importance for teachers. It has an immediate relevance in the conversation between Elaine and Stuart about the snails, in chapter 17 pp. 220–45. They constantly refer to the 'thingies' on the head of the snail, meaning the tentacles, two of which carry the eyes, while the other two act as feelers, sensitive to touch. The teacher does in fact introduce the word 'tentacles' into the discussion quite specifically, but the children do not use it. Should he have insisted on its use at this point? Douglas Barnes (1969) in *Language, the Learner and the School* also examines the use of specialist subject registers by pupils and teachers at secondary level, and finds that some teachers are more concerned with whether pupils can parrot the specialist register of the subject, than they are with the understanding of the processes involved.

SPOKEN LANGUAGE AND TRANSCRIPTION

This is discussed in more detail in chapter 17, pp. 242–3.

The addressor/addressee register is affected by the relationship of the speakers; for instance, their respective ages, their profession, their social status. Martin Joos (1962) in *The Five Clocks* describes five addressor/addressee registers (or **styles**, as he calls them), ranging on a continuum from *frozen*, through *formal*, *consultative* and *casual*, to *intimate*, each indicative of a certain kind of relationship between participants. The intimate style is that language which arises from a very close relationship in which the participants share so many ideas that the briefest exchange makes sense. A nod in reply to 'Hungry?', for example, can indicate to a wife that her husband is very ready for his tea. There are probably no examples of the intimate style on the tape you have, but there are examples of the casual style, where people within a particular social group do not have to spell out information as they would to a stranger. Elaine and Stuart's conversation when they are alone is of this nature; when they are alone the interchanges between them are brief and charged with expression.

ELAINE Shall I pick it up and get it off?

STUART You daren't.

ELAINE I dare.

STUART Go on then.

Stuart's 'Bloody hell' fully expresses his amazement at the mysterious behaviour of the snails, but it is not used until the teacher and visitor have left the room. The school was one in which the children were used to working in small informal groups, guided by the teacher, but even so there are subtle differences in the talk when the teacher joins in. It is the teacher who takes the initiative and directs the shape of the conversation by asking questions which the children answer, often very briefly. This trend is even more marked when the visitor joins in.

STUART Just like mushrooms.

VISITOR (*Surprised tone*) Mushrooms.

ELAINE AND STUART Yes (*Laughing*).

VISITOR Do they? Why do they look like mushrooms?

STUART That one does.

ELAINE I think they look a bit more like seashells.

VISITOR Aye (*tone of agreement*). They do look like seashells, don't they? Do you mean they're the same shape as mushrooms, is that what you mean?

STUART Mm, yes.

Clearly the visitor expects them to explain in detail how they have drawn comparisons between the snails, shells and mushrooms. This need to make matters explicit is part of the consultative style. There are no examples of the formal style on this tape, since it is a conversation between friends. The frozen style moves into the area of written language, and is not characterised by addressor/addressee interaction.

We need to recognise that the categorisation into these five styles suggested by Joos can lead to over-simplification and must not be used rigidly. Sometimes the language hovers between two styles, and it is hard to label it precisely. There are other classifications of spoken language which the reader needs to be aware of. These are to be found in *English in Advertising* by Geoffrey Leech (1966), and in *Investigating English Style* by David Crystal and Derek Davy (1969).

One of the problems for many children is their lack of experience of a wide range of social situations, and this unfamiliarity may make it difficult for them to establish an appropriate addressor/addressee relationship which takes into account the needs of the audience. This is well shown in the discussion in 'Cider with Rosie' (p. 271) when Mark becomes impatient with his own efforts to describe how he was lost on a walk. He needs to make this explicit for an audience unfamiliar with the incident, but is unable to do so and gives up impatiently.

> MARK ... there were an arch sort of thing and went inside there and then we turned somewhere and we got lost and found this building and we were scared to go in.

In contrast Judith is often more aware of her audience, as she shows when she recounts the details of her pony rides in sufficient detail to enable the listener to picture what is happening and to get an idea of the participants.

> JUDITH Well I/I was at a place called Dawden in ... near ... Nuneaton ... and ... em ... I was out playing in the field and a farmer came past with two great big horses ... can't remember whether they were shire ponies or ... em ... Welsh cobs, and ... em ... then he says, 'Would anybody like a ride?' because he was a very friendly farmer and we knew him well ...

4 Classroom attitudes to dialect and accent

Moving on to a different feature of spoken language, when you listen to the tape of the 'Snails' discussion you may notice that certain words are pronounced in ways unfamiliar to you unless you come from the part of the country where the tape was made. Two particular examples are Stuart's pronunciation of 'there' in 'That's gi'ing him a lift to climb on there', and the vowel sound in 'bloody' which is like that in the word 'push', rather than that in the pronunciation of 'honey' which some listeners may be more accustomed to. To use a technical term, when we speak of the sound patterns of the language, we are concerned with its **phonology**. Later on the same tape Stuart uses the word 'tabs' meaning 'ears', and this use of a particular word, or **lexical item**, marks his speech as belonging to a certain area of the country, as does his use of particular grammatical or syntactic structures. A further discussion of phonology, **lexis**, and **syntax** follows in chapter 5 on language acquisition and in the commentary on 'Ralph' in chapter 7. However, at this point in the book we are concerned to relate them to a consideration of **standard English, dialect, accent**, and **R.P. (received pronunciation)** – terms which sometimes cause considerable confusion.

Standard English is the term generally used to describe the form of English used by all educated English-speaking people. Although there may be very slight regional variation, and some variation in different English-speaking countries such as America or Australia, it is spoken and written with surprising uniformity. In the monumental *Grammar of Contemporary English*[2] stress is laid on the extraordinary worldwide agreement as to the nature of standard English, and the comment is made that agreement seems to be increasing under the impact of closer world communication and the spread of identical material and non-material culture. However, we all recognise that there may be different ways of pronouncing standard English. There is what is known as R.P., received pronunciation, which we can best describe as the kind of pronunciation adopted by BBC announcers, although we have to recognise that regional programmes have brought about some changes here. Received pronunciation does not reflect the pronunciation of any particular geographical area of the country, and is generally thought to have its origins in the great public schools over a century ago, since when it has been maintained and transmitted from generation to generation, mainly by people educated at public schools. Received pronunciation is generally seen as a prestige pronunciation, and in the past it gave entry to certain careers such as the Army. Standard English may also be spoken with a regional accent – a variation of the phonology or sound pattern of the language according to region.

17

In addition to their use of standard English, many people also use forms of regional speech known as dialect, which reflects the language of a particular area of the country. The dialect of any particular region will involve syntactical, lexical and phonological features which distinguish it from standard English.

Without necessarily being conscious of the fact, people use the dialect and accent which is appropriate to the particular situation in which they find themselves, so that they 'take on the colour' of the company they are with, and it is now being increasingly recognised that this is an important social skill, and that dialect is not a sub-standard form of language which its speakers should be ashamed to use. Attitudes to accent, particularly, do involve subtle social judgements. Certain forms of language (and by implication their speakers) have more prestige than others. In the hierarchy of accents, as numerous surveys have shown, R.P. has the most prestige, followed by some forms of Scottish and Irish, with the accents of towns and industrial areas such as Birmingham being relegated to the lowest place. As the Bullock Report points out, attitudes to accent, often unconsciously held, have important implications for educators.

> To criticise a person's speech may be an attack on his self-esteem, and the extent to which the two are associated is evident from the status accorded to accent by society at large ... We believe that a child's accent should be accepted, and that to attempt to suppress it is irrational and neither humane nor necessary.[3]

Where both dialect and accent are concerned, the aim should be 'not to alienate the child from the form of language with which he has grown up, and which serves him efficiently in the speech community of his neighbourhood', but 'to enlarge his repertoire so that he can use language effectively in other speech situations and use standard forms when they are needed'.[4] If only this had been the view when the author of this chapter, with a Midlands accent, suffered the humiliation, twenty years ago, of being rejected as a student by the principal of a training college with the words, 'You can't possibly teach with a voice like yours', then much unhappiness could have been avoided. After anxious efforts to eradicate this accent, the author came to realise after a number of years that although a Midlands sound might be strange to 'foreign' ears, it was not a barrier to successful communication in teaching, and it was therefore unnecessary to make drastic changes.

The test for any speaker is whether he can be easily understood in the context in which he is using a particular speech form. Those intending to teach need to be particularly careful that they do not, subconsciously, make assessments of pupils on the basis of accent and dialect, and reject those children whose speech does not correspond to their own. Geoffrey Thornton in *Language, Experience and School* emphasises this point.

> Devaluing a person's language, which is what you do when you accuse it of being inferior, is to devalue him. To do this within the society of the school is to weigh the scales against his chances of success. A barrier has been erected which he has to overcome, even if it exists only in the teacher's mind, a barrier which is not there for someone whose language is accepted for what it is . . . He doesn't have much success in school. Therefore others who sound like him aren't likely to have much success either, because their teachers come, unconsciously, to think that there are bound to be limits to what they can achieve.[5]

5 Features of spoken language

On page 9 we spoke briefly about some of the features of spoken, as opposed to written, language and we shall now take up these points in more detail. Spoken language relies for its meaning on **intonation** (the tones of the voice), as well as on **paralinguistic features** such as gesture and facial expressions. A good example of the former occurs in the transcript 'Helen at two years' (p. 113) in Helen's opening words, 'Leaving these 'namas on'.

These would be interpreted either as a question, 'Am I leaving these 'namas on?', or as a statement, 'I am leaving these 'namas on'. For the listener, the rising intonation makes it quite clear that Helen intends this to be a question, but for the reader it has to be signalled as a question by the use of a question mark.

The study of intonation patterns in English forms a very complex area, because as Halliday *et al.* (1964) point out in *The Linguistic Sciences and Language Teaching*, a particular intonation does not always signal the same meaning. A rising intonation may indicate, variously, a question, surprise, or indignation, depending on the relationship of the pattern with lexical items and syntactic structures.

Listeners will notice significant pauses between some words on the tape. The pauses are not always shown in writing. Research has been carried out into the significance of these pauses, known as **hesitation phenomena**, when the speaker may be taking time to think ahead, or to choose the correct word, or perhaps use an unfamiliar word which he is not quite certain about. Andrew pauses when he uses 'presume' in the discussion of 'Timothy Winters' (p. 253), and he also gives it special stress. His use of this unfamiliar word is noted and commented on by Mark, to Andrew's embarrassment.

The pauses between words are often filled by 'er' and 'em', known as **stabilisers**, or fillers, which serve to indicate to the listener that the speaker is pausing momentarily, has not completed what he intends to say, and is intending to continue. Carried to excess by a speaker who is desperately uncertain of what to say, the use of stabilisers can irritate the listener, who ceases to listen. Used with normal frequency, however, they are characteristic of every speaker's repertoire, and not, as some people feel, illustrations of 'sloppy' or 'slovenly' speech. The use of 'you know' and 'like' is also thought by some people to be a sign of poor speech, but these too are appeals for audience understanding and response.

Speakers may change structure in the middle of a sense unit, and start again to say something in a slightly different way.

STUART When that/eh up, can you notice anything on this?
(p. 226)

This change of structure is marked in the transcript by a diagonal line (/) which enables the reader to see where the renewal has taken place. It is also noticeable that speakers may repeat phrases and words, a process known in spoken language as **redundancy**, in order to emphasise important points, so that the listener is able to note these in the rapid flow of speech. **Initial markers**, such as 'Well', serve to mark the entry of a speaker into a conversation, while **terminal markers**, phrases such as 'see what I mean', and sometimes 'you know' (more often seen as a filler), signal to the listeners that the speaker has finished speaking. Andrew, in 'Cider with Rosie' has some interesting idiosyncratic terminal markers such as 'that's all there is to do with it', (p. 278) and 'like'. This latter is more common in the phrase, 'they'd took all the money, like'. In Andrew's phrase, 'starting a new life, like', (p. 275) 'like' has a more self-depreciating ring about it, as if he is afraid that the whole phrase sounds rather grand: indeed it *is* a significant statement in this discussion. Speaking and listening are reciprocal activities, with both participants playing different roles. Speakers, often quite unconsciously, rely on the facial expression of their listeners to indicate that what they are saying is being listened to, and sometimes listeners respond by muttering 'Mm' and 'Yes' as signals of their attention. These, and other similarly expressive

20

noises for this purpose, are known as **listener code markers**.

6 Transcription symbols used in this book

There are many different ways of representing spontaneous speech. At one extreme there are very detailed transcripts which use phonetic and other special symbols, and which consequently are not easily intelligible to the non-specialist. By contrast there are transcripts which have been so heavily edited in the interests of readability that they are too far removed from the original speech. (For details of a range of methods see A. Wilkinson (1965) *Spoken English*.) In this book we have attempted a compromise, bearing in mind that the transcripts need to be easily readable for the purposes of study. No matter how accurate we have tried to make these, it is likely that further details will emerge as the tapes are played.

A brief explanation follows of the symbols we have used. For the most part normal punctuation marks have been used conventionally with the following exceptions and additions:

.	Used at the end of a major sense unit (normally a sentence), but omitted at the end of an **utterance** when the next speaker interrupts, or follows quickly.
...	Used to mark a pause within or at the end of a sense unit. Pauses of four or more seconds have been noted in the transcript.
?	Indicates that a question has been asked, even though this may not be in the usual question form, but marked by intonation.
? Elaine ? tentacles	Where a question mark is used before the speaker's name, or before a word, this indicates that the identity of the speaker is in doubt, or that the 'reading' of a particular word is uncertain.
*	This marks an omission in the transcript as a result of poor sound.
( )	These enclose stage directions (*in italics*), where these are helpful, and in the case of Helen, the correct form of a word which she attempts to pronounce.
[ ]	These enclose an aside which is not part of the sense of the ongoing utterance. Sometimes in the Helen transcripts (chapters 8, 9, 10, 11, 12) the adults address each

other over her head about something other than her play, and on occasions repeat her words, as it seemed at the time of taping that she was saying something of particular significance which needed to be clear on the tape.

/   This marks a renewal, a further attempt at a word 'wh/what', or at a structure 'we go/we went'.

Generally we have not attempted the phonetic transcription of dialect. Such transcription can be difficult to read, and can suggest that speech is 'quaint' or unusual, when in context it passes unremarked.

'My' and 'yes' have been regularised, although we recognise that in spoken English they may, in fact, become 'me' and 'yeh'. As these latter forms are part of many people's pronunciation at certain times, there seemed little point in noting them unless this indicated a special use.

7 Suggestions for further work and discussion

a. Which greetings show language being used for the purposes of phatic communion? If you speak another language, or have someone in your group who does, you could make a comparison between English and other languages.

You might note here how a particular occasion and listener may make some greetings more appropriate than others in certain circumstances.

b. What topics of conversation in English, other than the weather, serve the purposes of phatic communion? Compare with other languages if possible.

c. It is possible to make study of the dialect of your own area by collecting examples of the special use of lexis, syntactical structures, and phonology. Then make a comparison with the dialect features of another area. This can be an extensive study, as dialect atlases show, but it is possible to take one or two words, structures or sounds and compare their use across the group. Check, for instance, on the different terms for 'splinter' and 'left-handed' used in the group. A simple introduction is provided in *Sociolinguistics* by Peter Trudgill (1974), chapters 5 and 7. Much more detailed is *Survey of English Dialects*, edited by H. Orton and E. Dieth (1962).

d. It is revealing to look at the dialogue in novels and plays to see how writers attempt to create the impression of spoken language. A range of writers should be selected, both historical and contemporary. Wilkinson's (1965) list of the features of spoken language in *Spoken English* is helpful for comparison between actual speech and created accounts. What features of spoken language do novelists and playwrights not attempt to reproduce?

e. Collect examples of speech from one person talking in three situations, e.g. child to friend, to teacher, to mother. What factors in each situation affect the language used?

f. Books to which it is helpful to refer include the following:
Doughty, P., Pearce, J. and Thornton, G. (1972) *Exploring Language* Arnold
Wilkinson, A. (1965) *Spoken English* University of Birmingham
Wilkinson, A., Stratta, L. and Dudley, P. (1974) *The Quality of Listening* Macmillan

8 References

[1] Wilkinson, A. (1971) *The Foundations of Language* OUP

[2] Quirk, R., Greenbaum, S., Leech, G. and Svartvik, I. (eds) (1972) *A Grammar of Contemporary English* Longman, chapter 1

[3] Bullock, A. (1975) *A Language for Life* Report of the Committee of Enquiry appointed by the Secretary of State for Education and Science, HMSO, 10.5

[4] Bullock, A. *op. cit.*, 10.6

[5] Thornton, G. (1974) *Language, Experience and School* Edward Arnold

4 Language and learning

---

1 Introduction

Imagine a world without human speech. Think of any well-known street in a large city where there was the usual noise of cars and buses, of hundreds of feet on the pavements, even perhaps the occasional sound of an aircraft, but where there was one familiar sound missing – the corporate hum of hundreds of simultaneous conversations. Or try to imagine the commuter trains converging on London, every compartment crammed with silent people, able to smile or frown their responses to others' gestures, but shorn of the power to communicate in any detailed or subtle way, and denied even the refuge of a newspaper behind which to shelter from the uncommunicating gaze of friend or stranger. Think of any one of those commuters returning home from a speechless day's work to an equally speechless evening, where even the television programmes were reduced to presenting the voiceless images that the name implies. Or imagine walking round a school where children were painting, making things, engaged in various kinds of physical activity, but where in classrooms there were no books for reading or writing, and not even the sound of speech from teacher or pupil. No doubt a good writer of science fiction could offer us not only a plausible explanation of how this universal lack of speech might have come about but an equally plausible working-out of its details and its consequences. In our less sophisticated way, any one of us – author or reader – could make an attempt to do likewise.

What none of us, amateur or professional, could begin to do, however, would be to envisage what this state of wordlessness would be like from the inside. All that you have read so far has obviously been made available in the form of language, something so familiar and taken for granted that it's difficult to stand aside from one's experience to assess how much of what one sees is seen in that way not only because the human perceptual apparatus is of a particular kind but also because the human language system predisposes its users to 'see' the world in a certain way. It's easy enough to continue the 'Imagine this ...' vein of the first paragraph, as an observer giving an external view of the situation, accepting the premise of cataclysmic word-loss and spinning out its implications with greater or lesser skill. 'Fancy', to use Coleridge's term, might be the power at work in such a case. But if it were 'imagination' that was required, no external observer's account would be enough: somehow the writer would, paradoxically, have to convey in words a view of a world totally unlike our own because it would be apprehended directly, without being mediated through language. Few of us would approach that task with confidence.

Yet if we think about it, the state of being pitched into a world full of a bewildering multiplicity of sense-impressions, faced with the task of making sense of it without the benefit of language, is one which we have all known at first hand. There was a time in our lives when we had no language, and if it would take a gifted writer to describe an imagined world that had known language and lost it, what would it take to transport us again to our pre-linguistic state, when the sounds of speech were so many noises, like all the other noises in our environment? It is not the intention of this chapter to attempt anything so ambitious, but what has been said so far is intended to stress something so obvious that it can easily be overlooked: we can take language for granted, as we can take for granted learning of language, and the part that language plays in learning.

2 Children's knowledge of language: the system
For these reasons, what follows will be based on a fragment of the speech of a child of twenty months, the same child whose speech will be heard on the cassette at various stages of her language learning. The very ordinariness of the fragment makes the point: more is going on than superficially appears to be. The comments will be concerned not only with her knowledge of the language system but also with what she has learned about the uses to which knowledge of the system can be put. Moreover, each point that is

made will be illustrated with examples from her speech at other times and from that of other children whose speech is discussed at greater length elsewhere in this book.

a. Words are more than labels

Here follow two short bursts of dialogue from transcripts on page 97.

a CHRIS Helen, what's this?
   HELEN Carrot.
   CHRIS Is it? What's that? What are those?
   HELEN What is it?
   CHRIS Helen, what's this?
   HELEN Water.
   CHRIS And what goes on water?
   HELEN Fish.
   CHRIS Fish?
   HELEN Water.

b CHRIS Where did the stone come from?
   HELEN Garden.
   JAN What else is there in the garden?
   HELEN Daddy.

One general comment is worth making before anything is said about any point in detail. If we ourselves were anxious to learn a language other than our mother tongue, especially one that was little known and not even written down, we could very well adopt the procedure familiar to linguists of choosing an 'informant' — someone proficient in the language and well-versed in the culture from which it sprang. Most children have access to just such informants in the shape of parents, and in many cases other children, but with the additional advantage that in this case the informants are personally concerned to ensure that the learner is successful. Thus in *a* the situation is a familiar one, familiar not only to everyone who has had anything to do with children, but familiar to this child. The activity is one that she has taken part in before — looking at a picture book and talking about it with her mother. Even before we look at her knowledge of language, we can see that she has already mastered one system of symbolic representation: she can 'read' a picture as a generalised representation of a class of objects, particular examples of which she has previously encountered. But at least the carrot that she is looking at (it is in fact a long red worm, but that only serves to confirm that the child really is generalising from a set of qualities) resembles in certain physical aspects the vegetable itself (is 'iconic', it could be said), which is more than can be said for the set of sounds that go to make up the word 'carrot' when the child says or hears it. In other words, Helen has already taken in her stride the arbitrariness of language symbols that have no necessary resemblance to the things they represent. Think what a gain it is for her that she can now store her experiences, scrutinise them, compare them.

To come down to matters of detail, however, what are we able to say about her knowledge of the language system? We could be forgiven for thinking that she can handle only one word at a time (apart from 'What is it?' which is best regarded as a formula, learned as a single unit), and this might well confirm the view that children begin to talk by naming things in their environment. But this would be to fall into several traps at once. One might question in general terms the supposition that a child interacting with the world in various complex ways should confine her use of the equally complex medium of language to the not very obviously useful practice of identifying, rather than commenting upon, features of her environment. When we look at the actual words she uses, we can be even more certain that a lot more than labelling is going on. 'Carrot' and 'water', it may be conceded, are certainly identifying things, but only in response to a form of question that invites just that. But there are no fish or pictures of fish to be named or labelled, and yet Helen also says 'Fish'. This is more than labelling: this child with her one word can show a grasp of a relationship and a sense of its being permanently true. Her mother was actually surprised to get the answer that she did: they had seen ducks on water that very afternoon, and like so many of us as teachers, she was asking a question to which she was expecting her own choice of answer. 'Fish?', she asks in surprise, and pat comes the answer confirming what the original monosyllable was meant to convey – 'Water'. What else?

It is much the same when we look at the two words she contributes to the second dialogue. Like the other words we have discussed, 'garden' would be classed as a noun in adult grammar (though we must be wary of assigning children's words uncritically to adult categories), but we can hardly say that a child is looking at a stone and labelling a garden. The different forms of question being employed by the mother require the child to show understanding of different relationships and qualities, and what is demonstrated here is how well the child can use this apparently slender resource of one word to do so. 'Daddy', on the other hand,

27

is an example of learning that is not yet complete. It is not simply a case of not knowing that Daddy is a 'who' not a 'what', but much more a matter of not realising that daddies are not permanent features of gardens.

The word-as-label view is too naïve and inaccurate to do justice to what children 'know' about words from a very early age. Children in infant school classrooms will sometimes compile simple dictionaries of words they need in their writing, but there are ways in which even the dictionaries they will eventually learn to use as adults are nowhere near as complex or subtle as the dictionaries in their heads. Take a simple word like 'rabbit', for example. It is easy enough to visualise a particular kind of animal as a consequence of hearing or reading the word, but one's knowledge goes far beyond that. Even describing it as an animal is already to go beyond mere description: 'animal' is a category to which 'rabbit' is being assigned, and a category, moreover, for which we have anything but a simple set of criteria. We certainly did not begin with such a category and then gradually learn different examples, nor is it likely that our parents deliberately set out to teach us this knowledge. For one thing they were probably unaware that the knowledge was there to be taught. In any case this is only a single example of a general characteristic of language, this hierarchical arrangement of words, whereby some are superordinate and others are in some sense included by them. Young children begin by overextending the meaning of words, so that, for example, all men are Daddy, and then they gradually refine their categories until Daddy is seen as one example not only of 'male, human' but also of 'male, human, in a particular relationship to another human being'. The words of a language have meaning partly because of their relationships with the other words in that language. The particular relationship that will have significance at any given moment will depend on the circumstances in which the words are used, and upon certain circumstances in the history of the user or hearer.

Thus to return to 'rabbit', most of us will at one time or another think of, say, fur, or droppings, or fecundity, or inability to play certain games, or particular characters in children's fiction, but not everyone who is asked to say what comes into their head when they think of rabbits is likely to say 'Union Jacks' unless, when they were children, they saw rabbits hanging up, flag-adorned, in markets. Such idiosyncratic associations are of course only part of our systematic knowledge of language, but a point worth making is that even our considerable systematic knowledge has been arrived at by idiosyncratic routes, however much it then qualifies as 'common knowledge'. Words are very much more then than inert labels, to be learned once for all as single items in a repertoire. Our language sets up a complex and elaborate set of relationships, and words are the points of intersection.

b. Children learning word meanings

It is knowledge of such relationships that Helen has already begun to build up, as can best be illustrated by looking at some examples of other children moving along the same path. But first, let us look at two examples from her own speech at a later stage. When she was two years old, her mother asked her where a child called Clare lived (p. 114), and answered her own question by saying, 'Clare lives in Nottingham, doesn't she?' Helen's revealing reply was, 'No, in house ... in house Mum'. For her at this stage, 'live in' implied being physically enclosed by a tangible dwelling, and 'Nottingham' failed to qualify. In the 'Lego farm' transcript (p. 155) we shall see another example of a concept in the making. 'Market' will occur more than once, and we might be tempted to say that this is a word that the child 'knows'. But, although she can recite 'To market, to market, to buy a fat pig' and has some notion of an association between farms and markets, it is obvious from her remarks – 'Build a farm called market', 'Build a farm called market field' – that she has only the vaguest inkling of the essential function of a market.

One of the transcripts (p. 170) contains another clear example of a concept in the making. Matthew, aged three and a half, is out for a walk with his family in Clumber Park when he sees something he cannot put a name to, and having mastered the 'What's this?' device for finding out things (as we all know, children are quick to turn the tables, and the much questioned child soon becomes the relentless questioner), he asks his father, 'Why do you have curtains in there?' Back comes the reply 'It's a dormobile'. Put yourself in the child's place, by imagining a similar situation in which someone's reply came as just so much noise, conveying nothing. 'Dormobile' for us is charged with meaning and not merely because we have long known what it meant. Captured in the word are the twin ideas of movement (the 'mobile' part) and of sleep (the 'dorm' part); we have already met words like 'dormitory' or 'automobile'. It is with one of the two elements in the new word that mother expands on father's reply,

MOTHER People sleep in them.
FATHER Shall we have one to sleep in?

29

They have to start somewhere. What more natural, therefore, than to start with the aspect in which this kind of vehicle differs so conspicuously from most others: being something to sleep in? But notice Matthew's eventual reply: 'I want a bed to sleep in.'

Dormobiles score over beds because they are mobile, but when it comes to sleeping – at this stage the only aspect presented to the boy – Matthew plumps for the familiar. This isn't the end of the story, however, for later in the conversation Matthew asks his father, 'Why do people sleep in dommobiles?' and thus the way is open for his father to deal with the mobility aspect.

There is another example of how we use words to help us to see different things in a common light in the conversation between Michael and his teacher in chapter 16. She has been sympathetically drawing him out, letting him talk about his fears, and after he has spoken of noise in the playground, and the noise of motorbikes, he mentions 'banging', but is quick to point out that 'that's something to do with noise, isn't it?' (p. 211). Here is a child who has not only learned an important principle in the organisation of his vocabulary, but is also apparently aware of it.

Nor will the first stage in the acquisition of a word and all that lies behind it always begin with the word itself. When you hear the 'Snails' conversation (chapter 17) you will probably be struck by the sheer volume of what Elaine and Stuart have to say: like all children at all stages, given the right encouragement, they will keep the conversation going with whatever resources they have mastered, and so, when they see a part of a snail for which they have no word yet, they simply fill in with a substitute:

STUART You know/you know them big things that's sticking up.
The experienced teacher who is listening to him accepts the paraphrase for the time being – the technical term can come later. Or take another example from the same transcript, when the boy asks: 'That's *glue* that they're leaving behind, i'n't it?' and the girl replies: 'No, it can't be because ... it's drying up again'. No-one would dream of asking a six-year-old to consider the criterial attributes of glue, but that is exactly what Stuart and Elaine are doing.

If we wanted an example from older children to show how we feel our way towards the manifold connotations of words that we think we know already, the discussion of 'Timothy Winters' in chapter 18 provides a very revealing one, while at the same time reminding us that learning can be very much a matter of sharing or pooling small areas of knowledge and experience. Bearing in mind

30

that the children are from a mining village, and are familiar with a building called a Miners' Welfare, let us look at the passage in which they are discussing the line 'He's not even heard of the Welfare State'.

MARK I've never heard of Welfare State

JUDITH I've not

MARK I didn't know there was a state called Welfare

TEACHER Mm.

MARK Did you? (To Julie)

JULIE No.

TEACHER Nobody's heard of the Welfare State?

ANDREW I have

MARK I haven't heard of a state called Welfare.

TEACHER You have, Andrew?

MARK I know there's er/ there's er fifty states, but I didn't know that was one of them.

ANDREW It's ... er ... they look after children. It's a Welfare ... er Children's Welfare.

TEACHER Mm.

ANDREW It's not a sort of ... a drinking place, it's where people stay when they're not wanted.

How often it happens that we meet a phrase that combines two words we know and yet we are baffled or at least put on the wrong scent. Here there are two false trails, and both are taken. First Mark goes for 'state' as part of America, a predictable mis-understanding, given the abstractness of the new phrase. It is Andrew, a shyer boy than the irrepressible Mark, who brings the group nearer to the real meaning, but he too is influenced by what one part of the expression has meant in his experience so far. However, he sees at least that the Miners' Welfare (a working man's club) is not the one intended, and his alternative, the Children's Welfare, does bring in the correct connotation of caring, as does his follow up 'a place where people stay when they're not wanted.' No one manages to master the meaning of the original phrase, at least not in this fragment, but it is interesting that in the ensuing discussion of how well different countries look after their old people Mark is moved to say that in Japan 'they haven't got many welfares', showing that Andrew's intervention has modified Mark's original view of the phrase in the right direction.

That this gradual refinement of one's ability to define words is a normal process in the acquisition of language is well illustrated by Andrew Wilkinson in *The Foundations of Language*, where he quotes definitions of words by the same child at different ages. The question 'What's a butterfly?' elicits from the child of three and a half 'It's a butterfly bun', in other words, a reference to another expression containing the same word used as a metaphor. At the age of eleven the same child is able to say, 'A butterfly is an insect which normally has many bright colours.'[1] Notice how she first assigns the butterfly to a category and then states a particular attribute, qualifying even that with the word 'normally'. Courtney Cazden quotes something similar from some work by Carson and Robin in 1960, in which children were asked to look at a picture of a wagon and say what it was. Some said that the wagon was a vehicle (categorisation); others, a car (synonym); others, 'a wooden thing with four wheels' (essential description); and so on.[2]

c. Syntax

Learning about language then is not easily to be separated from learning about the world. As Dale says: 'Learning about the referents of words is really a matter of learning about how the world is organised by human beings.'[3]

We must remember too that meaning is not merely a matter of vocabulary, but also of syntax, the patterns in which words are related – as many of us have found to our cost when we have tried to ask for directions in a foreign language. The young child may be able to accomplish a surprising amount with the single word (or **holophrase** as it has traditionally been called), but it is not until he has mastered the basic patterns of the language, like 'subject-verb-object' for example, that he can really begin to express and understand general truths, like 'dogs eat bones'. If words are more than labels, similarly language is much more than individual words.

3 Children's knowledge of language: its uses

a. Interaction

So far all we have been concerned with is the system that the young child is using. We must also look at the user of the system, and at the ways in which the system is applied.

However effective her use of the single word, Helen shows another ability: she delivers those one word answers in reply to lengthy adult questions, as though she can comprehend grammar that she herself is not yet able to produce. Many authorities would regard this as a feature of children's language development, though the claim has recently been disputed. What no one would dispute is that a single word can be put to effective use, as the following dialogue when Helen was twenty months old can confirm. As bedtime draws near, mother and aunt try the familiar strategies, but Helen is equal to their combined wiles (p. 99).

CHRIS Do you want a bath tonight, Helen?

HELEN No

CHRIS Do you want your hair washing?

HELEN No

CHRIS Are you going to bed soon?

HELEN No

JAN Doesn't big Dolly want you to read her a story?

HELEN No.

Whatever else is going on here, and however frustrating this may be to the adults involved in it, we can safely say that the child is learning a model of interaction through speech.

Learning the patterns of sounds or of structure may be one important target, but children are also learning the uses of language. We shall hear many examples of interaction in the 'Snails' dialogue (chapter 17), as the two children ask questions, or give one another orders.

b. Learning about the world

This brings us to an obvious but important connection between language and learning. Elaine and Stuart in chapter 17 are learning from each other in a way that they could not if they were given the same task to work at separately. By the time they have gone through the education system it is to be hoped they will be capable of formulating the right questions and suggesting appropriate answers when confronted by any form of learning task. En route to this goal, however, others will occasionally pose the questions; sometimes the teacher or, as here, their fellow pupils. For the child, there is so much to learn about the world that it will not be enough to base a reply merely on his own experience of it. Others have also had experience, and they can be questioned about it. 'Tell me' becomes a powerful instrument of learning. At first it may be simply 'Tell me what' (the names of things), but before long it's a case of 'Tell me why'. When Helen was just over two and a half, she was playing with a Lego outfit and some model figures, one of them a Red Indian (p. 154).

HELEN What's that, Mummy?

CHRIS It's a Red Indian.

HELEN Red Indian?

CHRIS Mm.

33

HELEN An what/an what does he do? What does that Red Indian do, Mum?

JAN Well could he be looking after some animals, do you think?

Later in the conversation the animals were to move to another farm and Helen's aunt, Jan, asked, 'Who's going to look after them at their new farm?' Helen's reply showed that she had learned something, if only to accept the authority of adults (p. 154).

HELEN The Red Indian.

Matthew's questions come thick and fast: his father asks plenty of questions and the boy seems to have picked up the habit. We may think that all we are doing is taking a child for a walk, a relaxing physical activity, but all the time there is an unremitting output of questions to be answered, not all of them simple. Take this small sample of Matthew's 'Why' questions. 'Why are these fir-trees broken?' 'Why do they [moons] shine at night-time?' 'Why do a lot of traffic here?' 'Why do you have towers on cafés?' 'Why haven't ducks/ducks got no eyes?' 'Why has he got big feet?' or these, that defy instant slick answers: 'What's under sky?' 'What's under clouds?' 'What do the ducks think?' 'What do moons do?'

Already at three and a half Matthew has discovered that there is much more to be learned than names of things, and he has come to expect adults to be able to tell him what he wishes to know, as have Elaine and Stuart, who show the younger child's faith in adult wisdom when they say, 'Well, we'll ask Mr Godfrey.'

What we should be noticing about some of the questions that these children are asking is that they are open-ended: they admit of more than one answer. There are times in classrooms when teachers ask questions to which they know the answers and in fact will reject any that are not what they predicted as being useful to the orderly presentation of facts that they have planned. While there will always be a place for this kind of questioning, it is to be hoped that it will regularly be supplemented by something more akin to the 'Why?' questions of the young child, so that learning can be associated not only with acquiring knowledge or skill but also with understanding and insight. There is a case for the staccato fusillade of quick questions and one word answers, but we must also hope to see questions like these: 'What kind of person do you think he is?' 'What leads you to believe he's like that?' 'Why do you agree with that?' – all taken from a single lesson in which the teacher deliberately abstained from steering the discussion in a predetermined way. In much the same way Matthew's father often counters the boy's question with another – 'What do you think it

34

is?' – to ensure that, first, Matthew is encouraged to think things out for himself, and second, that questions are an expression of a genuine need to find something out, and not just a habit, a reflex almost, that at least keeps the adult busy.

c. Learning about myself

The few words spoken by Helen in the extract from the dialogue at twenty months have shown something of her knowledge of the language system and its uses; but obviously, because she was only twenty months old, she had much more to learn about both. We have looked at the way the child learns about the world he inhabits, but, through what others say to and about us, and through that ability to contemplate experience which mastery of language confers on us, we also learn a good deal about ourselves. For example, in the Michael transcript (p. 212) he ends his recital of his various fears with 'I'm frightened of a lot of things'. Language enables him to generalise not only about events and processes in the world but about himself.

Similarly, while the four children are discussing 'Timothy Winters' (p. 251), Mark is accused of being rough, the criterion apparently being the fights he has; but Mark objects: his fights all took place 'last term' and last term does not count. Most of us have said things like 'I never was any good at . . .', a self-concept that language has helped us to form.

d. Displaced speech and make-believe

Apart from this ability to develop self-concepts, there are many things about the world that the child has not yet learned. As human beings we are very much constrained by the physical laws of the universe: we can obviously only be in one place at once and although we may choose whether to do certain things or not, we cannot prevent our actions from having certain consequences. At first a child is going to be very much bound by these constraints, to live in a here-and-now, but soon he will learn that language can help us, to a certain extent, to escape the bondage of space and time. We can use what Bloomfield called **displaced speech**,[4] refer- ring to things or people that are not physically present, or to events that have already or not yet taken place. Helen, at two years, has already begun to do this. When her aunt asks, 'You're going in Aunty's car?', she replies, 'Mummy's shopping basket', referring both to a future time and to an object that is not actually in the room. In the same way, when her mother asks her, 'Who came to play in your sandpit yesterday?', she can say, 'Emma', and in reply

35

to the further question 'Who else?, 'Baby ... uh ... got socks off ...' Once again it would be easy to be distracted by the imperfections of her syntax, without giving her credit for her grasp of displaced speech. It is this ability to focus on a sequence of future events that helps Stuart to envisage how he will go about the task of writing up his experience with the snails. 'Picture, writing, picture ... writing', he says as he visualises what is going to be done. There is another relationship that we need to grasp if we are to make sense of the world around us: that of cause and effect. At two years seven months Helen is beginning to understand this, judging by a reply such as 'No room' to the question 'Why can't they go in now?'.

Even this extended definition of learning still relies too heavily on matter-of-factness. We have seen many examples of children using language to ask serious questions about their environment, but obviously there is a less serious side to our language use. Displaced speech is not particularly daring as an escape from the constraints of reality. Children can do better than that. From a very early stage they take great pleasure in playing with the medium they are learning, with its sounds, its meanings and its structures, and, as any infant teacher knows, they are always willing to spend time in imaginative play. Look at this little sequence from an infant classroom, a corner of which has been fitted up as a hospital, complete with telephone. Admittedly, certain 'props' such as the telephone are helping the children to sustain their imaginary identities, but the real vehicle of their fantasy is their language.

NURSE Hello, Doctor ... someone wants you.

DOCTOR Yes.

NURSE This is ... Mr Jackson wants you.

DOCTOR What for?

NURSE About his daughter. She's ... She's ... Her heart isn't beating.

PATIENT I'm not breathing very well.

NURSE I know, and your heart isn't beating.

Sometimes the illusion breaks down and the doctor is referred to as 'David' or 'you twit'; sometimes the jargon is only partly remembered, as in 'He's nearly back to his normal'; and the patient is all too ready to double as scriptwriter − 'Pretend I turned over and died.' Shades of 'Force brandy down my throat'! Is this merely play, or is something being learned as these children try to enact what they have seen on television or heard other children talk about? Does this enable them not only to try out new expressions, but also to assimilate new experiences? Halliday's 'let's pretend' model is surely an important aspect of language and learning.[5] Counting snails may be one kind of activity, but seeing snails as 'giants' through a magnifying glass not only sustains a sense of excitement and wonder, but suggests a different point of view. Here is where the constraints can really be broken, where the laws of the universe can be set aside. And here is where literature can come into its own. Whether it is via realism or fantasy, literature can enable us to see the world from novel points of view, and to see it through the personalities of other people.

4 Conclusion

This has taken us a long way from the handful of words that were discussed at the beginning of the chapter. The aim has been to remind the reader that there is more to learning language than acquiring a set of sounds or words or structures, or even than learning how to use these appropriately in various situations. There is certainly more to it than simply learning about 'the world', unless we include ourselves in that phrase, and include the imaginary as well as the actual world. What should be stressed most of all, however, is the magnitude of every child's accomplishment.

In part two we shall hear Ralph on the tape (chapter 7), exemplifying some of the characteristic, and characteristically limited, repertoire of the as yet uncommunicating child. Following this there are recordings of Helen at the age of twenty months and older (chapters 8–12). As we listen to the recordings, or read the transcripts, we should try to ensure that their sheer ordinariness does not detract from the magnitude of the commonplace daily accomplishment of the normal child: learning to talk.

Part three reminds us that talking effectively is no inconsiderable feat, and can play a crucial role in our learning.

5 References

[1] Wilkinson, A. (1971) *The Foundations of Language* OUP

[2] Cazden, C. B. (1966) 'Subcultural Differences in Child Language: an Inter-disciplinary Review'. *Merrill-Palmer Quarterly of Behaviour and Development* **12**, 185–219

[3] Dale, P. S. (1972) *Language Development: Structure and Function* Dryden Press

[4] Bloomfield, I. (1935) *Language* Unwin University Books

[5] Halliday, M. A. K. (1975) 'Relevant Models of Language' in A. Wilkinson *Language in Education*, OUP

5 Studying the language of young children

1 Introduction

A four-year-old child stands in front of a mirror, smoothing down her new nightdress, and is heard to say, 'I can hardly believe my own hands'. Years before, her mother had plaintively said to her own long-striding father, 'Slow down, Daddy, you're out of my breath'. We have all had experience of this kind of children's language: suddenly out of the flux of daily chatter these happy accidents of creativity come to divert us and to stay in our memory. The book *From Two to Five* by Chukovsky (1963) is full of such instances. But remarks like those quoted above are only fragments of the language a child produces, and one could hardly base a study of language development on them alone.

It was suggested in the previous chapter that learning to talk was an achievement that no one should undervalue, but that it was nevertheless the commonplace achievement of virtually every child. Demonstrably, the new-born infant is unable to speak, but comes irresistibly to the point of being able to talk as we do. So much do we take for granted *what* we see happen that we also take for granted *how* it happens. How then does the child come to talk as we do? We can think of family resemblances in speech that extend not only to vocabulary and accent, but to voice quality as well. If we are prepared to explain the latter by physiological factors, we are probably inclined to think of vocabulary and accent as being 'just picked up', and to explain them in terms of successful imitation. For the student of children's language, however, nothing can be taken for granted, just as there can be no picking out only the interesting or comprehensible parts of what a child says. 'Everyone knows' will not be good enough: the concern will be to describe what really happens, and then to account for it.

But think of what that means, even in respect of the amount of material available. Take a two-year-old child, for example, and go through his talking day: play, mealtimes, walks, shopping, bathing, bedtime. Consider the problems of collecting all that he says, even with a tape recorder, and then making it accessible in some form of transcript that would really capture every aspect of his speech, let alone the complete environment of the speech. Even then, after all that effort, one's record would be 'one day in the life of . . .', and how much generalisation could one legitimately base upon that?

Next there would be the problem of interpreting whatever data was collected. It is one thing for parents to put an interpretation on something that a child says (the transcripts in chapters 8 to 13 will provide more than one example of adults doing just that, and will suggest that it is both a normal and helpful thing to do), but it is done on the spot, making best guesses in the circumstances, and parents are hardly unprejudiced observers. It is quite another thing to offer an explanation that will command the assent of others.

There is also more involved than matters of detail: judgements about language acts must be based on assumptions about the nature of language itself, and here there is no happy consensus. To many people, the question 'What is language?' seems as irritatingly irrelevant to a discussion of language use as the question 'What is football?' would be to a Manchester United supporter simply concerned to demonstrate how good his team was at playing the game. We are back to the problem of seeing something as familiar as language in a new light; and if an answer to 'What is language?' that starts with 'Well, you know . . .' might have to be good enough for the layman, it could not satisfy the serious student.

It is for such students that the standard reviews of language acquisition study are written, and those who would like a wider perspective than this chapter offers are recommended to read overviews like those of McCarthy (1954) or Bloom (1975). The main function of this chapter is to offer readers unfamiliar with the study of children's language something in the way of background against which to set the transcripts and commentaries in chapters 7 to 13. It is proposed to survey the field only in the sense of selecting certain broad themes rather than offering a chronological survey.

First there is an attempt to define the term 'language acquisition', which in turn requires a definition of language itself. Next, some reasons are given for studying the subject, followed by a section 'Perspective' in which the reader is offered

a a brief statement about trends in the field

b a list of the questions that have been the chief focus of concern

c information about the methods of study employed

d information about some of the areas of agreement in the field of language acquisition

e an introduction to theories of language acquisition.

Such an overview can do nothing like justice to so complex a field, and it is hoped that the interested reader will consult some of the books recommended in the final section of this chapter.

2 What is language acquisition?

a. Language defined

Dull though it may be to start with definitions, in this case it seems inevitable. Already, the term 'language acquisition' has been used in place of the earlier 'language development'. This, alone, calls for an explanation. Is 'language acquisition' only a fancy term for 'learning to talk', or is it a more subtle and comprehensive description? And what of a definition of 'language' itself?

If someone said to you, 'Let's discuss the different aspects of sesquipedalianism' you could be forgiven for thinking, 'Hadn't we better decide what it is first?' For 'sesquipedalianism' read 'language', and you will realise that, having earlier rejected 'Well, you know ...' as an acceptable answer to the question 'What is language?', we have still offered no suitable alternative. Let us look at one or two definitions of language to see what they have in common.

> Language is primarily a system of phonetic symbols for the expression of communicable thoughts and feelings.[1]
>
> [Language is] ... a system of arbitrary or conventional vocal symbols by means of which human beings communicate with each other.[2]
>
> A language consists of a number of linked systems, and structure can be seen in it at all levels.[3]
>
> A language is a structured system of arbitrary vocal sounds and sequences of sounds which is used, or can be used, in interpersonal communication by an aggregation of human beings and which rather exhaustively catalogues the things, events, and processes in the human environment.[4]

To begin with, there is a distinction made in most of the definitions between what language is and what it is used for. It is the former with which we are concerned at present. Notice that three of the definitions assume that language is primarily something that we speak rather than write. All living languages are spoken, but not all of them are written down.

The first important point of unanimity is in the use of the word 'system' (allied in two cases to the word 'structure'). Human beings make noises, and other human beings apprehend meanings as a result. This initially unlikely outcome is possible only because the noises are patterned, and the various contrasts that the patterning makes available have significance for any two people with access to the same system. This sounds all so very obvious to any language user: others talk and we hear them say things. Of course this happens. Or, to be more precise, we receive a set of signals and appear, instantaneously, to decode them. The signals are 'symbols', in the word of two of the definitions, and they are 'arbitrary symbols': there is no necessary connection between the words themselves and what they represent. Think of the word 'dog', for example, and its equivalent in other languages. Are we to say that any one of them is somehow more essentially 'dog-like' than another?

If there is to be effective contrast, then the items to be contrasted cannot be too numerous. Linguists would suggest that a system is 'closed' in the sense that it consists of a finite number of items, each distinct from each other, so that each item is defined in terms of its contrast with the others in the set. Suppose that the days of the week are a system. The meaning of 'Saturday' will lie in its contrast with six non-Saturdays, its position after Friday and before Sunday, and so on. Add a new day of the week ('Playday', 'Restday', 'Payday') and the meaning of 'Saturday' has been changed.

Every time we speak we are operating within systems of contrast in three areas simultaneously, as for example in the following remark made by a child of five about a boy in her class: 'He's so good at telling jokes he ought to be a chameleon.'

First there are contrasts in the sound patterns she is using. The malapropism makes the point very clearly: we would not find her remark amusing if we could not differentiate the /d/ and the /l/ sounds that for some speakers are the only parts of the pattern that make 'chameleon' and 'comedian' two distinct words. But every segment in the whole utterance offers the same possibility. 'He' contrasts with 'be', 'we', 'she', and dozens of other words differing

41

only in respect of a single segment. 'Tell' contrasts with 'sell', 'till', 'ten' (and many other words) in the first, second, and third segments respectively.

If we had heard her make the remark, we should also have heard (i.e. responded to, without necessarily being directly aware of) the rhythm of her utterance and the intonation that helped us to know that she was making a statement rather than asking a question. These are other areas of possible contrast in phonology.

When it comes to syntax, there are various systems operating to give the utterance significance. The girl is talking about one boy, not about several, and so has selected the singular ('he') from the **number** system. She is affirming something, selecting positive not negative from the system of **polarity**; she chooses present not past from the **tense** system, and so on. Grammar is an intricate network of related systems, selection from among the terms of which is as much a part of meaning as the more obvious contribution of the individual words.

In the third area, that of vocabulary and **meaning**, there are also choices being made throughout the utterance: 'good' where a synonym ('skilful' for example) or antonym ('bad') would be possible. Contrast will be less clear-cut here than between the smaller number of items in the system of grammar, but the previous chapter showed that words have meanings only in relation to each other, and to the situation in which they are used.

'Meaning' is itself a word that defies simple definition: what to the layman is self-explanatory, the linguist would need to consider under several headings.

There is, for example, the **referential theory of meaning**, which states that the meaning of a word is its referent. In this view, 'words are symbols that stand for something other than themselves, something in the world, namely their referents'.[5] In other words, if you look at a dog and say 'dog', then the referent is the animal referred to by the word, which represents, symbolises, means, 'dog', and can be used whether or not a dog is physically present to be referred to.

The **behavioural theory of meaning**, on the other hand, 'focuses on the use of language in communication. It postulates that the meaning of a word or expression is the set of responses that it produces in the hearer.'[6] This is obviously a complex area, needing further discussion. For the present, let us be content to call it **semantics**, thus completing the set of three elements within which patterning and hence contrast can be manifested.

These three elements will be the phonological, the syntactic, and the semantic. When we come to examine some of the trends in language acquisition study there will be examples of research centring upon any of these three.

There must be a word of caution here: all the definitions of language cited on page 40 are those of linguists, who might tend to look upon language as some form of code that can be seen separately from its users and the situations of its use. Psychologists, on the other hand, would offer a different point of view. Peter Herriot suggests three approaches to language: language as a system of sounds and symbols (the approach that we have been discussing so far); language as personal behaviour, an approach which 'involves the making of inferences from behaviour to psychological function'; and language as inter-personal behaviour, that is 'a means of communication in a social situation'.[7] One's view of language acquisition is obviously going to depend very much upon which of these three approaches, or any other, one adopts.

b. Language acquisition defined

If we return to the original question, 'What is language acquisition?', one answer would be 'Learning the code', that is learning the sets of patterns in phonology, syntax and semantics that make significant contrast possible. Another would add to this accomplishment the ability to match the utterance to the occasion – that is, to speak not merely grammatically but also appropriately with respect to both the situation and one's addressee. Such a view is reflected in the following definition: 'By the acquisition of language is meant the process whereby children achieve a fluent control of their native language.'[8] Here 'control' presupposes more than the ability to produce utterances in a vacuum. M. A. K. Halliday offers a richer definition when he says:

> We can see all the time, if we pay attention to what is said by, to, and in the presence of, a young child, how in the course of the most ordinary linguistic interaction he is constantly learning the structure of the environment in all its aspects, material, logical, institutional, and social. He is also, at the same time, developing his own unique personality.[9]

Depending on which of the approaches we take, we shall also give different answers to such questions as 'When does the process begin and end?'. It has been customary to credit the child of six with full knowledge of the structural patterns of his native language, but this could scarcely be true of his knowledge of the vocabulary items of the language, and much less of his ability to control the different registers of his native tongue so that his utterances were always appropriate to the occasion.

3 Why study the acquisition of language?

There are two groups of people we could expect to have a particularly strong interest in language acquisition: psychologists and linguists, whose fields have recently been brought together in the area of 'psycholinguistics'.

Language has attracted the interest of the psychologist for a number of reasons. Learning to talk is an everyday, easily accessible example of the learning process, and its study could throw light on the nature of the learning process in general. Then there is the fact that much of our learning takes place through the medium of language, and can also, perhaps, be monitored through language. There is a close link between language and thinking, and the child, with his concepts still in the making, could have something to tell us about the nature of the link. Child psychologists in particular will wish to relate language development to the child's development as a whole.

For the student of language there will be the fascination of seeing a child wrestling with a system that even the professional linguists have not yet been able to describe or account for completely. Anyone who has traced the development of the knowledge required to produce even an apparently simple utterance (asking a question, for example, or using a negative) will come to realise afresh the complexity of language as a whole. Studying the language of children may be one way of putting to the test new theories about the nature of language itself.

There will, of course, be others with a less theoretical interest in the topic. If there are norms and milestones in language development, then people with professional concerns for young children, such as teachers, speech therapists, doctors, social workers and the like, will need to know what they are.

4 Perspective

a. Historical

Following Bloom,[10] upon whose review this section is very largely based, one can divide the history of the study of language acquisition into four periods.

i. (*c.* 1882–*c.* 1929) The period in which the main studies were those of psychologist or linguist parents who kept diaries of the language development of their own children.

ii. (c. 1930–c. 1957) The period of the large-scale studies of the form of children's language with the aim of establishing 'milestones' of development.

iii. (c. 1957–c. 1969) The period in which, under the influence of Chomsky's revolutionary ideas of language, the concentration was on children's syntax and the knowledge that lay behind their ability to produce sentences.

iv. (c. 1969–   ) The period in which the emphasis has been on cognitive development and the relation between form and meaning.

i. The diary studies (c. 1882–c. 1929)

Studies of this kind were produced by linguists or psychologists who were interested in the language development of their own children, and who kept very detailed records of their speech over considerable periods of time, noting not merely what the child said, but, in many cases, details of the attendant circumstances also. Well-known examples are those of Preyer (1882), the Sterns (1924, 1928), and Leopold (1939–49). As Campbell and Wales (1970) say: '. . . the scientific study of child language has an important and thoroughly respectable heritage of observation and theoretical discussion'[11], and Braine says of this period that it 'saw a promising beginning made on the study of the development of linguistic structure'.[12]

ii. The normative studies (c. 1930–c. 1957)

According to Braine:

> In America, the behaviourist revolution brought [the first] period to an end and ushered in a long period of data gathering, mostly quantitative and mostly by psychologists, with only a little of the data gathered being of discernible linguistic interest. The behaviourist period lasted until the early 1950s, and during it useful communication between psychology and linguistics seems seems to have effectively ceased.[13]

He is referring to the tendency, described by Bloom, to disparage: 'information, however detailed and minutely recorded, gathered by a parent–investigator who, it was presumed, was necessarily biased in what he chose to record in his notes, and in what he overlooked as well'.[14]

The data required by the normative studies was of the sort that could be described statistically, and so one sees a concentration on the kind of things in the form of children's speech that can be counted and measured, like numbers of particular classes of words,

45

or the length of utterances. The chief result, according to Bloom, was the specification of 'milestones' of development: what can be expected from children at particular stages. Her objection to such milestones is that they make no allowance for the changes that can occur during one of the specified stages. The model of language used by the investigators of this period was that of structural linguistics, and so the child's language at the single word stage was described in terms of adult word classes, and later in terms of adult sentence types. There was no question of child language being autonomous, and the focus was very much on description and form.

iii. The work of the 1960s (c. 1957–c. 1969)

The third period, Braine tells us, 'began with the resumption of communication between the disciplines [of psychology and linguistics], and the subsequent emergence of the generative-grammar school of thought in linguistics has been a powerful stimulus to the present concentration on grammar acquisition'.[15]

This too was a reaction to the period that preceded it. People were not content with description, but wished to find explanations of how children could produce novel forms. This was very much a consequence of the advent of Chomsky's model of generative grammar with its insistence on the creativity of language and the idea of deep structures underlying the surface structures that we produce and hear. There is a further contrast between the studies of this period and the normative studies like those of Templin (1957) and that is in the number of children studied. The well-known work of this period, like that of Brown and Bellugi (1964); Braine (1963); Miller and Ervin (1964), is based upon the detailed study of very small numbers of children not beyond the age of three.

One important effect of the advent of **transformational-generative** grammar (T.G.) was to provide an alternative way of describing the adult model that the child was learning. The emphasis during this period was on accounting for the creativity of children's language use by attempting to write 'grammars' in TG terms for successive stages of the child's development. The child's language was being regarded as a system in its own right and not as an inferior version of the adult system. One consequence of this was that certain regularities in the speech of children were highlighted, and various attempts were made to characterise them (for example, Braine's **'pivot and open** classes' and Brown's **'telegraphic speech'**). Although Braine is right in saying that communication was resumed between psychology and linguistics, it is also true to say that there was no lack of conflict between the two disciplines during this period, particularly concerning the best way of accounting for the learning of language.

iv. Language development and cognitive theory (c. 1969–   )

It is Bloom's view that progress in the fields of both language theory and the study of language development combined to show that: 'The essence of language had to do at least as much with underlying meaning as with the surface form of linguistic representation.'[16]

As far as work in the study of language development is concerned, she points to the growing dissatisfaction with pivot grammar, which had attempted to describe the two-word utterances of children, such as 'allgone shoe', in terms of the pivot 'allgone' (one of a small number of words in fixed positions) and the open-class word 'shoe' (one of a much larger class of words that were used with pivots). Pivot grammar ignored meaning, had no correspondence with structures in the adult language, and made no allowances for any effect of what children talk about on their choice of words. Thus, in this fourth period, there has been concentration on 'the underlying semantics of early sentences', as for example Bloom's own work (1970) and that of Schlesinger (1971).

Bloom herself suggests two strategies for learning grammar: one by learning to use words like 'more' and 'my' to express relationships; the other by learning to juxtapose two words to signify relationships (as for example 'Mummy hat' for possession). This, she argues, shows that children have learned more than simply which words can follow which others in speech, and the issue becomes one of the relationship between cognitive development and language learning. Does the one determine the other, and if so, which? Thus, the beginning of the 1970s marked a major shift in research into language development, away from the description of child language in terms of language theory and towards the explanation of language development in terms of cognitive theory.

The other development that she spoke of was in language theory and here she is referring to the attempts to modify or replace Chomsky's syntactically-based model of language by one with a semantic base. She quotes work by Bowerman (1973) using generative grammar, and the 'case grammar' of Fillmore (1968), with its emphasis on semantic structure in terms of the meanings of noun forms in relation to verb forms. This can be seen as a promising model for the study of child language, in which noun forms predominate.

This has been all too brief a summary, which should be amplified by reading one of the surveys mentioned in section 5 of this chapter. The following headings are worth keeping in mind when reading either a survey, or the account of a particular piece of research:

Subject of survey or research: description or explanation
Number of children involved
Theory of language
Psychological theory
View of child language
Stage of development

b. Typical questions

One way of classifying the questions that are asked about the development of children's language is in terms of description, interpretation and explanation.

First there is the collecting of information about exactly what happens. Typical questions here are, for example:

'Is there a fixed order of acquisition of sounds or sentence patterns?'

'Do parents simplify their language when speaking to children?'

'At any given stage do children understand language in advance of that which they are able to produce?'

Next there will be questions about the conclusions which may be drawn from a particular piece of research or observation, or from particular data. Suppose, for instance, that a child produces a sentence pattern that in the adult grammar would express a **grammatical relationship** (say **subject/verb** as in 'Daddy come'). Is it reasonable to say that the child is aware of the same relationship or must we look for other explanations?

Finally, when all the evidence has been amassed and there is some degree of consensus about what happens and how certain facts should be interpreted, there come much more difficult and interesting questions like:

'If this is so, then why should it be so?'

'Given that a child acquires language in this order and is influenced by this or that factor, how is the learning carried out?'

In this section we shall look at some of the key questions of description (what happens?). There are two broad categories of speech that we could examine: the language that the child hears (the input); and the language that he learns to produce (the output).

i. Parental speech

Just how do parents and others speak to children? Typical questions would be:

> 'Do parents, and other adults, consciously modify their language, making it simpler, always grammatical, and highly repetitive?'
>
> 'Do they (parents and other adults) use "baby talk"?'
>
> 'Do they coach the child, picking up his errors, or insisting on little repetitive drills?'
>
> 'If so, does this vary at all with the social class of the parent?'
>
> 'Are there special problems for the child with deaf or dumb parents?'
>
> 'What other responses do parents make to their children's utterances?'
>
> 'Do they expand the primitive sentences that children produce?'
>
> 'Just how much do they talk to the child?'
>
> 'How vital for the child's language learning is the context in which the language is produced?'

These are some of the obvious questions that need to be answered. Not so obvious, but at least as important, will be questions about what the child makes of what is said to him. It would be easy to assume that what we hear when an adult speaks to us must necessarily be the same for a child. We should be forgetting that we have had to learn to process speech sounds, and we have no recollection of the stages by which we did so, any more than we can remember how we learned to see. One of the key questions will be how the child does process the speech he hears. Human language is very much more complicated than many of us realise (see, for example, Roger Brown's discussion of the use of 'a' and 'the' in *A First Language*),[17] and psycholinguists are interested in the strategies that children use to help themselves in mastering it.

ii. Children's language development

When it comes to the output (what the child learns to say and to understand), once again there are many questions, both general and particular, that need to be asked. Bearing in mind what was said earlier about taking nothing for granted, let us look at some of the general questions.

> 'Is it true that virtually every child learns to speak, irrespective of intelligence or background?'
>
> 'When does the process begin and end?'

'Is it as rapid as it is often said to be?'

'Is there some fixed order of acquisition, the only variations from child to child being in the rate of acquisition?'

'What criteria can we use to determine that a particular item has been acquired?'

'Is the process smooth and continuous?'

'Can children make themselves understood at whatever stage of their development?'

'Is it true that children learn first the things that they hear most often in the speech of their parents?'

'How much of the speech activity of children can be fairly described as imitation?'

'How much is constructed, rather than learned by rote?'

'How active are children in the language learning process?'

'Is children's language a simplified, modified version of adult speech, or is it an imperfect imitation, or is it something autonomous: a language in its own right?'

'If child language is autonomous, then what is the best way of representing the child's knowledge of language without having recourse to the categories of adult grammar?'

These are questions of production, mainly, but there are others to do with comprehension:

'Is it true that a child can understand constructions that he is as yet unable to produce?'

'If not, then what is the relationship between his production and his understanding of speech?'

Every question above can be applied to a child learning English, but obviously the same questions could be asked of any child learning any language, and there would be the further question of how universally true any of the answers would turn out to be.

What we have called the 'particular' questions will be those that are asked about particular aspects of language acquisition. Since children can make sounds before they produce actual words and sentences, let us begin with some questions about the acquisition of phonology.

If we take reception before production this time, there are such questions as:

'How soon does the child learn to distinguish the sounds of the human voice from the rest of the sounds in his environment?'

and there is one major supplementary question:

'How soon does the child learn to distinguish one speech sound or intonation from another?'

In the field of production there is the question already posed at the general level:

'Is there a fixed order of acquisition, a set of stages through which all children pass in the same sequence, even if at different rates?'

'If so, does this match in any way the ordering of the different units of phonology?' (In other words, does the child learn first the smallest building bricks, the individual sounds or **phonemes**, and last of all the largest, the intonation patterns?)

'Does every child babble?'

'Is babbling recognisably different for each child according to the speech community in which he finds himself? Do Chinese and English children babble differently, for example?'

'In the course of babbling is every sound that is produced relevant to the repertoire of sounds that will be needed to speak the target language?'

'Similarly, when it comes to learning the individual phonemes, is there a recognisable order of acquisition?'

'Must the child be able to produce a sound himself before being able to discriminate it in the speech of others?'

When we turn to semantic development, we must accept Dale's assertion that: 'In the competition for least understood aspect of language acquisition, semantic development is surely the winner.'[18]

The questions here are just as numerous as for phonological development, but suggested answers are not as readily forthcoming.

'What are the first words that children appear to use?'

'Are they similar in content for children the world over?'

'Does the child's use of an adult word necessarily mean that, for him, it has the adult meaning?'

'If not, is there any recognisable path along which the, perhaps initially restricted, meaning will develop?'

This last question applies not merely to the more obvious case of 'content' words like 'dog' or 'balloon' or even 'sympathy', but to the more elusive meanings that have to do with relationships between things – like those conveyed by prepositions such as 'in' or 'on', for example.

'When a child strings together two words as in "Dolly shoe", how can we know that a particular relationship, such as possession, is being signalled?'

'If such juxtaposed words do express various relationships, is

51

there a fixed order in which children learn to express them?'
Finally there is syntax, the area that has been the focus of so much attention since the early 1960s. Once again there is the question of the possible order of acquisition.

'Does every child go through the successive stages of one element/two element utterance?'

'Is it the case that at each stage the child is signalling certain relationships, first by merely juxtaposing two words in the normal English word order, and later by adding inflections like /-ed/ or /-ing/, or the "little words" like "is" or "with"?'

'Are these inflexions and "little words" themselves acquired in a fixed order?'

'And is the same true of the various sentence types and patterns?'

'How true is it that children can understand structures that are in advance of those that they are capable of producing?'

'Is new knowledge immediately detectable because it is expressed in novel forms and immediately takes over from the previous forms, or do the old forms persist for a while side by side with the new?'

The study of children's syntax has emphasised the difficulty of describing children's language in ways that will do justice to its productivity. So far in this chapter we have fallen into one of the major traps of language study, by speaking of language as though it were merely a matter of code (phonology, semantics, and syntax) without reference to the circumstances of its use. There must, therefore, be one further set of questions: those dealing with the child's ability not only to use a word or structure, but to use it appropriately with reference both to the situation and to the particular addressee. Unless, that is, one believes that the ability to allow for what Ervin-Tripp calls 'situation and setting'[19] is not developed until the child is of school age, and thus falls outside some people's definition of language acquisition.

The preceding list of questions, although typical of the areas of concern, is nowhere near complete, nor has anyone come up with all the answers. What is more, even if they did, the answers would give rise to further questions in their turn. Once you establish *what* happens, there is the question 'why?' or 'how?'.

Suppose it were established that certain things were acquired in a certain order by most of the children learning a particular language or, even more impressively, by most of the children in the world. Immediately one would ask:

'Why in that order?'

'Is an item learned early because it is in some way less complex, either grammatically or semantically, than others learned later?'

'If imitation turns out to play less of a part than was popularly supposed, and children were somehow "creative" in their language use, then what could be the explanation?'

If it were demonstrated that the child was somehow 'figuring out' the nature of the language to which he was being exposed, one would have to ask:

'What are the strategies or hypotheses that the child brings to this task?'

If it were proved that the child 'internalised' a set of rules that enabled him to go on using and understanding language for the rest of his life, then the following question would have to be asked: 'How is the necessary knowledge stored and made available for that apparently instantaneous and unreflecting use of language that we normally take for granted?'

Speculation about the nature of language acquisition could well lead one to consider whether this evidence related to a special case, out of pattern with other forms of learning, or whether the explanations that appeared to make sense for language might lead to a reconsideration of other forms of learning too. In that case, it might be profitable to place the learning of language in a wider context, by considering it in relation to cognition itself. One would then find oneself pondering the issues of the relationship between thought and language.

c. Methods of study

When it comes to the collecting of examples of children's language for study, there are at least two possible approaches, to be employed either independently or in conjunction.

We can be present as the child talks in the course of his daily routine, and collect whatever he says over a series of visits. This corpus of utterances, together with whatever additional information we have managed to record about the situation (other participants, accompanying actions, facial expression, etc.), will then be available for analysis and discussion.

A quite different approach would be to set up a situation, using toys or pictures, and to elicit responses to prepared questions or instructions.

The first is the **naturalistic** approach, and is exemplified by the diary studies, and by much of the work of the 1960s. The second is the experimental approach, exemplified by Jean Berko's work on morphology (Berko, 1958).

In this study, Berko tested children's ability to use various morphemes productively, with the help of pictures and nonsense words. Thus, if a child was shown a picture of 'a wug', and could then say of another picture that there were 'two wugs', it was argued that he had generalised the function of the plural morpheme, since presumably he had never heard either 'wug' or 'wugs' before, and was not merely repeating learned items from a repertoire.

In the field of syntax, the experimental approach has an example in the work of Carol Chomsky (1969). Wishing to examine the assumption that, by six, the child has learned the patterns of syntax, she set out to test children's understanding of various structures. For example, when she showed children a blindfold doll, and asked the question, 'Is this doll easy to see?', she was given the answer 'No' by the younger children, and 'Yes' by the older ones – the inference being that children learn fairly late that the subject of 'see' in this kind of structure is not the expected one.

These two studies illustrate another possible contrast in approach. Since 'language acquisition' means not only 'learning to talk' but also 'learning to understand', studies may differ in their concern with either producing or understanding speech.

Returning to the contrast between naturalistic and experimental approaches, there are other points to be made. It is, perhaps, misleading to lump together the diary studies of the late nineteenth and early twentieth centuries with the work of the 1960s under the heading of the naturalistic approach. The diarists were working alone, and whatever skill they brought to their task of recording, they were still basically writing things down. The workers in the 1960s, on the other hand, had the benefit of working in pairs, and with tape recorders, so that one of them could concentrate on the situation in which the speech was produced. In the intervals between their visits to the children's homes they could discuss the material with each other, and with others, so that fresh minds were brought to bear on the problems. Where necessary, they could supplement their observations by carying out some simple test. The alternative was experimental studies of the kind mentioned above, in which the experimenter could make use of prepared apparatus to elicit certain structures or words more systematically than would be possible in the naturalistic setting, where the failure of children to produce certain items might be no more than the accident of there being no stimulus to evoke them at the time of the visit.

When Donaldson and Wales (1970) wished to study the child's understanding of 'more' and 'less', for example, they tried to ensure that it was both possible and natural for such words to be used. The three- and four-year-old children were shown model trees with hooks on them. Some hooks were empty, and some had 'apples' on them. The children were then given spare 'apples', and instructions such as, 'Now make it so that there are more apples on this tree than on that tree'.

This is a good example of taking nothing for granted. No doubt to a casual observer there would have been evidence that some of these children had been using the words with understanding, but the experimenters set out to see whether this was really the case. But the test material need not always be something concrete: where the focus is upon, for instance, the child's understanding of words to do with time, the experimenter can present sentences containing such words as 'before' and 'after'.

What other variables are there apart from number of children, nature of approach, and focus on comprehension or production?

One will be the age of the children studied. For example, one could concentrate on what has been called the **prelinguistic stage**, when the child has begun to move along the path of language learning, and is doing more than make mere noises but is not yet producing what is to most of us recognisably language. When it comes to the linguistic stage, there is the choice of looking at the pre-school child, or at schoolchildren who have supposedly 'acquired' language before coming to school, and who now need to refine and develop their control over it.

Two more simple points need to be made. The first is implicit in what has already been said about the different approaches. If we are concerned to show development (change, and presumably also increased skill or knowledge), we can compare a child either with himself or with others. In the first case we should be doing what the diarists did: recording one child's output, and examining the records for examples of change. The alternative strategy (what Bloom calls 'the normative studies')[20] is to observe and compare large numbers of children of different ages and backgrounds. In both cases the aims and assumptions are similar: children move from lesser to greater proficiency, and it should be possible to demonstrate the stages through which they pass.

The second point concerns the dangers of describing, however sketchily, a list of studies as though they were written in a vacuum.

Some attempt was made, in the first section of this chapter, to suggest that behind the particular observations or experiments of individual workers there lay theories of the nature of language and of language learning that helped to shape them. In addition to giving details of particular researches, a genuine overview would also have to acknowledge the influence of certain theoretical works. It would, for example, distort the perspective if one were unaware of the influence of Chomsky on McNeill, for example, or of Jakobson on the whole field of the study of the acquisition of phonology.

d. Describing children's language: points of agreement
It is notoriously easier to ask than to answer questions, and there would be no point in pretending that one can reel off the answers to the questions that were listed in section 4 b of this chapter. Instead it is proposed to keep to the headings used in that section and to offer answers, in general terms, which would meet with general agreement.

i. Parental speech
Let us start by looking at how parents talk to children. We might expect to find that parents somehow simplify their language when speaking to children, but there has not been a lot of investigation to find out whether they actually do so. Dale (1972) quotes the findings of Phillips (1970), who recorded the speech of a group of mothers in two sets of circumstances: talking to the experimenter, and talking to their children at play. When speaking to the children, the mothers' speech utterances 'were shorter, contained fewer verbs and modifiers, and included a smaller variety of verb forms than when talking to the experimenters'.[21]

About adults' reactions to children's utterances there is a great deal more evidence. There are three familiar processes: prompting, echoing, and expansion. Thus, if the adult asked a question in the form normal in adult grammar ('What do you want?') and got no reply, he would prompt by rephrasing the question in a way easier for the child to understand ('You want what?'). This is **prompting**. **Echoing** is not unlike prompting, in the structures that it produces. Suppose that the child said something like, 'I'm eating bik'. A typical response could be, 'You're eating what?' The third reaction, **expansion**, is the most well-known and the best documented of all. A child says, 'Doggy bark', and the mother immediately says something like 'Yes, the doggy is barking', an adult version of what she imagines the child meant. In many cases there will be more than one possible meaning in the situation in which the child spoke, and the mother's expansion serves in part to check which meaning was intended. This is not to say that the mother is coaching the child in grammar. As Cazden says: 'No one has suggested that parents expand with any conscious tutorial intention. It seems simply to be one spontaneous way of keeping the conversation with the young child going.'[22]

Even those parents who imagine that they do regularly correct the grammar of their children may be deceiving themselves, according to Roger Brown (1973), who believes that:

... what parents generally correct is pronunciation, 'naughty' words, and regularised irregular allomorphs like 'digged' and 'goed'. These facts seem to penetrate parental awareness. But syntax, the child saying, for instance, 'Why the dog won't eat?', instead of 'Why won't the dog eat?' seems to be automatically set right in the parent's mind, with the mistake never registering as such.[23]

Brown believes that parents are much more concerned with the truth of what the child is saying than with the accuracy of his syntax, a belief that readers can bear in mind when studying the Helen transcripts (chapters 7–12) or when next they talk to young children.

ii. Children's language development

If we now turn to children's speech, it seems sensible to begin with answers to what we called the particular questions, so that there will be some clear trends to comment on when it comes to possible answers to the general questions. One thing needs to be borne in mind: though the elements of language are separated into the phonological, semantic, and syntactic for the purposes of discussion, it must always be remembered that in actual use there is no such separation. The child who made the remark about the 'chameleon' (p. 41) was using contrast in all three areas simultaneously. With that word of caution we can begin by looking at what is generally agreed about the child's acquisition of the sound system of his language, that is, his phonological development.

Before listing, in chronological order, what appear to be the child's achievements, we should be clear about what exactly it is in the field of phonology that he must eventually acquire. What are the possible contrasts available to him in the sound system of his language?

First there are the contrasts between individual segments. If ten speakers from different parts of the United Kingdom were asked to say the word 'mate', for example, it is more than likely that they would pronounce the **vowel** in different ways. Their pronunciation would differ in respect of that particular segment. On the other hand, there would be enough similarity between speaker and speaker for us to say that we had heard the same word in each case, and not 'meet' or 'mite'. That is, there would be a collection or family of different **phones** that all make up the same **phoneme**. It is the contrast between phonemes that children must learn to detect in the speech of others and to produce – with communicative intent – themselves. Phonemes are defined by Hartmann and Stork as 'a class of sounds treated as equivalent by a language'.[24] David McNeill describes a phoneme as 'a meaningless sound used to distinguish meaningful messages'.[25] Take as an example, 'We were drinking tots [or lots] of rum'. Here the phonemes /t/ and /l/, though meaningless in themselves, vitally affect the sense. In the case of vowels the stream of air used in speaking is virtually unobstructed in its outward passage, whereas in the case of **consonants** there is obstruction at some point in the vocal tract above the glottis. There are other contrasts within the general categories of vowels and consonants. Take the words 'fun' and 'gun', for example, and the consonants with which they begin, /f/ and /g/ respectively: /f/ is produced at the front of the mouth, it is a **continuant** (we don't stop the flow of air completely), and it is **unvoiced** (there are no vibrations of the vocal cords); /g/, on the other hand, is a back consonant, it is a **stop consonant** and it is **voiced**. If instead of 'gun' we had chosen the word 'sun' there would have been the same things to say about the /s/ as about the /f/, but we should have had to go into further detail about how the two sounds were made (by what use of which parts of which speech organs the sound was produced) to differentiate them further.

There are three main areas of contrast, then: where a sound is made; how it is made; whether or not it is voiced. There are other contrasts to learn about vowels. Because we have learned to make and detect contrasts in consonant sounds, we can differentiate between the two statements:

'He bought his wife a chop'.

'He bought his wife a shop'.

However, there are contrasts that extend beyond the single segments of the phoneme. We can recognise syllables (any speaker of English is unlikely to have difficulty in saying how many syllables there are in 'bigamy' or 'elementary'), and we can stress some more than others, as witness such familiar schoolroom exercises as 'Use the word "refuse" in two different ways'. Ask any native speaker of English to pronounce such a series of words as 'photograph', 'photography', 'photographic', and he will shift the stress systematically and without thought, according to strict rules that he does not know that he knows. The child must learn the contrasts in **stress**, then.

Finally there is intonation. On paper the utterance 'You've won the pools' looks like a statement, but any of us can deliver it as a question merely by changing the intonation pattern when we say it. Every time we speak or listen, it is partly through these contrasts in individual phonemes, in stress, and in intonation, that meaning is being conveyed; and it is the task of every child to learn them.

The reference to meaning in the last sentence is particularly important when one is considering what is generally agreed about the child's acquisition of phonology. Children are making sounds from the outset: what is at issue in the debate about pre-speech and speech is not merely the making of sounds that contrast in any of the ways outlined above, but making sounds that contrast significantly and convey an intended meaning. A child may make sounds that correspond to phonemes in adult speech or to the 'tunes' that signal questions or statements, but unless there is communicative intent, he is no more talking than a parrot is. As long as sounds are being made without deliberate or meaningful use of contrast (even if they are sounds that occur in normal speech), there is no question of the child's performance being linguistic. The distinction between the pre-linguistic and the **linguistic** can be borne in mind as we look at what the child achieves in the first year of life.

No one would dispute that the first sound the child utters is the cry at birth, and equally no one would ascribe to the child at this point any intention to communicate. For at least another two months the same kind of cry will be the main sound, to be supplemented eventually by what Lewis (1936) calls the comfort and discomfort noises. These, again, are involuntary sounds made because of the child's physical state. Such sounds may tell us certain things about the child, but this is very different from saying that the child is telling us anything: we are still a long way from intention to communicate. During this time (as early as the second week of life according to some authorities) the child appears to respond selectively to the sound of the human voice, in contrast with other sounds in his environment.

The next significant development is that the child begins to show

59

greater variation in the pitch of the sounds he is making, continuing this tendency in the next stage, that of **babbling**, a process that appears to take up a good part of the second six months. We are all familiar with this kind of 'scribble talk', in which the child uses unintelligible combinations of sounds that still seem a little like language because they preserve the intonations of normal speech. It has been suggested that this is a kind of vocal play, possibly a bridge between the pre-linguistic period and genuine speech. Ervin-Tripp (1966) suggests that the sounds are at first vowel-like, to be supplemented later by consonant-like sounds made in the throat and at the back of the mouth. Voicing comes later, and a common feature is reduplication of syllables, as in 'dada'. She stresses that babbling includes sounds and sequences of sounds that are not found in the speech of the parents. It is generally agreed that babbling is what has been called 'a self-directed activity', carried out by children playing with sounds, experimenting with them, not attempting to set up some form of interaction with others – though the listening adult may well try to initiate some form of 'dialogue' that will be a model of interaction to come. Many writers stress the discontinuity between the babbling stage and later stages in that there is no apparent connection between the sounds produced in babbling and the phonemes that will have to be learned in the language proper. In fact it has been pointed out that children will produce sounds in the babbling stage that will be among the last to be produced in their speech, and even some that just do not occur in the language they are learning. The final stage of the pre-linguistic period is marked by the child's obvious comprehension of what is being said to him, and by what appear to be increasing attempts to imitate what he hears.

Of the areas of contrast, then, it seems that children gain some control over the 'suprasegmental' elements like stress and intonation before the 'segmental' ones like phonemes, but this is not to say that at this stage they have mastered the system of intonation: the contrast only becomes linguistically significant when it is used to signal meaning. In the same way, much has been written about the order of appearance of particular sounds in child speech, but we must be careful not to confuse such sounds with phonemes. When we hear a child saying 'dadada' in his pram, irrespective of audience and situation, we can credit him with the ability to utter two distinct sounds. However, this is not the same as his having acquired two phonemes that he can use in contrast with others to form words. It is generally agreed, in fact, that in the first year of life children begin by producing vowel-like sounds at the front of the mouth and gradually begin to make such sounds increasingly farther back, while their consonant-like sounds start at the back and are gradually moved forward. This contrasts with what appears to happen in the second year of life when the first phonemes acquired are likely to be a front consonant and a back vowel (as in 'mama' or 'dada'), and differentiation proceeds in the reverse direction.

The development of a system of phonemes by the child clearly illustrates what would be accepted as a general principle of language acquisition, namely that children produce their own systems. Adult English calls upon forty-three phonemes, all of which the child must eventually acquire. One possibility could be for children to master each of these in turn. What appears to happen is that children set up their own limited sets of contrasting phonemes, none of which is an exact replica of any in the adult system. Such a set could exemplify one kind of contrast like consonant/vowel allied to another kind of contrast, front/back, producing front consonant/back vowel. Velten (1943) drew attention to this: his child had a word 'ba', with the first consonant /b/ being a front consonant, and the vowel /a/ a back vowel.

Then a further contrast could be added, like voiced/unvoiced. Thus, more than pure imitation is involved: it is as though the child had grasped a general principle. Once such a process is under way, there is the problem for the child of producing his versions of adult vocabulary, and again there appears to be a predictable path of approximation. As well as there being a probable order of emergence of individual phonemes in a child's speech (e.g. stops like /p/ and /b/ earlier than **fricatives** like /f/), there are also modifications of sounds that occur in clusters such as /sp/ and /sm/: 'poon' for 'spoon' and 'thmoke' for 'smoke'.

In summary, therefore, one could answer some of the questions posed earlier as follows: there does seem to be a fairly invariant order of acquisition of the sound system of the language that can be described in two stages, the pre-linguistic and the linguistic. Of the former, Ervin-Tripp has this to say:

'Within this period of a year or so, three stages have been noted: first a period of organically based sounds; next, extensive vocal play and babbling; and finally evidence of imitative behaviour and speech which seems intentional because of its situational distribution.'[26]

It is not the case that children first acquire the smallest unit – the phoneme – and then go on to the 'suprasegmental' like the intonation patterns. In fact, during the pre-linguistic period, the child appears to play with these patterns, as well as with particular sounds. As for the linguistic period, there is again an order of acquisition of particular phonemes, though such a description can be misleading if it conveys the impression of the child laboriously imitating an adult system, one item at a time, rather than using the general principle of phonemic contrast to set up systems of his own. The whole process is nothing like as continuous as may be supposed: babbling is universal, but there is no evidence to show that it is connected in any direct or discernible way with the development that occurs in the linguistic period. Finally, there is some evidence that children can understand speech before they can speak themselves.

We come now to what was described by Dale (1972) as 'the least understood aspect of language acquisition', semantic development. His view is shared by others, among them David McNeill, who speaks of it as 'at once the most pervasive and the least understood aspect of language acquisition'.[27]

It is not that there is any shortage of data – collecting and counting children's words has always been a popular activity – but that there is no generally-accepted theory that satisfactorily describes even the adult's knowledge of the semantic system of his language. Vocabulary alone, of course, will be inadequate to account for meaning, as was pointed out in the previous chapter (p. 32): syntax, too, plays its part. There is the further complication that cognition is involved. As Dale says:

'Learning a word meaning is basically a problem of concept formation.'[28]

One has only to consider the contrasting views of Piaget and Vygotsky on the relationship between language and thought to realise how complex an area this is, and how great the divergence of opinion can be. Certainly, in the last five years, the problem has received increasing attention.

In such a complex area, what has the child to learn? A repertoire of words, certainly; but more than that, an increasing number of meanings for each word, and an increasing number of relationships between words. There must also be some way of combining the meanings of the separate words when they are used in sentences. We may begin with the first words that children acquire. These will not necessarily be accurate versions of adult words, as a glance at almost any of the studies will show. What matters is whether the child is consistently producing a sound pattern in a particular context in such a way as to convince the adult that a particular meaning is intended. When a child at the zoo referred to all four-footed animals that he saw as 'mum', it was reasonable to assume that he had both a criterion for classifying them, and a word for expressing the category that he had created.

If we consider that young children the world over spend the first year of their lives under much the same constraints – dependence on adults, and restriction to their immediate environment, which includes people as well as objects – it will not be surprising if the first words that they use come from a fairly restricted set of possibilities: words for objects in the immediate environment, for things in pictures, for food, for parts of their bodies, for the people closely related to them. One crucial factor could be what has been called 'perceptual salience': things in the world have colour, distinctive size, shape, texture; they can move or make noises; and the child's attention may be drawn to any of these attributes. The child's vocabulary development is thought to move from the concrete to the abstract.

Once a child begins to use words, there are two questions to be answered:

1 What is the relationship between the word as the child uses it, and as an adult uses it?
2 How is the child's meaning developed?

As to the first it is natural to assume that there will be some overlap between child and adult use, since both have the same environment and the same senses with which to perceive it. But if we think back to the 'rabbit' example (pp. 28–9), and to others in the previous chapter, it could be the case that children are engaged in a lengthy and complicated process of building up a dictionary, of a kind far more complex than many of us suppose. It is mere commonsense to assume, therefore, that at first the 'entries' in a child's dictionary will be few and rudimentary, and that there is little likelihood that when we hear him use a word he is using it with anything like our sense of its manifold potentialities. The differences usually singled out in the literature on this subject are two: **overextension** and **narrowing**.

The first is one we have all encountered. 'Doggy' says the child, as a dog runs by, and we assume that there is one word mastered, until perhaps a cat or a horse or a cow is similarly greeted, and we realise that, like the 'mum' already quoted, this item represents a generalisation about four-footed animals and not a label for a single species. This brings out what is stressed in the literature, that **ostension** (pointing to things and saying their names, and encouraging children to repeat the name words) is not as simple a process as it appears. We, the adults, with our language learning behind us and unaware of the complexities of language, happily point to a duck and give it its generic title, 'seeing' it now as language has helped us to see it. The bill, the webbed feet, the ability to swim, and to fly, the fact that it is a bird, and that it is in particular a mallard: these and many other attributes of the creature before us are available if we wish to refer to them, just as the word 'duck' has other meanings for us unconnected with birds at all. But to the child, with the whole set of attributes to choose from, it is by no means as obvious that what is being pointed out is the whole creature. See something, and make a noise to refer to it: that is a principle children may have grasped and be working on, but that they should always hit upon the same attribute as the adult with his wider choice would be too much to hope for. The same will apply to the adult seeking to interpret the child's meaning correctly.

No wonder then that the literature on the subject is full of examples of overextension. Here are a few taken from a table produced by Eve Clark:

'fly'	First applied to a fly, and then successively to: specks of dirt; dust; all small insects; his own toes; crumbs of bread; a small toad.
'bird'	First applied to sparrows, and then successively to: cows; dogs; cats; any animal moving.
'mooi'	First applied to the moon, and then successively to: round marks on windows and in books; round shapes in books etc.[29]

In the first example it is size that is the basis of the child's category, in the second example it is movement, and in the third it is shape. A recent example also based on shape is that of a child seeing some Calor Gas containers and saying 'Billy cans'.

In contrast to overextension we have the other process of narrowing, in which the child restricts the reference of a word in a way that the adult would not. There is the instance of the child who had two words for milk depending on whether it was in a cup or in a bottle, or another child who rejected her father's use of 'white' to describe paper, because she used the word to signify milk. Both processes illustrate once again that children's language development is an idiosyncratic and an active process, far removed from passive imitation.

The picture, then, is one of progressive differentiation of the child's categories until they correspond to those of the adult and all the types of relationship are employed and understood; not simply **synonymy** and **antonymy**, but **inclusion** or **hyponomy** also (i.e. the relationship between 'animal' and such words as 'horse', 'cat', 'elephant').

Precisely how the development takes place is by no means certain. It has been suggested that at first the child is using words to express some need ('more' or 'up' for example), rather than to describe or refer to something, and that development will consist partly in making this transition. Dale suggests that the three stages of symbolic development proposed by Piaget are also good descriptions of early semantic development. These are:

1 The pre-symbolic stage in which there is no substitution of one action or object for another.

2 A symbolic stage in which, while symbols are used, they are personal to the child, and not shared with others. (He gives the example of a child who pretends that a piece of cloth is a pillow. Here there is one thing symbolising another, but you will remember that when we looked at definitions of language (p. 40) the symbols of language were said to be arbitrary in that they had no necessary resemblance to what they symbolised.)

3 A stage at which signs are used that are both shared and arbitrary.[30]

As for the methods by which the child is helped to develop his vocabulary, pointing has already been discussed; and defining words is not thought to be either as frequent or as helpful as might be supposed. One device that can be seen throughout the transcripts in this book is that of the child questioning the adult, and this may well be more effective than the converse, because so often the adult appears content to elicit the word he himself uses, and to leave it at that, whereas the child can follow up the answers with another question.

One point of agreement in the literature is that semantic development is, by contrast with the frequently asserted speed of syntactic development, a very slow business. This is not surprising when one considers that what is to be learned is so complex.

Finally, in this consideration of answers to questions about particular aspects of language acquisition, there is syntax, the area that has received so much attention during the last fifteen years. There was a time when it appeared to be enough to chart increases in the average utterance length of children at various stages – as if one could ever hope to learn much from any method that lumped together utterances different in structure and intention merely because of their not very interesting identity of length! But all that has changed. If semantic development is little understood partly because there is a lack of well-developed models of semantic knowledge, the study of syntactic development suffers from no such disability. Whatever one's view of Chomsky's model of language, it is indisputable that it suggested to students of children's language development new and potentially fruitful ways of looking at the subject, and its influence, whether direct or indirect, as rival models are proposed and applied to the field, has scarcely abated. This in itself leads to a difficulty in the writing of a summary. When it comes to the section on theories of language acquisition, there can be no question of omitting Chomsky's views. But to do justice to his model of transformational–generative grammar would require half a book, let alone half a chapter, while potted summaries can be scarcely less daunting and nowhere near as effective. The reader should be aware, therefore, that what follows will be as accurate as can be, without attempting to enter into the full technicalities of what has been a major shaping influence.

There is one further problem, and that is the word 'syntax' itself. So far we have been looking at sounds and, on the whole, the meaning of individual words, both areas familiar enough for us not to be worried by the technical terms 'phonology' and 'semantics'. 'Syntax' is another matter. We may have heard it at school, probably linked with 'grammar', and could well find it not only rather uninteresting but also unclear. Quite simply, it means the arrangement of words in sentences to express relationships and, however vague and imperfect we feel our conscious knowledge of it to be, our unconscious, unreflecting knowledge of what turns out to be a highly complex area is correspondingly detailed and elaborate. It has to be for us to use language effectively.

Here are a few examples of what we know without necessarily having been taught. Which of these two arrangements of words would you regard as normal English?

Of the was hosepipes banned use.

The use of hosepipes was banned.

The first is meaningless, but the second is an acceptable sentence because its word order is the normal one and therefore signals a meaning to us.

Next look at the following sentence:

Birds lay eggs.

and decide who does the action of laying. Obviously the birds. But why 'obviously'? Because we all know that birds lay eggs, it may be argued, and that is a matter of knowledge of the world and not of syntax. In that case, try the next example:

Arprins gaboon skronties.

Who or what performs the action of 'gabooning'? Obviously the arprins. But this time it is not because of our existing knowledge of arprins that it is obvious, since they were unknown to both reader and writer until they first appeared on this page. The knowledge that helps us so confidently to make the arprins the performers of the action is our knowledge of syntax, in this case of word order. Skronties get gabooned, and gabooning is what arprins do, and assigning arprins and gabooning and skronties to their roles in sentences is what human beings can do, because in English, and some other languages, word order signals the grammatical relationships between subjects and verbs, and between verbs and **objects**. We need never know the word 'subject' or 'object', or have much success with the grammar exercises of the classroom, but subjects and objects in their relations to verbs we nevertheless manipulate all our lives without having to think about it.

Word order also signals other things. When we were discussing the child's acquisition of phonology, we suggested that one way of signalling a question was by using a particular intonation. Another is by changing the order of words in the sentence.

Consider the following sentences:

The man in the mask was never captured.

Was the man in the mask never captured?

If the second sentence had been printed without the question mark we should still have known that it was a question because of the order of the words. Grammarians can write extremely complicated rules to show the relationship between sentences like the two above, but speakers of English can produce such sentences without knowing *how* they do it.

Take this sentence and produce the corresponding question form:

The many people in the audience who had no sympathy with

his views were beginning to grow impatient.

So far, so simple. Now try to explain *how* you did it, imagining that you are explaining the rule to a foreigner, and you will realise that what you have learned is more complex than you thought. 'Learned' is the important word here, because this is something that you were not taught.

Word order is one way of expressing the relationship between words in sentences. We are also accustomed to using what we called earlier the 'little words' like 'in' and 'of'. But there is another set of signals that we use. If someone said to you, 'What is the meaning of "horse"?' you would find no problem in giving an answer, nor would you if the word was one less obviously concrete (like 'more'). But suppose the question had been, 'What is the meaning of "-ed" or "-ing"?' These are not words at all, but parts of words, and yet we use them also to express our meaning. In the sentence, 'I wanted to go home', we know that the wanting happened in the past because of the **morpheme** /-ed/, in the same way as in 'The kettle's boiling', the /-ing/ is one of the signals that the action is ongoing as the person speaks. It will be helpful in understanding the summary that follows if we keep in mind these two devices for expressing relationships: word order and the use of morphemes.

Having already considered what is agreed about the order of acquisition in phonology and semantics, we shall begin with the same topic in relation to syntax. To the question, 'Is there a fixed order in the acquisition of syntax?' the provisional answer can be 'Yes'. It is true that all children go through the stage of using one-word utterances, passing on to sentences made up of two and then three words. It is also the case that at first they express the various relationships, both syntactic and semantic, simply by juxtaposing words in normal order and without using inflexions. When children begin to use inflexions there is, according to Roger Brown (1973), an order in which they learn to do so. When their sentences become longer and more complex there is a discernible path of development for such processes as asking questions or using negatives. We can look at some of these stages in more detail, starting with the use of one word at a time.

Immediately there is a problem, not because there is any dispute about whether children do begin to speak in this way, but because we have been discussing syntax in terms of relationships between words in sentences, and here we are looking at single words. The traditional approach has been to class these utterances as one-word sentences on the grounds that parents treat them as such when they hold a conversation with their children. The usual term for what have been variously described as 'sentence-words' or 'sentence-like words' is holophrase, and there is the corresponding expression **holophrastic speech**. A holophrase has been defined as 'a word which expresses on its own the meaning of an entire sentence'.[31]

In the words of Halliday 'the lexical item forms by itself an utterance that is functionally independent and complete.'[32] David McNeill tells us that holophrastic speech 'means that children are limited phonologically to uttering single words at the beginning of language acquisition, even though they are capable of conceiving of something like full sentences.'[33] There is no agreement at all about what grammatical knowledge these single word utterances represent.

Let us begin, therefore, by stating what is less controversial. Most writers agree on the time at which the child begins to employ holophrases – about twelve months – and accept that this will be immediately after the babbling stage, and that babbling and the use of holophrases may overlap. The single words themselves will not belong exclusively to a particular class, like nouns, and will often be said with an intonation that suggests that a statement or a question or a command is being produced. Children will often use the words to express their emotional states. While it is important not to equate the holophrase with some simple naming process, naming will be one of the things the child will learn to do with the single word. Bloom also suggests that the child goes beyond this when he learns to use a word like 'Mommy' to refer to a number of different items that are connected with the mother, the inference being that the use of the single word is evidence that the child has formed an idea of possession.

This brings us back to the question of interpretation, and hence to controversy. Roger Brown, for example, does not share others' optimism about demonstrating that children have semantic intentions which are more advanced than their linguistic expression. 'However, some very clever people are convinced that it can be done, even that it has been done. I myself think that as of 1971 it still has not been done.'[34] For him the danger is of over-interpreting the data. Adults, in the same situation as the child, who is in any case constrained by the here and now of the physical environment, are responding to all the elements in the situation, and not to the child's one word only, and may be crediting him, without justification, with skill in communicating (and even with the intention to communicate). There are others who would claim otherwise.

If we imagine a sentence as having two elements – one the topic (the subject that is announced), and the other the comment (the statement that is being made about it) – then in an adult sentence like 'The postman came today', 'the postman' would be the topic, and 'came today' the comment. One view of the holophrase is that it is really a comment on an unstated topic, unstated for the reason that it is palpably there to be commented upon.

You may have noticed that, in discussing the holophrase, which is an element in the child's development of syntax, we have made various references to semantic intentions. This shows that the dividing line between the two areas is less clearly drawn than might be imagined and also reflects the recent trend in the study of the early sentences of children to concentrate on the relationship between linguistic and cognitive development. It is important to realise that the holophrase, far from being uncontroversial, is likely to be the subject of a good deal of further investigation and speculation. (See Bloom, 1973.)

It is when children first begin to put words together to form primitive sentences that interest and controversy increase. Here are some typical utterances taken from several different sources in the literature: those in (a) are imitations of adult remarks that have just been addressed to the children, while those in (b) are spontaneous:

a.

Read book.	See cow.
This book.	Big one.
Is broken?	Fraser unhappy.
This ring.	No shoe.

b.

Baby high chair.	Sweater chair.
Sat wall.	No wash.
See ball.	Throw daddy.
Mommy sock.	More outside.

It is immediately obvious to any adult speaker of English that these are child utterances of the kind that we are accustomed to hearing from children between the ages of about eighteen and twenty-four months. What is more, there appears to be no great difference between the two lists in the respects in which we can now discuss them.

70

First of all, even without full details of the situation in which they were uttered, we can form a pretty good idea of what the various children were trying to say. These are not random juxtapositions of words. They certainly do not sound like the English that we ourselves speak, but one feels that the two forms are not unconnected. For one thing, these utterances preserve the normal order of words, and this is an important way of signalling relationships between words. For another, they are obviously made up of vocabulary items from the adult system.

In what ways, then, do they differ systematically from adult English? The best way of settling this question would be to do with any of them what, as adults in contact with children, one would do without thinking: expand them. Thus, we might have such expansions as:

child	expansion
Read book	You're reading a book?
Throw daddy	Throw it to daddy
Baby high-chair	Baby's in the high-chair.

There may also be many other different expansions, such as 'Read book/Read the book to me'.

If we try to decide what we are supplying in these expansions, we shall find several of the things that were discussed when syntax was being defined. The 'little words', for example, like 'a' and 'the', 'in' and 'to', and the morphemes like '-ing'. We should be doing in reverse what we do when writing a telegram – putting back the very words that then we would miss out – hence Brown's characterisation of this kind of speech as telegraphic (Brown and Fraser, 1963). This might lead us to believe that the relationship between child and adult language is merely one of imitation to model, but although we must believe that there is certainly a systematic relationship between the two, there is more to it than that. Such expressions as 'More outside', like so many in children's speech, are inventions rather than bad imitations, and the creativity of child speech is generally acknowledged.

Suppose we adopt what Jean Aitchison calls the 'Let's pretend he's talking Martian' technique,[35] and try to discuss the grammatical aspects of the utterances without reference to their meaning. What grammatical knowledge can we ascribe to these speakers? To answer this we need to look briefly at our own grammatical knowledge.

It was suggested earlier that, as native speakers of English, we have to be able to understand the grammatical relationships between words in sentences. It is time to be a little more specific. When we look at a list of words such as 'man', 'eat', and 'shark', they may have meaning of sorts for us, but it is only when combined into certain patterns that they become really meaningful, as in 'The shark ate the man,' or 'The man ate the shark.'

Word order tells us that in the first sentence it is the shark, in the second sentence the man, that does the eating. We are dealing with two grammatical relationships here: subject of verb and object of verb. The subject in the first sentence is 'The shark' and the object is 'the man'. In the second sentence it is the other way round. Once again, this is not a matter of conscious knowledge to be tested in the classroom, but of something that is essential to our production and understanding of sentences. If we take the following list of words: 'rabbit', 'rain', 'New York', 'impetuosity', 'gold', and try to determine what they have in common, we might well classify them in various ways according to what they mean. But put them into sentences as follows: 'A rabbit lives in a burrow', 'Rain stopped play', 'New York is in America', 'Impetuosity will be your undoing', 'Gold is more precious than silver', and we can say something about them that, as in the 'arprins' sentence on p. 67, does not depend on our knowing what they mean: we can say that they are all the subjects of their respective sentences. In other words, we are classifying them by relying on an abstract criterion.

The point of this brief excursion into grammar is to make it possible to answer the question, 'What grammatical knowledge can we ascribe to the children who produced the two-word sentences on page 70?' With the usual warnings about the dangers of over-interpretation, we can examine them for evidence of the child having acquired a knowledge of grammatical relationships. For example, 'This book' and 'This ring' might both have 'This' as subject of an unstated verb ('is'). In 'Read book' and 'See cow' and 'See ball' the pattern could be verb/object. Presumably, when the remarks were made the listening adults reacted to them in ways that would have suggested to us as observers whether or not they thought the utterances expressed these relationships.

All that has been said so far reflects an attitude of treating the child's language as something worthy of consideration as a system in its own right, whatever its relation to adult language, and this is very much in the spirit of the work of the 1960s, when there was a great concentration on finding the best ways of representing the systematic divergencies of child language from the adult forms. One well-known, but now less acceptable, formulation was that of Martin Braine, whose pivot/open description was very influential. He was drawing attention to the fact that the words in children's speech at the two-word stage seemed to fall into two categories, a small class of words that were used frequently, apparently in fixed positions (the pivot class), and another class with more members that occurred less frequently (the open class). Although there have been various objections to the accuracy of his description since it was first formulated, it did serve to draw attention to certain regularities in child speech that any description and theory will have to take into account. Roger Brown's 'telegraphic' characterisation has also been influential, although he has since advanced good reasons for rejecting it. The other, and probably the most, influential approach has been that of transformational-generative grammar which has led to the search for knowledge of the underlying structure of sentences and of the operations that lie behind the production of negatives, passives, interrogatives and so on.

If we go back to the list of two-word sentences on p. 70, and ask what else there is to say about them in terms of relationships expressed, it may seem that the earlier formulation of grammatical relationships expressed by word order and other devices such as morphemes exhausts the possibilities, because word order and grammatical relationships have been discussed, and in these sentences there are no morphemes like /-ed/ or /-ing/. And yet few of us would feel that what has been said so far does justice to the communicative ability of the children quoted.

Are there not other relationships that these children are also capable of expressing? This is exactly the question that certain people began to ask themselves about the data that others had characterised in the ways mentioned, with deliberate exclusion of semantic considerations.

In 'Big one', for example, is it possible that the child has grasped the idea of modifying one word by preposing another? Is 'No shoe' not evidence that the idea of non-existence is being expressed? And what of 'Throw daddy'? No one would suggest that daddy was to be thrown, in which case is not 'daddy' the person to whom something must be thrown? Similarly, in 'Sat wall' is not 'wall' the place where someone sat?

The point to note is that our expansion of these utterances would express the suggested relationships by using such devices as prepositions ('*on* the wall', '*to* daddy'), but apparently the child has grasped the relationship before he has mastered the linguistic means of signalling it.

That is why there was dissatisfaction with the pivot/open classification which could group together two expressions because they consisted of juxtaposed nouns, whereas, as the above examples make clear, they might express quite different semantic intentions. There is a sentence in the literature that has become famous — 'Mommy sock', quoted by Bloom[36] — because a child used it to express two quite different things. In one case it was clear from the context (which is so often part of the message) that possession was signified (i.e. 'Mommy's sock'), while on the other occasion the child meant 'Mommy is putting my sock on for me'. This is further illustration of the current trend, to see the division between semantic and syntactic as blurred, and to look beyond purely linguistic considerations to the cognitive development that may underlie linguistic achievement.

Such an approach would encourage us to look for relationships to be expressed partly by word order or word juxtaposition, like those just quoted, but also by the use of particular words like 'more' or 'no'. Here is a list of eleven kinds of structural meaning suggested by Brown as being characteristic of the two-word sentences of what he calls Stage 1 (defined as the period in which the child's mean length of utterance rises above 1·0 word and ends at 2·0). He divides them into 'operations of reference', where a constant term precedes another word, and 'relations', where there is no repeated word and an abstract semantic relation is expressed by juxtaposing two words.

1 Operations of reference
   Nominations: 'That' (or 'it' or 'there') + book, cat, clown, hot, big
   Notice: 'Hi' = Mommy, cat, belt
   Recurrence: 'More' (or 'nother') + milk, cereal, nut, read, swing, green
   Nonexistence: 'Allgone' (or 'no-more') + rattle, juice, dog, green

2 Relations
   Attributive: Adjective + Noun (big train, red book)
   Possessive: Noun + Noun (Adam checker, Mommy lunch)
   Locative: Noun + Noun (sweater chair, book table)
   Locative: Verb + Noun (walk street, go store)
   Agent–Action: Noun + Verb (Adam put, Eve read)
   Agent–Object: Noun + Noun (Mommy sock, Mommy lunch)

Action–Object: Verb + Noun (put book, hit ball)[37]

This shows how unrevealing it would be to classify utterances merely by specifying the kind of words of which they were composed: look at the second group and see how many different relations are expressed by the noun + noun configuration, for instance.

What is happening in the classification above is that the utterance is being treated as it would be by a parent, who would attribute a meaning to it like 'possessive' because of the context in which it was made. There is a distinction to be made between grammatical relations, like subject/verb, and what Brown calls semantic roles, like agent/action, but the distinction would take many pages to explain. It is sufficient to be aware of the important trend in the study of two-word sentences towards looking at the meanings expressed by the structures used by children.

Roger Brown (1973) sees these meanings as extensions of what Piaget calls 'sensori-motor intelligence', the achievement of which, according to Piaget, is to 'construct reality', so that the child has meanings available for representation in language symbols when he begins to construct his first sentences.

Whether one speaks of grammatical relationships or semantic roles, it is not difficult to predict what will happen when children begin to put three words together. For one thing it will be possible to produce the pattern subject–verb–object, as in these children's sentences: 'I | giving | food.' 'Doggy | chase | me.'

For another, one would expect to see developments in phrase structure. Compare these two sentences, one from a child, one from an adult:

Dolly eat that.

The river burst its banks.

In terms of pattern they are identical – subject–verb–object – but look at the phrases representing the elements 'subject', 'verb', 'object':

subject: 'Dolly' / 'the river'
verb: 'eat' / 'burst'
object: 'that' / 'its banks'.

The telegraphic appearance of the child's sentence is due in part to the fact that each phrase in it consists of one word, whereas we find the adult sentence normal because of the greater elaboration of the phrases that go to make it up. The child's first phrase, 'Dolly', is a **noun phrase** consisting of the single noun: the adult uses a noun but qualifies it with 'the'. One would expect to see the process of expanding the noun phrase as one of the next stages in the development of children's language, and this turns out to be the case. Braine quotes the following examples showing that such a process takes place. He calls them 'replacement sequences', because the child first uses the more rudimentary form, and then replaces it with the fuller one.

Truck fall down.   Big truck fall down.
Yellow balloon.   Two yellow balloon.[38]

Other examples, but this time of development over a longer period, are these from Brown and Bellugi. The left-hand column shows expressions in which a noun is used as an element, while the right-hand column shows how a noun phrase is now being used in the same way.

Noun positions	Noun phrase positions
That (flower)	That (a blue flower)
Where (ball) go?	Where (the puzzle) go?
Adam write (penguin)	Doggie eat (the breakfast)
(Horsie) stop	(A horsie) crying
Put (hat) on	Put (the red hat) on

N.B. the words within the brackets were not in brackets in the original.[39]

It should be clear from all that has been said about these early sentences that at this stage, as at every other, children are behaving in anything but a haphazard way. It is as though they are constantly looking for regularities in the language that they are learning and systematically building up productive rules. You will probably have noticed that the expressions in the noun-phrase list above contain the morphemes and 'little words' that were missing at an earlier stage, and it is believed that this is the feature of the next stage. According to Roger Brown (1973), children begin to 'modulate the meanings' within sentences by using such devices as morphemes (e.g. /-s/ for plurals and /-ing/ to signal the present progressive of verbs, as in 'going'), the verb 'to be' (e.g. 'It's a truck') and prepositions like 'in' and 'on'.

So far the sentences have been mainly **simple sentences** making statements. From now onwards the chief developments will be of two kinds: first the child will learn to produce other kinds of simple sentence, such as questions or negatives; next will come the combining of sentences in various ways. Further details of some of these processes will be given in the commentaries on the Helen transcripts (chapters 8–12), but before leaving the area of syntax we can stress two points yet again.

When we looked at the growth of word meaning for children we noticed that over-extension was common. Something similar happens when children are learning grammar: they tend to generalise a rule and then apply it inappropriately. Adding '-ed' to signal past tense works well for the many **weak verbs** of the English language, like 'walk' for example, but when it comes to the **strong verbs** like 'swim' or 'come' we have to use a different system. Children regularly begin by saying 'came' and 'swam', but pass through a stage when the influence of the other, and more productive, rule is too strong, and forms like 'comed' and 'swimmed' are common.

That is one example of the child's rule not conforming to our own, but there are other examples that show much more strikingly how children seem to grasp a principle in advance of controlling the normal linguistic means of expressing it. The use of word order at the two-word sentence stage comes into that category, of course. The emergence of the negative is another case that has been studied in detail, and it has been shown that children pass through clearly marked stages, in the course of which they say things that are not imitations of adult English. Klima and Bellugi studied the negatives of the Harvard children Adam, Eve and Sarah, and observed the following phases:

1 'No sit there.'   Put 'no' in front of the whole sentence
2 'I no want envelope.'   Put the negative word after the first noun phrase
3 'You didn't caught me.'   Put the negative as the third element in the sentence, after an auxiliary like 'did' or 'can', or after 'to be'.[40]

Children are not so much playing a game badly as working out the rules of the game. One thing that we must be on the look out for is any sign that, though the same resources are being used, the child has begun to use them to express a new function. As Slobin says, 'new forms first express old functions and new functions are first expressed by old forms.'[41] Bloom pointed out that the children she studied used one word – 'no' – in three ways.

Nonexistence: 'No more juice' ('The juice has gone')
Denial: 'No truck' (Her mother had stated that there was one)
Rejection: 'No dirty soap' (The child did not want the worn soap).[42]

The answer to the earlier question, whether there are discernible stages in the acquisition, must be 'Yes', therefore, but that does not mean that the stages are clear-cut and separate. In all the literature one can find instances of the coexistence of new and old forms, until the new form takes over.

There is one question that we have not considered at all so far, and that is the relationship between what children can understand and what they can say. It has been customary to say that children's comprehension of speech is in advance of their production, but increasingly of late one finds assertions to the contrary. Martin Braine sums up his discussion of the question as follows: 'In summary, the data reviewed seem to indicate rather conclusively that there is no large difference between sentence reception and production, insofar as the control of grammar is concerned. The possibility of a small difference in favour of reception is still open, but it is clearly going to be difficult to demonstrate.'[43]

It only remains now to return to the general questions about language development in the light of what has been said about particular aspects.

Does virtually every child learn a language? Yes.

When does the process begin and end? Rather earlier and later than has been supposed, if we remember on the one hand what we said about the child's response to adult speech and apparent understanding of it before using words, and on the other, the slowness of development of word meanings and Carol Chomsky's findings about children's understanding of syntax.

Is there a fixed order of acquisition? To a very large extent, yes: think of what was said about the acquisition of both phonology and syntax, for example.

Can children make themselves understood at each stage? Emphatically, yes. Not only do adults appear to assume that children intend meanings every time they speak and, as Roger Brown (1973) points out, children appear to take it for granted that they will be understood, but we have noticed that children seem to be able to get by with whatever set of resources they have currently acquired.

Is children's language an imperfect imitation of the adult model, or is it autonomous, a language in its own right? Certainly it is not mere imitation because there are far too many examples of patterns that children could not possibly have heard from adults, and we must credit them with some degree of the creativity that is an essential feature of all language use. But neither is children's language entirely *sui generis*: one can see in it a systematic relationship to the adult form.

Whatever the differences of opinion about details of the process there is general agreement that human language turns out to be highly complex, and the child's achievement in learning it considerable.

e. Theories of language acquisition

The previous section was an attempt to answer the question 'What is acquired?', because one cannot answer the question 'How?' until the 'What?' has been agreed upon. We can now look briefly at two contrasting theories of how language is acquired. The trouble with short summaries is that where opinions are so divided, nothing short of detailed discussion of conflicting points of view will have much value, particularly where the divisions have been deep and the controversy often bitter. In this case there has been a division between those who see language learning as one example of learning as a whole, and therefore to be accounted for by some form of 'learning theory', and those who accept the contention of Chomsky and his followers that language learning is different in kind from other learning, and thus requires a different explanation. We have what Staats calls 'the cognitive–learning schism',[44] between those with a bias towards linguistics and those with a bias towards psychology. Readers are advised to consult the various formulations for themselves, with the warning that there is a tendency in the literature for one side to set up 'straw men' versions of the rival position, the more easily to demolish them.

Let us remind ourselves of some of the facts which any theory of language acquisition must account for. We are often told that man is the talking animal, that language is species-specific: only man uses it. It is also alleged that all children learn to speak, irrespective of their intelligence, without specific teaching, and in a surprisingly short time. There is, too, as we have seen, an order in which language is acquired, and although each child en route to the goal has a different input, the system acquired is the same in all cases. That system is productive in the sense that we could not hope, in the first few years of life, to acquire a repertoire of sentences that would somehow keep us going for the rest of our lives.

The theory must account for the creative aspect of language. Learning to talk, unlike learning to walk (which is also something that we cannot do at birth, but eventually learn to do), does not happen simply with maturation but requires that children are

79

exposed to the speech of other human beings. Only then is it true
that children just cannot help learning to talk.

If we consider learning to be signalled by some change in
behaviour, we can think of various factors that might bring this
change about. There is first of all the kind of behaviour that is
called instinctive. A new-born puppy crawls to its mother's teats
and begins to suck; she has just nipped open the sac in which the
pup was enclosed. In neither case would we regard this as learned
behaviour, but would rather attribute the actions of both creatures
to something they had inherited through their genes. On the other
hand, the same pup will not need to burn his nose twice to learn
that the fireguard is hot; this is something that he learns by being in
contact with his environment. Most people would accept that both
nature and nurture contribute to learning. The dispute will be about
the respective roles of the two factors.

Stimulus-response (S.R.) theories will give the role of experience
pride of place, with learning happening as the consequence of
response to stimuli in the environment. Some versions of the theory
will stress reinforcement as being an important factor. If a
particular response results in some form of reward then that
response is more likely to follow the same stimulus again. As
applied to the learning of language, learning theory sees the child as
a blank page that will gradually be written on in response to
various encounters with the environment. Imitation is regarded as
playing an important part, with the child's imitations being
reinforced by greater success in communicating his needs, or by the
pleasure afforded him by his mother's approval.

The full account is obviously more elaborate and sophisticated
than this, and would reflect most parents' ideas of language learning, with much emphasis on imitation, practice, and correction.

The weakness in this position, for its opponents, is the view of
language upon which it is based. If language is indeed a set of items
sequentially produced, and one can build up associations between
successive items, then an S.R. model of learning has its obvious
attractions. But suppose the model of language is wrong.

Those who support Chomsky's view of language acquisition
would point to several features of language that call for explanation.
One, creativity – the ability to innovate – has been discussed
already. Another is much more revolutionary, and hence more controversial. Look at these sentences:

The missionary was ready to serve.

The police were told to stop drinking after hours.

They fed her dog biscuits.

I object to your driving.

The chances are that you will simply have read them and assigned a meaning to them. Now look at them again and try to assign two meanings to each. They are, in fact, ambiguous. As speakers of English, one of our many abilities is that of hearing (or reading) the same set of symbols and, even with no context to guide us, extracting two different meanings from them. According to Chomsky, every sentence has not just the self-evident single structure that we say or hear, but two structures, a **deep structure** and a **surface structure**.

It is the surface structure that we hear (or see), and it is the underlying deep structure that tells us what the sentence means. The deep structure can be accounted for by the operation of certain rules; other rules will map them into the surface structures. Thus, in the ambiguous sentences above we could say that there are two underlying deep structures for each surface structure.

Here is another argument. You will remember that when discussing the acquisition of syntax we discussed the question of grammatical relationships and looked at some straightforward examples like 'Birds lay eggs'. The kind of sentences that Chomsky asks us to consider are more interesting. Take these, for example – probably the best-known in the literature:

John was easy to please.

John was eager to please.

We could break them down like this:

John | was | easy | to | please

John | was | eager | to | please

and say that they were identical in structure. But if we ask ourselves the question about grammatical relationships, it is a different story.

In the first sentence someone else will do the pleasing; in the second it will be John. This would mean, according to Chomsky, that the two sentences had different deep structures, in one of which 'someone' would be shown as subject, while in the other one John is the subject.

But if this is true, it would mean that as children we heard only surface structures, and yet we acquired a knowledge of the deep structures that underlie surface structures without their being directly accessible. The knowledge that enables us to produce and understand new sentences is stored in the form of 'rules' of a highly specific kind – and not of a kind that would necessarily be expected.

81

If we look at some **declarative** sentences, and then at the **interrogatives** that correspond to them (in Chomsky's terms these would be two surface structures derived from the same deep structure) and try to see the relationship between them, as was suggested on p. 68, we shall arrive eventually at an understanding that there is no simple permutation of single words, but a switching of larger elements. Thus, in:

The man in the mask | was never captured.

it is 'the man in the mask' that changes place with 'was' in the interrogative form:

Was the man in the mask never captured?

while in:

The people in the audience who had no sympathy with his views | were beginning to grow impatient.

it is 'the people in the audience who had no sympathy with his views' changing place with 'were' that makes the interrogative.

The different sets of words preceding 'was' and 'were' respectively are both noun phrases, and so fulfil the conditions for operating a 'rule' such as:

Find the word that follows the first noun phrase and move it to the front of the sentence.

The point that is being made is that to perform this operation and others, as we do many times a day and certainly not merely with sentences we have produced or heard before, we need to 'know' the structure of sentences, because the operations are **structure-dependent**. According to Chomsky such operations are not necessarily simpler or more efficient than others requiring no such knowledge. Once again we have the situation that children need to be able to recognise the constituents of sentences, even though no one has shown them how. They do this as a result of knowledge ('competence' as Chomsky calls it) they have built up merely by being exposed to human speech.

Such a feat of abstraction, so the argument would go, would be possible only if children were pre-programmed to expect the language they were learning to fall within a particular class, using certain elements (like noun phrase) and performing certain operations (like transposing) upon those elements. Since a child will learn whatever language he is exposed to, the programming will have to be such as to make this possible, and one would expect therefore that the apparently diverse languages of the world would turn out to have more in common than has been supposed.

The theory is in fact closely linked with the idea of language universals: language, being the product of the human mind, should bear its imprint; and study of the different languages of the world should show that the elements and operations referred to just now are to be found in all of them. It is not a case of a child being born with an inbuilt grammar of any particular language: what is innate, according to this view, is knowledge of the general form that the elements and operations can take, so that the child's task is then to work out how the language he is learning expresses them. He will thus end up by having internalised a 'grammar' or set of rules that will enable him to go on producing and understanding language for the rest of his life.

How would such a view help to account for some of the features of language and language acquisition that we have been discussing? All children learn language, it would be argued, because they are all born with the same inbuilt knowledge of its form and, however diverse the input to different children, they will all arrive at the same set of productive rules. This will be done unconsciously, unlike a puzzle-solving process, and will not therefore depend on a particular level of intelligence. The much-cited speed of language acquisition will be more comprehensible because of the child being equipped with a 'blueprint' of language in advance.

The fact that, at the time of writing, there is no incontrovertible evidence of other animals learning language as we have defined it would be accounted for by their not being programmed genetically to do so. The creativity of language would be explained by the nature of the rules that were eventually acquired: they would be such that an infinite number of different sentences could be produced.

What we have been looking at is a greatly simplified version of what has come to be called, by its opponents in particular, the **innateness hypothesis**. Chomsky (1959) first proposed something like it in his review of Skinner's *Verbal Behavior*, and has elaborated it in many publications since. It has always aroused controversy. Many would reject it out of hand as 'mentalistic': some have enthusiastically accepted it *in toto*: there are others who are in sympathy with the strictures on behaviourism and structural linguistics that are very much part of Chomsky's proposal, and who are ready to concede that there are language universals without accepting that this necessarily entails innateness. The debate has often been conducted with great acrimony, and this brief account has not done justice to the complexities of the argument.

It is important to realise that more is involved than accepting one position or the other, even if there were only two positions available: there would be nothing implausible in assuming that a child could have an innate predisposition to learn language and still carry out some of his learning by processes described in traditional learning theory. Whichever argument one accepts, there would still have to be an explanation of the way in which the child goes about the task, and here it is worth looking at the set of strategies proposed by Slobin (1973) and summarised by Aitchison (1976) in the seventh chapter of *The Articulate Mammal*. See also the relevant section of Bloom (1975).

5 Further reading

a. Language in general

A good simple introduction that is both interesting and accessible is: Wallwork, J. F. (1969) *Language and Linguistics*, Heinemann.

There are two books, one English and one American, that combine scholarship with liveliness and wit: Quirk, R. (1966) *The Use of English*, Longman, 2nd edition; Bolinger, D. (1968) *Aspects of English*, Harcourt, Brace & World; and one 'classic' that has triggered off an interest in language for so many readers: Sapir, E. (1921) *Language*, Harcourt, Brace & World.

b. Models of Language

Probably the best simple but not oversimplified introduction to transformational-generative grammar is to be found in: Lyons, J. (1970) *Chomsky*, Fontana, which will also be useful when one is considering Chomsky's views on language acquisition. A more detailed treatment is to be found in: Greene, J. (1972) *Psycholinguistics*, Penguin, after which the determined reader could move on to Chomsky himself, perhaps starting with his appendix to Lenneberg (1967).

As far as the systemic model is concerned, and it is only fair to point out that this important model has not been dealt with in this book, there is: Berry, M. (1975) *Introduction to Systemic Linguistics*, Batsford.

c. Language acquisition

i. General introductions

Not an introduction at all but simply a book that any parent or teacher will enjoy is: Chukovsky, K. (1963) *From Two to Five*, University of California Press.

Of the introductions proper, pride of place could well go to: Dale, P. S. (1972) *Language Development: Structure and Function*, Dryden Press. This is a clearly written and well-organised book with good chapter summaries and short excerpts from relevant authors at the end of each chapter, so that one can test one's understanding of Dale's own presentation against the words of the originals. Highly recommended.

Rather more specialised, because it is an introduction to psycholinguistics, but very readable and stimulating is: Aitchison, J. (1976) *The Articulate Mammal*, Hutchinson. This has the recommendation that it was written by someone who has had to teach the material and therefore knows how to present it.

ii. Overviews

There is a short article by Elizabeth Ingram in: Fraser, H. and O'Donnell, W. R. (eds) (1969) *Applied Linguistics and the Teaching of English*, Longman, that makes a useful starting point, like so much else in the book.

For the more detailed overview there is a wealth of choice. One could try McCarthy (1954), Ervin-Tripp (1966), Braine (1971), Bloom (1975) (details in *Bibliography*, p. 303) or others listed in Slobin's 1972 version of *Leopold's Bibliography of Child Language*.

iii. Collected articles

Here are two of the many available that could be a starting point:
Rogers, S. (ed.) (1976) *Children and Language: Readings on Early Language and Socialisation*, OUP
Ferguson, C. A. and Slobin, D. I. (eds) (1973) *Studies in Child Language Development*, Holt, Rinehart & Winston.

iv. Particular emphases

Since Roger Brown has pioneered so much of the work in the field of syntactic development, it is reasonable to recommend: Brown, R. (1973) *A First Language*, Allen & Unwin.

For the more recent emphasis on semantic roles there is Bloom (1970) and Schlesinger's article in: Slobin, D. I. (ed.) (1971) *The Ontogenesis of Grammar*, Academic Press.

There is no simple account of recent work in the field of phonological development. It is still worth consulting: Lewis, M. M. (1963) *Infant Speech*, Routledge and Kegan Paul.

To offset the tendency to concentrate on American works and to divorce form from function, one ought to look at: Halliday,

M. A. K. (1975) *Learning How to Mean: Explorations in the Development of Language*, Edward Arnold. Readers will find it refreshing in the originality of its outlook and more than worth the effort of following its arguments.

If we move on to the overlap between language and cognition, there are:

Cromer, R. F. (1974) 'The Development of Language and Cognition', in B. Foss (ed.) *New Perspectives in Child Development*, Penguin

Hayes, J. R. (ed.) (1970) *Cognition and the Development of Language*, John Wiley.

v. Theories of language acquisition

On the transformational-generative side there is Lyons (1970*a*) and Chomsky's many statements of his own position, particularly in: Chomsky, N. (1965) *Aspects of the Theory of Syntax*, MIT Press; and (1968) *Language and Mind*, Harcourt, Brace & Jovanovich.

There is a powerful statement of the behaviourist view in: Staats, A. W. (1971) 'Linguistic–Mentalistic Theory versus an Explanatory S.R. Learning Theory of Language Development', in Slobin. In the same book one can find 'An Overview of Theories of Grammatical Development' by Susan Ervin-Tripp.

One would also recommend Herriot (1970); and for a statement of the biologist's position: Lenneberg, E. H. (1967) *Biological Foundations of Language*, Wiley.

There are in addition various relevant journals, in particular the *Journal of Child Language*.

6 References

[1] Sapir, E. (1921) *Language* Harcourt, Brace & World

[2] Potter, S. (1960) *Language in the Modern World* Penguin

[3] Barber, C. L. (1964) *The Study of Language* Pan

[4] Carroll, J. B. (1953) *The Study of Language* Harvard University Press

[5] Dale, P. S. (1972) *Language Development: Structure and Function* Dryden Press

[6] Dale, P. S. (1970) *op. cit.*

[7] Herriot, P. (1970) *An Introduction to the Psychology of Language* Methuen

[8] Lyons, J. (ed.) (1970) *New Horizons in Linguistics* Penguin

[9] Halliday, M. A. K. (1975) *Learning How to Mean: Explorations in the Development of Language* Edward Arnold

[10] Bloom, L. (1975) 'Language Development Review' in Horowitz

et al. (eds.) *Child Development Research IV* University of Chicago Press

[11] Campbell, R. and Wales, R. (1970) 'The Study of Language Acquisition' in J. Lyons (ed.) *New Horizons In Linguistics* Penguin

[12] Braine, M. D. S. (1971) 'The Acquisition of Language in Infant and Child', in Carroll Reed (ed.) *The Learning of Language* Appleton

[13] Braine, M. D. S. *op. cit.*

[14] Bloom, L. *op. cit.*

[15] Braine, M. D. S. *op. cit.*

[16] Bloom, R. *op. cit.*

[17] Brown, R. (1973) *A First Language* Allen & Unwin

[18] Dale, P. S. *op. cit.*

[19] Ervin-Tripp, S. M. (1966) 'Language Development' in M. Hoffman and L. Hoffman (eds.) *Review of Child Development Research* Vol. 2 Ann Arbor: University of Michigan Press

[20] Bloom, L. *op. cit.*

[21] Dale, P. S. *op. cit.*

[22] Cazden, C. B. (1966) 'Subcultural Differences in Child Language: An Inter-disciplinary Review, in *Merrill-Palmer Quarterly of Behaviour and Development* 12 185–219

[23] Brown, R. *op. cit.*

[24] Hartmann, R. R. K. and Stork, F. C. (eds) (1972) *Dictionary of Language and Linguistics* Applied Science Publishers

[25] McNeill, D. (1970) *The Acquisition of Language: The Study of Development Psycholinguistics* Harper and Row

[26] Ervin-Tripp, S. M. *op. cit.*

[27] McNeill, D. *op. cit.*

[28] Dale, P. S. *op. cit.*

[29] Clarke, E. (1974) 'Some Aspects of the Conceptual Basis for First Language Acquisition' in R. L. Schiefelbusch and L. L. Lloyd (eds) *Language Perspectives, Acquisition, Retardation and Intervention* Macmillan

[30] Dale, P. S. *op. cit.*

[31] Hartmann, R. R. K. and Stork, F. C. *op. cit.*

[32] Halliday, M. A. K. *op. cit.*

[33] McNeill, D. (1969) 'The Development of Language' in P. A. Mussen (ed.) *Carmichael's Manual of Psychology* Wiley

[34] Brown, R. *op. cit.*

[35] Aitchison, J. (1976) *The Articulate Mammal* Hutchinson

[36] Bloom, L. (1970) *Language Development Form and Function in*

Emerging Grammars MIT Press

[37] Brown, R. (1970) 'The First Sentences of Child and Chimpanzee' in *Psycholinguistics, Selected Papers* The Free Press

[38] Braine, M. D. S. *op. cit.*

[39] Brown, R. and Bellugi, U. (1964) 'Three Processes in the Acquisition of Syntax' *Harvard Educational Review* **34** 133–151

[40] Klima, E. S. and Bellugi, U. (1966) 'Syntactic Regularities in the Speech of Children' in J. Lyons and R. J. Wales (eds.) *Psycholinguistic Papers* Edinburgh University Press

[41] Slobin, D. I. (1973) 'Cognitive Prerequisites for the Development of Grammar' in C. A. Ferguson and D. I. Slobin (eds.) *Studies of Child Language Development* Holt, Rinehart and Winston

[42] Bloom (1970) *op. cit.*

[43] Braine *op. cit.*

[44] Staats, A. W. (1974) 'Behaviourism and Cognitive Theory in the Study of Language: a Neopsycholinguistics' in R. L. Schiefelbusch and L. L. Lloyd (eds.) *Language Perspectives, Acquisition, Retardation and Intervention* Macmillan

PART TWO
Learning to talk

6 Introduction to part two

Part two consists of transcripts of young children, and commentaries on the transcripts. We start with Ralph at six months, move on to Helen, whom we see at various ages and thus can see developing, and end with Matthew out for a walk in the park. Different readers will, of course, use the section in different ways. It is suggested that the order in which the children are presented is the sensible order in which to hear them speak, but this does not necessarily apply to the order in which overview and commentaries should be read. Some readers may prefer to leave the overview until they have sampled the speech of actual children. In the same way there could be different strategies for using transcripts and commentaries. It was our intention in providing the commentary to do what one would do with groups of students: give them a chance to read or listen for themselves first and to form certain impressions before hearing what others have to say. On that basis one would prefer readers to read the transcript and listen to the tape before reading a particular commentary, but provided that they do read both, there is room for other approaches.

7 Before the first word: Ralph from six weeks to six months

---

1 Introduction

It is time to turn from generalities and theoretical speculation to listen to the sounds of an actual child at what we previously called the prelinguistic stage. Before you listen to Ralph on the cassette it would be as well to refresh your memory of what was said in the previous chapter about the acquisition of phonology. Remember that children have to acquire control over contrast in two areas: what we called the segmental phonemes, those families of sounds that build up the words we utter (thus there are three phonemes in 'dog' and 'fill' and four in 'spot' and 'trim'); and the suprasegmental phonemes – those, like stress and intonation, that extend beyond individual segments to syllables and to the child's whole utterances. Remember too that in the process the child was not passive but took an active part. As you listen, therefore, keep an ear open for any signs that Ralph is beginning to develop control over particular sounds (it would be inaccurate to speak of 'phonemes' at this stage because there is no question of Ralph using them in significant contrast) or syllables, or intonation patterns. Notice too the nature of the interaction between the child and the adult, and ask yourself whether there is any evidence that he is trying to communicate.

1█ 2 Six weeks: early sounds

Listen first to the sounds that Ralph is making at the age of six weeks. He cries, screams, breathes heavily, coughs, makes sucking noises, just as all babies do, English and other nationalities. It could be argued that to make some of these sounds he is using his speech organs, and even that some of the sounds resemble the sounds of English speech, in that they are produced by outgoing breath, relatively unobstructed, like vowels. Perhaps too the different sounds signify differing things to he adults who hear them. Is Ralph comfortable, or is he in pain? Certainly we hear the adult talking to Ralph as though his noises had significance. But that would be to confuse 'having significance' with 'intending to convey a meaning'. We can say that a lowering sky is a sign that it is going to rain, without imputing to the clouds an intention to communicate anything. Ralph may make sounds that have meaning for us, but it is unlikely that they have meaning for him. Even so, think what is going on. If he is ever to figure out the contrasts that we spoke of, then evidently he needs to hear them often, and in this part of the tape he is doing just that. He is also hearing himself make noises, as he does certain things with certain parts of his anatomy, and this will also be essential feed-back if he is ever to learn to make particular sounds just as he requires them. We could also say that he is being given a model of normal human interaction through speech: perhaps the speech sounds that he is hearing are so many noises at this stage, but at least he will quickly learn to associate people with speech. As for his interlocutors, it seems that people just cannot help talking to babies. It is as though we feel that it is very important to treat the child as a person from the very beginning, and to initiate what will be a life-long dialogue as soon as we can. Adults do it, but so do children: we must have heard quite young children talking affectionately to unresponsive baby sisters or brothers, with no sense of frustration.

2.3 Sixteen weeks: how adults talk to babies

If we move on to the sixteen weeks stage on the tape, there are already some significant changes. Not only is there an increased repertoire of sounds, but we now seem to have some sounds produced apparently in response to the speech of others. He laughs and makes other sounds when his mother talks to him, and he also seems to respond to the 'oo' sounds that he hears. We ought to be listening carefully now to the 'input' that the child is receiving. Just how normal is it? Is it the so-called 'baby-talk' that adults are said to use when talking to very young children, and if so what are its features? According to Susan Ervin-Tripp, the characteristics of this linguistic style are 'special phonological patterns, syllable repetition, reduction in consonant clusters, and special vocabulary, with probably a simplified selection of the syntax. Also, adults often employ a special voice quality in addressing children.'[1]

Here are some of the things that are addressed to Ralph on the tape:

'What are you doing?'

'You're a good boy, aren't you?'

'I shall get you.'

'Yes, you're lovely.'

'Are you talking to me?'

'Do you like that? Shall I do it again?'

'I'm coming to tickle you.'

'Are you laughing at your shoes?'

Presented like that on paper, they certainly do not seem to be 'baby talk' in the sense defined above. There are no special vocabulary items such as 'moo-cow' or 'puff-puff', or such modifications of pronunciation as 'ickle' for 'little', for example, nor would one say that the syntax, though not complex, is in any way unusual. But on the tape it is another story: no one hearing those utterances could be in any doubt that they were addressed to a child (or possibly an animal). Why are we so certain? Largely because of what Ervin-Tripp calls 'special phonological patterns', in this case what was referred to as 'tunes' on page 59. Listen to them and try to decide what it is that marks them. Take, for example, 'Yes, you're lovely'. Try saying it as you normally would, and then compare it with the version on the tape. Is that rising intonation at the end of 'lovely' normally used when we make statements? Another point that is missed in the bald list of examples is the amount of repetition that is taking place. If Ralph's task is to pick out contrasts both in tunes and in individual sounds, then this constant repetition is going to help him considerably, just as later it will help him to sort out the 'rules' of the grammar.

It is also worth noticing that already at this early stage there is a certain amount of teaching going on, in the sense that when Ralph appears to reply to an adult utterance, there is a delighted response to the happy accident, which presumably acts as reinforcement. And what of imitation? In this part of the tape at least, the imitation is more of, than by, the child. For example, notice the way in which the adults join the child in a kind of unison when he is making certain speech-like sounds. The commonsense answer to the adult's question 'Are you talking to me?' is 'Hardly', but once again there is a kind of interaction going on that foreshadows genuine conversation. And if we revert briefly to Ralph's own repertoire, there is certainly a feeling that he is acquiring greater control over his speech organs, and can make and repeat separate sounds, some of which will perhaps be incorporated into his speech later. In terms of contrasts he shows variation in pitch, in individual sounds and in the duration of particular utterances. If we were, inaccurately, to apply adult criteria to his speech we might say that he was producing something like a vowel sound, and that the next important contrast would be the introduction of a consonant.

3.4 Six months: babbling and interaction

Precisely such an introduction is what can be observed in the next part of the tape – the six months stage. There was a model already available to the child at sixteen weeks when the adult produced a series of sounds something like 'wa wa wa', which was not only rhythmic (one area of importance to the learner), and repetitive (also important, as we have already seen), but also offered a contrast between vowel and consonant. Now, at six months, Ralph can produce such 'syllabic reduplication' for himself, first in a not absolutely indisputable 'ye ye ye' but later in a quite unmistakable 'da da da'. This is babbling and it represents a great advance. To produce such an utterance a child must be capable of detecting the rhythmic quality of speech addressed to him, of controlling his speech organs with enough accuracy to produce the same sound again and again, and of monitoring his own performance as he does so. The effect on adults is often quite dramatic. There is always a tendency to treat the child as a communicating human being, as we have seen, but the usual reaction of an adult who hears a child's 'da da' is to repeat it in a kind of conversation. What we have on the tape is the other situation: the mother says 'br br' and the child responds with 'da da'. Perhaps 'appears to respond' would be a fairer statement, bearing in mind the usual temptation to credit children prematurely with skills that we very much wish them to acquire. Even so, one could just as easily fall into the opposite trap of discounting the child's performance as imperfect imitation, instead of adopting the more constructive approach that would see any kind of performance, albeit imperfect, as an indication of some sort of knowledge or ability. If Ralph is really responding to 'br br' with 'da da' (or a similar pattern), then he has learned quite a lot. First he can respond ('talk back'); secondly he can detect the adult's repetition and rhythmic pattern; and thirdly he can produce a pattern identical in rhythm and very similar in some of its other elements. The repertoire of areas of contrast is growing: pitch, rhythm, and individual sounds. There are still various sounds that we can class as accidental or incidental, like that caused by blowing or sucking, just as not all the input is straightforward speech; for example what is Ralph to make of his mother's whistling? And why is it that there are certain sounds such as 'raspberries' which we consider perfectly acceptable when we are talking to babies, but would scarcely ever use at other times? One senses that Ralph's control over the sounds that he makes is increasing, because even non-speech sounds, such as laughing, can be delivered in single units. It is the sense of greater deliberateness that helps us to feel that Ralph is approaching something that we shall be able to call speech. The cries, coos, and gurgles seem to be much more under the child's control, and on occasion he even seems to be listening to himself. And of course we must remember that the tape records only the sounds made by adult and child whereas in the actual situation there would have been all manner of facial expressions and gestures accompanying the speech and helping to convey the message. The important thing to notice is the length of the exchange between child and mother, in which it is hard to say who is imitating whom at any given point, but easy to hear that, meaningful or not, Ralph's contribution is not random. 'Scribble talk' perhaps, but getting nearer to speech as we know it.

5 Suggestions for further work and discussion

Points for discussion
i. Do you agree that all the sounds at the six-week stage on the tape are involuntary? If so, how are they being caused?
ii. What are your opinions on baby talk? Does it have a harmful effect on a child's language development? Does it hold children back? How would you set about proving your case?
iii. If we are right to ascribe to Ralph, at the six-months stage, control over a sequence like 'dad', how does that fit in with what was said in chapter 3 about children's phonological development?

Follow-up activities
i. We have made several references to phonemes. Check your understanding of the term by attempting the following exercise:
   a. Here are several words followed by a number in brackets representing the number of phonemes in each word:

fish (3)   photography (9)   ascertain (6)
child (4)   would (3)   revive (3)

Remember that we are discussing the sounds of speech and not counting letters. Nor are we counting syllables.

b. Now try to work out the number of phonemes in each of the following:

Empire   ape   scissors
filth   respectable   psychic
octopus   villages   innumerable
jonquil

ii. Listen to other babies at the same stages as Ralph, and see to what extent the picture is the same.

iii. Listen to adults talking to babies and decide what are the special characteristics of this kind of speaking. Do the same for young children talking to their baby brothers and sisters.

iv. Observe a very young baby for evidence of a selective response to the human voice. (Some of the articles in *Child Alive* edited by Lewin (1975) may help here.)

v. Record, or make up (or both), some baby talk and then examine it for its relationship in phonology, syntax, and vocabulary, to normal English.

6 Reference
[1] Ervin-Tripp, S. M. (1966) 'Language Development' in L. W. Hoffman and M. L. Hoffman (eds.) *Review of Child Development Research.* Vol. 2 Ann Arbor: University of Michigan Press

8 A word at a time:
Helen at twenty months

1 Transcripts†

Looking at a book; playing with stones from the garden; examining the tape recorder; looking at a toy cart and donkey; eating sweets; building houses and castles with bricks.

1 Looking at picture of a long red worm in a book

CHRIS Helen, what's this?

HELEN Carrot.

CHRIS Is it? What's that? What are those?

HELEN What is it?

CHRIS Helen, what's this? (*Pointing to picture of water*)

HELEN Water.

CHRIS And what goes on the water? (*Expecting answer 'ducks' as some had been seen that afternoon*)

HELEN Fish.

CHRIS Fish?

HELEN Water.

2 The stone

CHRIS Look, there's that little stone, isn't it? Where did the stone come from?

HELEN Garden.

JAN What else is there in the garden?

HELEN Daddy. (*He had been pushing her on the swing*)

† For an explanation of transcription symbols, see p. 21.

JAN Daddy's been in the garden with you, has he? What have you been playing with in the garden? (*No reply, although she knew the word 'swing'*)

3 *Tape recorder*

HELEN Nanette . . . What's that? (*Pointing to the microphone*)

JAN Well it's the microphone.

HELEN What's that?

DAVE You talk into it, Helen.

HELEN What's that? (*Pointing to tape recorder*)

JAN It's the machine

CHRIS Helen, say 'machine'

HELEN Machine

CHRIS Very nice

JAN And what do the wheels on the machine do? (*We discussed this the day before*)

HELEN Round, round, round, round.

CHRIS What are these? (*Trying to distract her by holding up her socks*)

HELEN Socks.

CHRIS Whose socks?

HELEN Henen's (*Her own pronunciation of her name*)

4 *Toy cart and donkey*

CHRIS What's that?

HELEN Don dey

CHRIS And what are these?

HELEN Wheels

HELEN (*Singing and tipping sweets in and out of the cart*) Henen's Henen's

JAN Helen's sweets

HELEN Sweets, cart. Ooh oh

5 *The book again*

CHRIS What is this, here?

HELEN Pic pic

CHRIS A picture, that's right

CHRIS (*Pointing to a picture*) What's this man got on his face, Helen?

HELEN Glasses

JAN What's he got on his head?

HELEN Hat

6 *Bricks*

CHRIS Helen, what's Daddy built for you? (*Pointing to a pile of bricks*)

HELEN Castle

CHRIS A castle, lovely

HELEN Sweetie, sweetie

Hou. Hou. Hou. Hou. (*'House', looking at bricks*)

CHRIS A house. It's tall, isn't it?

HELEN Tall

CHRIS Do you want a bath tonight, Helen?

HELEN No

CHRIS Do you want your hair washing?

HELEN No

CHRIS Are you going to bed soon?

HELEN No

JAN Doesn't big Dolly want you to read her a story?

HELEN No

2 Introduction

Whatever the textbooks say to the contrary, for most parents the first linguistic landmark is likely to be the child's use of a recognisable word, that is a word that they would use themselves. There will be false scents before, when the chance resemblance of the child's utterance to an English word is seized upon as evidence of prowess probably beyond his competence, and conversely there will possibly be 'words' that are not recognised as such. For example, a child who consistently said 'ferf' every time she saw a fly could be said to be using a word even though it was not the normally acceptable one. The fact that there is still some way to go in mastering the adult version of a particular word is less important than the clear evidence that she has learned a general principle which will result in the production of a flurry of words before long. But, anxious as we are to have a genuine two-way conversation with our children, it still is a great day for most of us when our child says his 'first word'. The trouble about using the expression 'word' is that it may blind us to what the child is really doing. For us words are self-evidently single units, the bits between the spaces on this page, for instance, things that go to make up sentences where the real communication goes on. We have stereotypes of painful word-at-a-time conversations between speakers of different languages, with liberal helpings of sign language and constant misunderstanding. The picture is very clearly one of inadequacy, of inferior substitute for something taken for granted as preferable. If we are tempted to carry over this attitude to our study of the language of young children, we shall do them less than justice.

3 Helen's use of single words

This can be illustrated from the transcript of Helen at twenty months, for which there is unfortunately no recording available. It has already been referred to in the second chapter, and some of the points made there will be touched on again. Before examining the transcripts in detail, however, look again at the discussion of holophrases in chapter 5 (page 69). We can then examine Helen's utterances in the transcript to see how they fit in with what was said earlier. It should be pointed out first that there are always dangers in generalising from particular samples, not simply because they are, as in this case, very small, but also because the nature of a particular situation is itself very much a constraint upon the speech that is likely to ensue from it. In this transcript most of the initiative rests with the adults, who, characteristically, in their efforts to keep the child talking use well-tried rituals which give the child every chance to make not merely a response but an acceptable one. Helen has looked at books before, probably at this book, and has probably answered the same questions. In fact it is a case of questions, questions all the way. Consider our own replies to a series of questions: they might well tell others something about our ability to understand language, but we would not rely upon them to indicate our full powers of expression. We certainly would not answer questions in the full sentences that would be appropriate on other occasions. In other words, in reply to the question 'What's this?' although we might not say just 'Carrot', 'A carrot' would be quite acceptable.

Assuming, however, in spite of such warnings, that Helen's replies do represent the current limits of her syntactic knowledge, what can be said about them? A plain list might be less than revealing: 'carrot', 'water', 'fish', 'garden', 'Daddy', 'machine', 'round', 'socks', 'Helen's', 'don dey', 'wheels', 'cart', 'pic pic', 'glasses', 'hat', 'castle', 'tall', 'no'; because it seems to confirm the doubtful assumption that children begin to speak by using nouns as labels. This is where the nature of the situation comes in. Given that the adult is calling the tune, by asking one question after another, the child has no alternative but to reply with what in the adult grammar are nouns. (The only examples of spontaneous speech are in fact slightly different: 'What's that?' and 'Henen's'.) But are these nouns simply labels? 'Carrot', 'water', 'socks', 'don dey', 'wheels' are all replies to the 'What's that?' type of question and could be said to be identifying, but in the case of other words it is not so straightforward. 'Fish' might be said to represent something like 'Fish go on water'; 'Garden', 'Stone came from garden'; and 'Daddy', 'Daddy is in the garden'. Such interpretations are highly suspect in that they credit the child with knowledge it cannot be proved that she possesses, but this is the problem with the holophrastic stage. The very fact that the conversation goes on so smoothly shows that the adults must be assuming that the child's single words have something of the sense suggested; and Helen's apparent ability to understand the adult's utterances suggests that she is capable of processing more than one word at a time. Perhaps we are assuming that she is responding to all of the elements in the adult utterance when in fact it is only a particular item that is triggering off her responses. Otherwise we must assume that she is capable of understanding grammar that is more complex than anything she is able to produce.

4 Understanding what the grown-ups say

It is worth looking in more detail at the structures that she apparently does understand. It has been pointed out that they are very often questions, but notice the various forms these take. In addition to the basic 'What's this?' question and its variants such as 'What are these?', there are other questions of the 'Wh' type (in which a word such as 'who' or 'which' or 'what' is used, and the answer cannot be a plain 'Yes' or 'No'). To reply 'Fish' to the question 'What goes on the water?' presumably requires a response to more than the 'Wh' word alone. Perhaps Helen is giving an association to the word 'water', but it is at least possible that she has understood the whole phrase 'goes on water'. Similarly the reply 'Round, round' may be remembered association to an experience with a tape recorder previously, a kind of verbal pointing, but it is also possible that she really understands the whole of the question 'And what do the wheels on the machine do?' Even more impressive is her reply to the question 'Whose socks?', for she not only understands the question but appears to be able to use the possessive morpheme, judging by her spontaneous use of 'Henen's' later on. Again the question 'What's this man got on his face?' appears to demand an understanding of the whole utterance, unless the child is responding to the adult's pointing as much as to what is said (though there is no evidence of pointing to elicit the next reply, 'hat').

101

5 What the child is learning

What else can be said about what this child is learning or has learned about the business of talking? The model of human interaction is becoming well established. The adult contribution may be very much a matter of question after question, but at least this gives the child the chance to make good use of her as yet limited resources, and to feel a part of the ongoing situation. She is learning to take part in a conversation, in which she is made to feel that her contribution has some value. She is under no illusions about the importance of performing well, because the adults take pains to reward her acceptable responses with praise ('Very nice') or confirmation of her accuracy ('That's right'). In a sense the whole dialogue could be seen in the light of a lesson, or the testing of a repertoire. Helen will learn from this and a hundred other such conversations not only a store of words or of structures but also the important lesson that we can use language to find out things, by asking others who know more than we do about certain things. She has already learned to ask the question 'What?' and will soon acquire the more searching question 'Why?'. For the present she accepts the role that is assigned to her of respondent rather than initiator, but that will change before long.

6 Suggestions for further work and discussion

Points for discussion

a Examine the adults' contribution to the dialogue and consider whether they:
i. expand the child's utterances, and if so, how
ii. ignore 'errors' (e.g. mispronunciation) and reward the 'truth value' of what Helen says
iii. give any evidence of 'coaching'.

b What particular structures do you think Helen is learning, or likely to learn, in this conversation?

Follow-up activities

a Think of other situations in which a child of this age might be expected to talk freely.

b Record such a child in such a situation and compare your transcript with the one here.

c A group of students could compare transcripts in respect of
i. the child's single words
ii. the child's understanding
iii. the parents' expansions.

d Compare this transcript with those in Bloom (1973).[1]

7 Reference

[1] Bloom, L. (1973) *One Word at a Time: the Use of Single-Word Utterances before Syntax*, Mouton

9 Nother one:
Helen at twenty-one months

---

1 Transcripts†

Extracts from an hour's taping at breakfast: riding her bike with big Dolly; playing with truck with yellow wheels; hitting a marmalade jar; looking at a book.

1 Putting the doll on the bike and trying to push it round
   HELEN Handles. (*Trying to fix the doll's hands to the handlebars*) Pedals.
   HELEN Henen ride. (*Climbing on*)
   HELEN Dolly in. Dolly in. (*Lifting the doll on the bike*)
   HELEN Henen ride (*Now riding round*) Both.
   JAN Yes you're both riding round.
   HELEN Bye. Bye again. (*Being pushed and wanting it to go on*)

2 Playing with the truck, rolling it along
   HELEN Henen do it. Henen do it.
   CHRIS Where is it? (*It had fallen on the floor*)
   HELEN Down there. Daddy.
   CHRIS Where's your Daddy?
   HELEN Bed. In bed. Bed. Bed.
   HELEN Nut off. (*Banging wheels of truck and turning screws*)
   CHRIS Mummy will take the nut off.
   HELEN Table. Nut out. (*Pointing to the shaft which held the wheels*)
   CHRIS It's a large screw.

† For an explanation of transcription symbols, see p. 21.

JAN Where's it gone? (*The shaft fell on to her chair*)
HELEN Chair, chair.
JAN Yes, it's fallen on the chair.

3 *Marmalade jar with golliwog on the side*
HELEN On off. On off. (*Wanting to take the golliwog off*)
CHRIS Yes it's on, and you want it off.
HELEN Mummy do it. On. On. On. (*Put the lid on*)
JAN What do you want me to do?
HELEN On. On.
JAN Put it on.
HELEN Lid on.
CHRIS Put the lid on.

4 *Helen coughing*
CHRIS I'll have to give her some of that medicine again.
HELEN Cough. Spoon. Spoon.
CHRIS Yes, I'll go and get a spoon. (*Going out of the room*)
HELEN Upstairs. Upstairs.
CHRIS She thinks I've been upstairs for it.

5 *Looking at a book*
JAN What are these? (*Watches*)
HELEN Ticks. Ticks.
JAN What's that? Have you seen this golly?
HELEN Henen's
JAN Helen's got a golly
HELEN Home
JAN I thought you'd brought him with you.
HELEN Nother one (*Wanting a page turned over*) Nother
HELEN Knife. Daddy's spoon. Henen's spoon. Nother spoon.
  (*Pointing to picture of cutlery*)

6 *Also heard*
Daddy do it.   (Daddy push the swing)
Daddy come.   (Daddy come and push the swing)
Daddy *coming*.   (Difficult to be precise about the meaning. Said
              when Daddy was lying in bed and Helen wanted
              him to come down as well.)

2 Introduction: from holophrase to two-word 'sentence'

It is worth looking at this transcript, though the tape is not available, because it shows the difference that a single month can make in the process of learning to talk. How simple and obvious it is to say that where before Helen was using a single word to make herself understood, now she can put two words together. And how dull and unrevealing! If all that we can point to is a not unpredictable sequence of one word followed by two words and so on, then we are forgetting the very principles that were invoked in the earlier chapter on Ralph. What we were looking for then was communicative intent; what we should be looking for now in addition is communicative skill. If Helen can use two words at a time, for what purposes is she using them and in what different relationships to each other do they stand? There were instances at the previous stage when she used two words in succession, but it seemed reasonable not to treat them as words in construction, because of the way in which they were said (e.g. 'Sweets. Car.') In the present extract there are many two-word utterances that the adults respond to as though they were sentences, and they do so because in the child's grammar that is what they are. It is not a case of imperfect imitation, as though the child's utterances were an inferior version of what adults say, but of a different system for expressing some of the relationships which can be expressed in the adult grammar.

3 Some two-word patterns in Helen's speech

In chapter 3 we discussed the two-word 'sentence' stage and saw instances of children expressing grammatical relationships, such as subject—verb, or semantic roles, such as agent—action, by juxtaposing two words. Are there similar instances in the Helen transcript? She has certainly begun to master the subject—verb or agent—action pattern, judging by the repeated 'Henen ride' and 'Henen do it' and the three 'Daddy' examples, and it would be a mistake to think that the absence of other patterns, such as verb—object, from this very small sample means that she is incapable of producing them.

There are other two-word patterns, however, that she does produce and that are worth looking at. Take 'Dolly in', for example, which she says as she lifts her doll on to the bike. Is it noun plus adverb, or is that to fall into the trap of trying to account for children's speech acts purely in terms of our own grammar? Is there a 'Put' or 'Let's put' to be understood before the word 'Dolly', as though the child were half-remembering the previously heard adult utterance or supplying the missing element in her head? The short answer must always be that no one can ever know: this is one field where the informant cannot be questioned about her use of language and we are left to make the best available guess. But, however we attempt to classify or analyse the utterance, we are in

106

no doubt as to its meaning: once again we have the child making the best use of her available resources and the adults perfectly willing to accept her version of the language. It is the same with 'In bed', where the sequence 'Bed. In bed. Bed. Bed' illustrates how a child moves from holophrase to fuller statement. Had she said simply 'bed', we might have called it a holophrase and suggested that it signified a location, and showed that she could interpret the question-word 'Where?' The immediate expansion to 'In bed' shows that we would have been right to assume that a location was implied, because the added word is a preposition, the kind of word that serves to signify relationships, often relationships in space. Even so, unless one heard her produce other phrases using 'in' and other nouns with 'in', it would be unsafe to assume that she was really using the word meaningfully. Can we be sure that Helen connects this 'in' with that in the 'Dolly in' example already discussed? There are other similar patterns: 'Nut off', 'Lid on', which suggest that she has mastered a pattern that is genuinely productive for her, since she can vary both the words in it. Whether such patterns are a result of imitation must remain an open question. Granted the mother says 'Mummy will take the nut off' after Helen's 'Nut off' – the typical expansion that plays such a prominent part in adults' responses to children's speech – but presumably the sequence could have happened before the other way round, and Helen's utterance could then have been regarded as a reduction, reproducing the words most recently heard. But in that case what are we to make of the sequence:

JAN What do you want me to do?
HELEN On. On.
JAN Put it on.
HELEN Lid on.
CHRIS Put the lid on.

Admittedly the adult helpfully expands the 'On. On' to 'Put it on' but the child's response is not 'It on' but 'Lid on', where she genuinely seems to be creating her own phrase to express her meaning. Notice how the mother rounds off the little lesson by expanding the child's final version. It may well be the case, as Cazden suggests, that parents do not 'expand with any conscious intention' but 'simply to keep the conversation going',[1] but nevertheless what effective teaching this procedure can be!

Finally in this examination of indisputably two-element utterances, there is 'On. Off', transparent in its intention but not easy to analyse in adult terms. It is another revealing sequence showing how children at times appear to be practising a newly acquired structure, almost for the pleasure of showing that they have acquired it. After 'Nother one', an example of that semantic role which Brown would call 'recurrence', like 'more milk', we have this: 'Knife. Daddy's spoon. Henen's spoon. Nother spoon.' Once again she is pointing to pictures in a book, and once again the pictures serve to remind her of the objects they represent, but what should be catching our eye now is the way in which she is ringing the changes on the word before the fixed noun 'spoon'. In teaching English as a foreign language, we often give the student a kind of language drill known as a substitution table. A particular structure can be practised: a fixed frame of words, such as 'This is a ———— house', is provided, and the learner concentrates on supplying a single item in the gap, thus practising the same pattern many times but partly varying its composition. If parents ever started to do the same with young children, then Helen's little sequence would be a possible drill for adjective-noun or possessive with noun. A month ago she could say 'Henen's' appropriately; now she can be even more specific. The whole sequence reminds one very much of some of the extracts in Ruth Weir's fascinating book *Language in the Crib*, in which she presents her children's pre-sleep monologues: they too seem to be deliberately trying things out, rehearsing their current repertoire.

In considering these examples of two-word utterances it should not be forgotten that not all of what Helen says in this transcript can be so classified. She still makes effective use of single words; effective because they serve to keep the conversation going:

JAN Where's it gone?

HELEN Chair.

and:

JAN Helen's got a golly.

HELEN Home.

and there are some 'sentences' which appear to consist of three elements, e.g. 'Henen do it' and 'Mummy do it'. It could be argued that once again we have evidence of undoubted syntactic knowledge because the child is using the same verb with different subjects, but it is the use of the word 'verb' that is begging the question. Does Helen know that 'do it' is two words, or is it for her still a single item? Once again the answer must be that we cannot know for sure, because the child would not understand the question. As always, we should be cautious in generalizing from slender evidence.

108

4 What the language is being used for

We began by rejecting the approach that would be satisfied with simple statements about a gradual increase in the length of children's utterances, but there is a danger that in moving on to discuss how the various two-word utterances differ in the relationships they express, not enough consideration has been given to what must always be at the forefront of our minds: what the child is using the language for. When everything has been said about subject, verb, object, and so on, we have still been considering only the means to certain ends. What of the ends themselves? Sometimes it seems that the words are not much more than an accompaniment to what Helen is doing ('Henen ride', 'Dolly in') or perhaps a way of ensuring that what she is doing will not go unremarked (and the adult's reactions do tend to support that interpretation: 'Yes you're both riding round'). At other times, however, she is using language as a way of getting things done, as, for example, when she says 'Again' when she wants to be pushed again. One is reminded of Washoe the chimpanzee, sitting in a tin bath and signing 'More', so that someone will push the bath again. This is what would be called by Halliday **instrumental model**, ('I want'), or perhaps the **regulatory model**, ('do as I tell you'). His paper 'Relevant Models of Language' (1969) is invaluable as a guide to looking at the language of young children from the viewpoint of its diverse functions, and it will be referred to more than once in these pages.

We see the same model again when Helen says 'Henen do it', 'Nut off', 'Nut out', 'On off', 'Mummy do it', 'On. On', 'Lid on', 'Spoon', 'Nother one'. Notice that these utterances fall into several different categories according to the criteria employed so far in discussing them, but in considering their effectiveness as communication it is probably what they have in common in terms of function that is most important. She also shows on several occasions that she really has grasped the connection between 'Where?' and location, as she says 'Bed' or 'Chair', and she can independently produce 'Upstairs' when her mother goes out for a spoon. She has already shown that she realises that there is some connection between coughs and the spoons that are used to administer the medicine. Similarly when Janet says 'Helen's got a golly', Helen can say 'Home', a good example of displaced speech and a perfectly acceptable continuation of the conversation. There are still instances of the question and answer ritual, but increasingly one has the feeling that this child is capable of initiating discussion and not merely continuing it. If Halliday is right when he says that 'dialogue can be viewed as, essentially, the adoption and assignment of roles',[2] then Helen is obviously beginning to acquire greater skill in dialogue.

5 Morphemes: the shape of things to come

Before leaving this transcript it would be useful, bearing in mind what is to follow, to return to a final point about Helen's grammar. We have several times used the word morpheme when discussing expressions like 'Henen's'. While it is true that English is largely uninflected and that relationships are usually signalled by word order and 'little words', there are instances, and 'Henen's' is one of them, where a change in the structure of a word itself conveys some information – in this case that Helen owns something. It is the segment represented by 's' in print that we have been calling the **possessive morpheme**. Morphemes, as we mentioned in chapter 3, are the smallest units of English grammar. The larger units are probably more familiar to most of us: we could recognise, if not define, a **sentence**, a **clause**, or a phrase, and certainly a word. Sentences are composed of one or more clauses; clauses of one or more phrases, and so on. The morpheme, too, is the constituent of another unit, in this case the word. Thus in the word 'beautiful' there are two morphemes: 'beauty' and 'ful'; in 'paintpot', two: 'paint' and 'pot'; in 'disgustingly', three: 'disgust', 'ing', and 'ly'. You will notice that in some cases what we are calling a morpheme is also a word, and such morphemes would be called **free morphemes**, while those that appear only as parts of words are called **bound morphemes**. According to that definition, therefore, 'Henen's' would consist of a free morpheme ('Henen') and a bound morpheme, ('s'). She also uses the **plural morpheme** when she says 'handles' and 'pedals', or it would be more accurate to say that she appears to use it, since unless we heard her use the singular and the plural forms appropriately in context we could not be sure. Researchers interested in children's morphology, as this area of grammar is called, use nonsense words to test whether children really do have a productive rule for using a particular morpheme.

Helen's morphology is as yet rudimentary, but although she can communicate pretty well with the resources at her command, 'communication pressure' will see to it that as she wishes to signal ever more complex relationships she will need to acquire ever more delicate nuances in her grammar. We can manage to a certain extent without some bound morphemes and some of those short and apparently insignificant words like 'of' and 'to' and 'the', but it is surprising how great a part they play in our communication. We can expect that along with an increased repertoire of sentence types, of vocabulary, and of language functions, we shall soon be seeing in the language of this child the use both of the 'little words' and of the various morphemes that in English signal the plurals, and so on.

6 Suggestions for further work and discussion

Points for discussion
i. Suggest interpretations for the 'Daddy coming' remark.
ii. Compare the expansions in this transcript with those in the previous one.
iii. Does the transcript bear out what was said in chapter 3 about the word order of the children's two-word sentences?
iv. Would you regard the sentences like 'Henen do it' as consisting of two or three elements?

Follow-up activities
i. Read Bloom (1970) on two-word sentences.
ii. Read Halliday (1969) on 'Relevant Models of Language'.
iii. Record the same child that you recorded at the one-word stage and consider what development appears to have taken place.
iv. It might be useful at this point to ensure that you really understand the meaning of morpheme. The following sequence is intended to help.

a Here is a definition of morpheme, taken from Berry: 'The morpheme is the smallest grammatical unit and therefore there are no smaller things from which it can be constructed.'[3]

b Here is a list of words, with their constituent morphemes shown in parentheses:

drinker	(drink er) (2)
telling	(tell ing) (2)
reappear	(re appear) (2)
reappearance	(re appear ance) (3)
reappearances	(re appear ance s) (4)
unforeseeable	(un fore see able) (4)

c The following list shows the number of morphemes in each word, without indicating what they are. Decide how each word is made up:

111

boats	(2)
disarming	(3)
perfectionist	(3)
stupidly	(2)
unprepossessing	(4)
disbeliever	(3)
blackboards	(3)
antidisestablishmentarianism	(6)

d How many morphemes are there in the following words?

ex-policeman
predestination
rarefy
bluebottles
discontinuity
unimaginably
reconstituted
immobility

e Remember that some morphemes (e.g. horse, rare, police) are also words. These are free morphemes. Others are used only as parts of words (e.g. -s, -ing, dis-, un-). These are bound morphemes. Which are the free, and which the bound, morphemes in *d*?

f Morphemes can coincide with syllables, but this need not be the case. Consider 'fatherly' and 'kites' for example:

fatherly	3 syllables	2 morphemes
kites	1 syllable	2 morphemes

Compare morphemes and syllables in *d*.

g Read the discussion of morphemes in Berry (1975) and Jean Berko's article in *Word* (1958).

7 References

[1] Cazden, C. B. (1966) 'Subcultural Differences in Child Language: An Inter-disciplinary Review', in *Merrill-Palmer Quarterly of Behaviour and Development* **12** 185–219

[2] Halliday, M. A. K. (1975) *Learning How to Mean: Explorations in the Development of Language* Edward Arnold

[3] Berry, M. (1975) *Introduction to Systemic Linguistics* Batsford

10 Playing in earnest:
Helen at two years

1 Transcript†

Transcript of tape made during an hour's play one morning. Most of the language is closely linked with the play situation and therefore difficult to transcribe because it accompanies activity — an imaginary breakfast situation — very closely.

HELEN Leaving these 'namas on.

CHRIS No, you're not having your pyjamas on, you're going to get dressed now.

HELEN No, don't want to

CHRIS Don't you? Do you want to go shopping?

HELEN Pease.

CHRIS Do you want to go in Aunty Janet's car?

HELEN Pease.

JAN You're going in Aunty's car?

HELEN Mummy's shopping basket.

CHRIS Yes. We'll take a shopping basket. Shall we take the push-chair?

HELEN ?Thank you.

CHRIS Shall we take the pushchair?

HELEN Pease ... in Aunty Nanny's car ... Get pushchair in Aunty Nanny car.

CHRIS Well, I think you can.

★   ★   ★   ★

CHRIS Who came to play yesterday, Helen?

HELEN Care. (Clare)

† For an explanation of transcription symbols, see p. 21.

CHRIS Clare? No, Clare didn't come did she?

HELEN No.

CHRIS Where does Clare live? Clare lives in Nottingham, doesn't she?

HELEN No in house . . . in house Mum.

CHRIS Mm . . . who came to play in your sandpit yesterday?

HELEN Emma.

CHRIS Yes, and who else?

HELEN Baby . . . uh . . . got socks off . . .? She . . . got socks off. (*Emma had taken her socks off*)

★ ★ ★ ★

HELEN I'm making some din . . . I'm making some dinner.

JAN You're making some dinner. What are we going to have for our dinner?

HELEN I'm putting some milk in

JAN Putting . . . milk in?

HELEN ** (*Wants the microphone moving off the tin it is standing on as she wants to use the tin for a table*)

JAN Oh I'm sorry, extremely sorry, on the tin, right.

HELEN ** That's it. Got some milk in **

JAN We're having milk, are we, for our dinner? What else?

HELEN Putting that in cup. Little **. Putting that in cup.

JAN Putting it in the cup.

CHRIS Pour Aunty Janet a cup of tea.

JAN Yes, I'd love a cup of tea.

HELEN * cup a ta. Nother cup of tea? Can't have a cup of tea. Baby having cup of tea? (*This may mean 'Can Baby have a cup of tea' – she is upstairs*)

CHRIS If you want.

HELEN Upstairs.

CHRIS She isn't upstairs is she?

HELEN *

CHRIS Give this baby a cup of tea. * floor. (*Adults laugh*) She looks as though she needs one.

JAN Oh, on her head?

HELEN I diving (giving) food.

JAN You're giving her food? . . . What/what food does she like?

HELEN * like these. Like *. Diving some milk. Cup. That's it.

JAN You've given her some milk out of the cup, have you?

CHRIS Would you like to give your dolly a biscuit, Helen?

HELEN Pease . . . on/on Mummy's plate . . . That's it.

JAN Switch on, Mama.

GRANDMOTHER I haven't switched the kettle on, have I?

HELEN *

JAN ?Up.

GRANDMOTHER Are you having a cup of tea?

HELEN No.

GRANDMOTHER Oh dear.

JAN No. Are you going to have some porridge this morning?

HELEN Round and round. (*Referring to the turning spools of the tape recorder*)

JAN Round and round. Yes.

HELEN Mama's. (*Referring to the tape recorder*)

JAN Is it Mama's or Nanette's — the machine?

HELEN Mama's.

JAN Is it?

HELEN What's that? What's that?

JAN It's the little wheels going round.

GRANDMOTHER I think she thinks because it's here it's mine.

HELEN ?Round and round and round. Wheels. Wheels.

CHRIS Who made it for you? (*Not clear what this refers to*)

JAN Who made that, Helen?

CHRIS Who made these wheels for you?

HELEN ?Wheels

CHRIS Oh it's got porridge on. Lift it off. Who did it for you?

HELEN *

CHRIS What does it do?

★   ★   ★   ★

CHRIS Helen, what did Aunty Margaret give you?

HELEN **

JAN What/what did you have to eat at Aunty Margaret's? Bread and . . .?

HELEN Butter.

JAN Bread and butter. Lovely. And did it have anything on it? Bread and butter and . . .

HELEN Jam (*Emphatically*)

JAN Jam. Oh lovely. And did you have a cup of tea?

HELEN Mmm. Cup of tea and milk.

JAN Cup of tea with milk in. Very nice.

★   ★   ★   ★

(*Playing with a large box which she climbs into*)

HELEN I'm going in likkle box. (*Makes a noise like a car driving off*)

JAN You're standing in your box, are you?

HELEN **

JAN What are you doing? What are you doing?

HELEN ** I'm sitting down . . . Helen sitting down.

CHRIS You're sitting down, are you?

HELEN Another cup of tea.

JAN Have another cup of tea while you're sitting down. Do you have sugar in your tea?

HELEN Mm . . . I've got tea leaves in that.

JAN You've got your tea leaves in that. [Those tea leaves have made a big impression, haven't they?]

HELEN I've got tea leaves in it . . . got tea leaves in box.

JAN But what's/what's this?

HELEN ?A likkle knife.

JAN A little knife

HELEN Cutting * get butter out.

JAN Cut a piece of toast then.

HELEN My toast. My toast **

[JAN Yes, she wants the real thing.]

DAD Isn't that a slice of toast alongside Dolly?

JAN Cut a piece of toast. Cut this piece of toast . . . Cut that piece of toast in two. What are you going to have on your toast?

HELEN Butter **

JAN Butter and what else?

HELEN Let dolly sit down **

JAN Let dolly sit down.

DAD What kind of butter do you want on your toast? (*She usually has peanut butter*)

JAN What kind of butter?

HELEN Eating some butter

JAN What's your favourite butter? What does Daddy/what sort of butter does Daddy put on in the morning. In the morning Daddy puts . . . ?

HELEN On some butter on.

JAN What about peanut butter?

HELEN Cutting it.

JAN You're cutting it, yes. Who's going/who's going to have some?

HELEN Daddy and my Mummy.

JAN And Mummy. Daddy and Mummy to have toast

DAD Give this to Aunty Janet to eat

JAN Lovely. Have a sandwich. Oh delicious, delicious.

HELEN Henen cutting that up . . . licious.

JAN Delicious

HELEN Can do (go) in dere (there, meaning the pram). Henen's
   baby in there.

JAN Your baby's in there, is she?

HELEN Lifting baby out.

JAN As well . . . yes.

HELEN (*In doll's voice*) Oh don't hold my arm·. . . don't hold my
   leg . . . don't hold my leg.

[JAN Don't hold my leg or my arm.] (*An aside made in case the
   tape wasn't clear*)

JAN Whoops a day.

HELEN In box ** in box ** Again

JAN Thank you. Oh delicious. (*Pretending to eat toast*)

HELEN Again . . . again. (Repeat the word)

JAN I haven't got my toast yet. Thank you. Delicious . . . now
   you have a piece . . . what do you say?

HELEN ?elicious

JAN Delicious, that's right.

HELEN Baby's having some.

JAN Will baby have a piece? What does she say? What does
   she/baby say?

HELEN Mm . . . what baby say? Eating toast . . . licious. *** I'm
   cutting that with * I'm cutting it with that *.

CHRIS Are you?

[JAN What is she doing?

CHRIS I don't know.]

HELEN I'm sitting in box *** I'm cutting my tea.

JAN You're cutting your tea up, are you?

HELEN **licious

JAN Delicious.

HELEN Knife

JAN Yes. You'll need your knife, won't you?

HELEN *elicious, elicious

JAN Delicious

HELEN ** cutting toast. Cutting toast on the stairs.

JAN You're cutting toast on the stairs, well you don't cut it there
   do you?

HELEN No, no haven't.

JAN What else do you have for your breakfast?

HELEN Marmite

JAN Marmite. What else do you have?

117

HELEN Oh baby * have some, baby's having some.

5 JAN Baby's having some, good. What are you going to give baby
for her breakfast?

HELEN Likkle Marmite

JAN Marmite, very nice. Anything else?

HELEN Likkle butter

JAN Butter. She says she's hungry. What else can she have?

HELEN Likkle ** peanut butter, pemate, playmate in ?stool,
having playmate, having playmate. (*These were probably all
attempts at 'peanut', although at the time, as the subsequent
remark shows, it was thought she said playmate.*)

[CHRIS Having playmate.]

JAN She's a playmate, is she? Very nice. She says she's very
hungry. What else can she have?

· HELEN Likkle lettuce, lettuce.

JAN Lettuce, very nice . . . Lettuce, yes. Is there anything else?

HELEN Likkle lettuce. Having likkle lettuce. Having likkle lettuce
** having my lettuce. Baby's having some in minute.

JAN Baby's going to have some in a minute.

HELEN Baby's having some, baby's having some.

JAN Shall I just help you? That's right. Are you all right? . . .
Can you manage?

HELEN I'm buttering some toast. *** She's cutting it. ?She's
cutting it?

JAN You're cutting it. Where are you making the toast? Where
do you make/where do you make the toast?

HELEN In titchen.

JAN In the kitchen, you do, that's quite right, on the toaster,
don't you?

HELEN Toaster *

JAN Yes.

HELEN *

JAN And what will you do after you've had your breakfast?

HELEN Do some butter on my toast.

JAN Butter on your toast, yes.

HELEN ** Having mine, that's mine, that's mine, and that's mine.

JAN That's yours, is it?

HELEN **

JAN Oh I don't think you have cars for your breakfast, do you?
What about cornflakes?

HELEN Cornflakes

JAN Could you have some cornflakes in that little dish?

HELEN Mm

JAN Yes, look, cornflakes. I like cornflakes.

HELEN Like some cornflakes ... Baby like some cornflakes. (*Screams*) What's that?

JAN It's a picture. Nothing to worry about. Baby likes cornflakes, does she?

HELEN Mm.

JAN What do you have on your cornflakes?

HELEN Likkle butter.

JAN Not butter on cornflakes. You have sugar, don't you?

HELEN Sugar on my cornflakes.

JAN You have sugar on your cornflakes, do you? And do you have milk on?

HELEN Mm. One toast. Have one toast.

JAN Yes, go and fetch the toast from the kitchen, then.

HELEN ** [*Muttered adult conversation about whether recorder was working*]

HELEN * on my * cornflakes. On my toast.

JAN You've got your toast, have you?

HELEN ?Just? you cut it up.

JAN You're going to cut it up, are you? ... Good.

HELEN Butter on ... butter.

JAN Put butter on.

HELEN Putting butter on my cornflakes.

JAN You're putting butter on your ...?

HELEN Cornflakes.

JAN On your cornflakes, are you?

HELEN Butter on my cornflakes.

JAN And how do you eat your cornflakes? What do you eat cornflakes with?

HELEN Knife, cornflakes.

JAN A knife, that's unusual.

HELEN Putting some milk in.

JAN Put milk in.

HELEN Some tea leaves in there.

2 Let's pretend

What strikes us immediately about this transcript, especially the long sequence when Helen is playing in the box, is that she is no longer responding to others' questions all the time but actually initiates many of the exchanges. It is she who has the first word with her 'I'm going in likkle box', and though there are times when we appear to have reverted to the question and answer ritual, there are many instances where it is her utterance that elicits the adult's response rather than the other way round. We may have 'What's this?' followed by 'A likkle knife', but we also hear 'Henen's baby in there', followed by 'Your baby's in there, is she?'

Nor should we fail to realise that the stream of talk, however mundane its subject matter, is no simple running commentary. There is no tea, no butter, no cornflakes. All we have is one box, one child, and the child's imagination, supported by three things: her knowledge of the world of real tea and cornflakes; her knowledge of the language that helps her to represent or half-create that world; and the willingness of three adults to enter into her world of make-believe. We are firmly in the area of Halliday's imaginative model ('let's pretend'),[1] where the child is amusing herself, and at the same time having intensive practice in the use of language appropriate to certain situations. The adults, with no sense of unease or condescension, join in her game, and take the child as seriously in the make-believe kitchen as they would in a real one. A genuine interchange develops, the adult taking up the child's remarks, asking interested questions ('Your baby's in there, is she?'), or responding to the proffered food ('Delicious').

That very word 'delicious' reminds us that children can enjoy words just for their sounds. Helen repeats the word after a fashion, and asks Janet to repeat it for her, trying out her own versions with increasing success. It is well known that children develop such an interest early. 'Ginger. Ginger', said a four-year-old with lingering relish. 'That's my favourite word.' For Arnold Bennett it was the word 'pavement'. 'Chimborazo, Cotopaxi had stolen me away', wrote the poet, and, for one reader at least, though the gist of the poem remains in the memory after many years, those evocative place names are the only details that stay fresh.

We spoke in an earlier chapter about adopting roles in speech and predicted that Helen would soon cease to be merely a respondent. Besides initiating conversation in her own persona she can also endow her doll with life and individuality, merely by speaking in an assumed voice, not because she necessarily believes the doll to be alive, but because she knows that people do speak, sometimes, in idiosyncratic ways. It will be a simple step from this to the kind of role playing that we can see in any Wendy House, a form of play that children seem to be able to take seriously although they realise that it is only make-believe. But listen to her talk in all its volume and variety and think how much practice she is getting in using her language.

3 The contribution of the adults

Before we look in more detail at how her language is developing we ought to consider the role of the adults. How do they talk and listen to her, and how might this affect the development of her speech? They still ask their fair share of questions, but with differing purpose and effects. There are questions like 'Do you want to go shopping?' where the answer is not as predetermined as it is with the 'What's that?' kind. Others give the child the chance to say something ('Who came to play yesterday, Helen?', or 'Where does Clare live?') and will encourage the development of displaced speech. This will help her to take a more active part in conversations by making it possible for her to discuss more than the restricted here and now. The adults also use questions in the make-believe situation, both to show a spirit of participation and to encourage Helen to develop her own suggestions ('Do you have sugar in your tea?' and 'What are you going to have on your toast?'). There is another form of question very much like the prompt that was described in chapter 5. Janet several times uses structures like 'Bread and butter and ———?' so that Helen can supply the missing word. There are other examples on a part of the tape that is not represented on the transcript, where they collaborate in a similar way to recite nursery rhymes.

Another technique well in evidence is 'expanding'. Let us look at some examples:

Child	Adult's expansion
I diving food.	You're giving her food.
Putting that in cup.	Putting it in the cup.
Helen sitting down.	You're sitting down, are you?

Helen is at a transitional stage in her grammar when she is still producing some of the 'telegraphic' utterances that we noticed at an earlier stage. One characteristic of these utterances is the systematic omission (or non-production) of certain items such as the articles ('a' and 'the'), forms of the verb 'to be' (in expressions such as 'You're giving'), and prepositions. When parents and other adults hear such utterances they usually respond by repeating what the child has said, with these items inserted. In the transcript a similar response follows even a correct utterance, as when Helen says 'I'm making some dinner' and Janet replies 'You're making some dinner'. The intention of this reply is presumably to show an interest in what the child has just said and perhaps to confirm that the message was understood because correctly constructed. We shall be examining the 'I'm making' kind of construction when we look at the development of Helen's syntax in section 3; and an input of this kind, closely related to an actual situation, with one correct form followed immediately by another, may well be of importance to a child with the rule to learn.

In the same way, there is a lot of repetition in some of the adults' remarks. Look at this, for example:

> JAN Cut a piece of toast. Cut this piece of toast ... Cut that piece of toast in two.

It is not only the repetition of 'piece of toast' that is important, though such repetitions must play a part in the child's learning of phrase structure, but notice how Janet rings the changes on the word before 'piece': we have 'a', 'this', 'that'. A child will eventually work out that certain words are classed together because they have the same **privileges of occurrence**, i.e. can occupy the same position in a sentence. For example, 'eats', 'dislikes', 'steals', 'describes' can all fill the slot in 'He — the food'. This practice of ringing the changes in context must help in the discovery of the rule. The procedure is reminiscent of the substitution table exercise mentioned in chapter 6.

There is no implication that in producing such a sequence Janet was consciously coaching Helen (it was delivered quite spontaneously as part of the conversation), but there is a good example in the transcript where the chance to teach does arise and is accepted. When Janet first says 'delicious', it is the appropriate adult response to the food that she pretends to be eating. But she says the word twice and with great expressiveness, and Helen's attention is caught by it. Her attempt to say the word herself leads Janet to ask 'So what do you say?', when Helen is 'eating'. Helen is being offered a clear model here of which words can be used appropriately in which circumstances. If you listen to the tape you will hear Janet's delight when Helen uses the word again and that must have reinforced the 'lesson'. Now with the bit between her teeth, Janet tries to consolidate the acquisition of the new word when she notices Helen assuming the persona of Baby, and tries to get Baby to use the word too.

If little has been said so far about the adults' corrections to

Helen's speech, it is for the good reason that they rarely make any. Had they wanted to, they could have found plenty to pick on in her pronunciation, but their corrections are reserved for the truth of what she says. Clare did not come yesterday, and we do not have butter on cornflakes or eat them on the stairs.

Two more points can be made about what the adults say to Helen, both connected with the nature of their language. First there is the naturalness of their speech. One school of thought believes that people express themselves in complete sentences, and in writing they usually do. In speech, however, it is a different matter. When Helen asks whether Baby can have a cup of tea, her mother's reply is 'If you want', and that is natural English. The second point is that, as Helen's speech develops, the adults may well credit her with greater understanding of their own language and may use more complex sentences. When Janet says, 'She says she's hungry' she is using a two-clause sentence (She says || she's hungry), something that Helen herself cannot produce at this stage, but which she is apparently expected to understand.

4 The development of Helen's language

a. Phonology

One consequence of Helen's linguistic development is, paradoxically, that we begin to notice her 'mistakes'. It is as though now that her language is beginning to approximate to the adult system, we are more inclined to judge her by the standards of that system rather than, as we have been doing and should still do, in terms of her own. Thus it would be over-simplifying and misleading to list her errors as though she were attempting, not very successfully, to imitate adult speech. One could start by looking at the examples of deviance in the field of phonology: 'Pease', 'Care', 'nother', 'likkle', 'Henen', 'licious', 'titchen'. It is a predictable list, in the sense that most of us have heard children say things like this and would regard them as typically child-like. They do in fact fit in pretty well with the textbook account of the acquisition of phonology. There is substitution of /k/ for /t/ in 'likkle', for example, and the reverse in 'titchen'; the omission of /l/ in consonant clusters in 'pease' and 'Care'; and in both 'nother' and 'licious' the child is omitting an unstressed syllable. We could look more profitably at how much of the sound system of English she has already mastered. We saw Ralph beginning to acquire the intonation patterns of English and some control of rhythm, but he

123

had yet to begin to learn individual phonemes. Helen, on the other hand, has acquired virtually all the phonemes and is now refining her perception and production of them in various combinations. One could think of several reasons why particular phonemes or combinations of phonemes should cause problems. In order to produce language at all we have to control our speech organs with great precision, accurately hitting very small targets to produce significant contrasts, and, as with any other physical movement, this will need practice. There is, too, the question of feedback: a major factor in learning to make phonological contrasts is hearing others and ourselves producing them.

When a child produces what is on the face of it an error, that is to say, a divergence from the adult system, he has often got more right than wrong. In the field of syntax, for example, the child who says 'swimmed' is wrong in assuming that this particular verb is a weak one (i.e. it forms its past tense by the addition of the -ed morphemes), but, what is more important, he does at least have some notion that there are past tenses, and he has mastered one common way of 'realising' them. In other words, there could be more profit for him in having this productive rule at his disposal (he has not heard *swimmed*, he has made it up) than in having mastered one 'correct' item in a repertoire. For this reason some writers would refer to such an over-generalisation as a **virtuous error**. It is a useful phrase for teachers to bear in mind, because it encourages us to look for the positive side of what could be simply dismissed as substandard performance. It can apply to miscues in reading, for example, when instead of merely correcting or noting errors we can look for the causes, and find at times that the child is reading more effectively than the surface blemish may indicate. Or we can approach errors in written English as evidence of partial accomplishment and as indications of the next steps to be taken. To come back to Helen and her pronunciation, we could notice that if her task is to differentiate the features of English phonemes, then /k/ for /t/, for example, is not very wide of the mark. After all they are both consonants, and stop consonants at that, and they are both unvoiced. And if we listen to our pronunciation of 'delicious', noting where the stress appears to be placed, we can understand how Helen came to hear and then say 'licious'. She has enough control over the systematic contrasts in stress and intonation for the adults to be able to understand her.

All this stress on phonology is in any case distorting our reaction to the dialogue. We have constantly stressed that when children talk to us we hear, but scarcely attend to, differences in pronunciation because we are more interested in what they have to say. If we are to pay attention to the form of Helen's language rather than to its function, then there are more interesting things to say about her syntax. When we last saw her, she was emerging into the two-element utterance stage, and we noted that she was able to make herself clear without using inflexions or the 'little words'. What is the position now? We can find examples of patterns which are very much like those of the earlier stage, such as 'Got socks off' or 'Putting that in cup', where, by adult standards, there is a missing element. (It has been suggested that young children regularly miss out the subject at first — 'I' in this case — because it is obvious to them that they are the performers of the action they are describing.) At the same time there are other utterances which are beginning to sound very much like normal English, such as 'I'm putting some milk in,' and 'I'm making some dinner'. You will remember that at the previous stage, when Helen was expressing various grammatical relationships with her two-word patterns, we predicted that she would soon progress to relating three elements. It is such patterns that we are describing as 'normal English'. Before, you will remember, she could produce the subject-verb combination ('Henen ride'), and in chapter 5 examples were quoted of other children's use of other combinations of two elements (such as verb-object). In 'I'm making some dinner' we now have not only the subject-verb-object pattern, but also some of the inflexions and 'little words' that were missing at the previous stage. This use of additional elements, together with sentence structure, provides us with two areas where we can look for further development.

b. Sentence structure

The first point about Helen's sentence structure has already been made. There are many of her utterances that are indistinguishable in their grammar from those of adults: 'I'm making some dinner', 'I'm cutting it with that', 'I'm putting some milk in', 'I've got tea leaves in it'.

All of these display the subject-verb-object pattern, and two of them a fourth element which will be discussed in the next chapter. But there are others which show how she is learning to do more than just make assertions or ask questions. Do you remember that series of 'No's' with which she thwarted the adults who wanted to pack her off to bed? Four months later she has a wider repertoire of negatives: 'don't want to', 'Can't have a cup of tea', 'don't hold my arm'.

She has learned that 'don't' and 'can't' can be used for saying 'No', in this case for different forms of rejection.

When it comes to the inflexions and little words, quite an advance has been made. Taking the words first, there is clear evidence that 'in' is now used frequently: 'in house', 'in likkle box', 'Get push chair in Aunty Nanny car', but the articles ('a' and 'the') are not: 'a cup of tea' and possibly 'A likkle knife' are the only exceptions. The position with the inflexions is more interesting and can best be discussed when we look at the next area of development, that of **phrase structure**.

c. Phrase structure

The different elements that go to make up sentences also have their own structure. The early utterances of young children have their stripped-to-the-bone look partly because of the number of elements of which they are composed, but also because those elements usually consist of single words. Take 'Doggy bite' for example. Its pattern is subject-verb, both subject and verb consisting of single words: 'Doggy' and 'bite'. An obvious path for development will be the elaboration of the single words into phrases. There are many examples of this in the transcript: 'Mummy's shopping basket', 'My toast', 'some butter', 'cup of tea' (unless that is really a single item), or these, which show a development from Helen's previous use of single words to show where things were: 'in Aunty Nanny's car', 'in that', 'in it'.

These last three show another aspect of Helen's development: if she can use both 'it' and 'that' in the same slot as 'car', then on the 'privilege of occurrence' argument she is beginning to build up a class of pronouns. Remember too that there is another way of looking at word combinations such as 'my toast' and that is as expressions of semantic roles such as possession ('my toast') and attribution.

There is one conspicuous development which is closely connected with the kind of situation which the transcript records. As we have seen, Helen talks incessantly in her make-believe kitchen about what is supposed to be going on. Both she and the adults are constrained in their choice of verb forms by the current nature of the situation. If someone says to you 'What are you doing?', the answer might be 'I'm reading a book,' but not 'I read a book'. We call forms such as 'I'm reading', 'he's sleeping', 'they're coming next week', the **present continuous** or **present progressive**, and the

126

transcript abounds in them, both in the full forms of adult grammar and in Helen's mixture of those and her own variants.

Consider what is needed to form the present continuous, in such examples as 'The sun is shining', 'Your slip's showing', 'They're turning off the water'.

One model of grammar would propose a 'be+ing' rule, because we need to use a form of the verb 'to be' in front of the verb stem ('shine', 'show', and 'turn', in the examples just given) and '-ing' after it. A child has to learn to associate the '-ing' ending with ongoing activity, and to choose the appropriate form of 'to be' to match the subject. It seems from the transcript that Helen has already mastered the rule, if we look at such utterances as, 'I'm making some dinner', 'I'm going in likkle box', 'I'm sitting down', but if we look more closely, there is plenty of evidence of more rudimentary forms such as, 'Putting that in cup', 'Baby having cup of tea', 'Eating some butter', 'Henen cutting that up'.

Apparently it is the '-ing' that is acquired first and the 'to be' part later. If we think about the contracted forms like /'m/ and /'s/ that we use in speech ('I'm going', 'He's leaving') and how they must sound to the learner, tacked on as they are to the end of stressed words, it is hardly surprising if they do not register at first. Most of Helen's normal forms are those with 'I'm', although even that form is not completely secure yet, judging by 'I giving food'.

If we look at the abundance of examples of the present continuous in the transcript, we realise how much repetition children are subjected to merely because of the situations in which adults talk to them. There will be a similar example in chapter 13 when the swans' arrival is greeted with a flurry of '-ing' forms. Not that all the input is helpful. If we are learning to associate '-ing' with present action, such remarks as 'What are you going to do?' may introduce a complication for which we are not yet ready. One realises too how odd the language of some early reading books must sound to children who have regularly taken part in conversations like this one. What are they to make of 'Mummy smiles at baby', when they know that people just do not talk like that? Since we know that prediction has a part to play in the reading process, we may as well ensure that children can profit from their existing knowledge of language.

The present continuous is the verb form which is needed when we are talking about ongoing action, but in displaced speech Helen must also be able to talk about the past. Here the important form will be the **present perfect** (not 'be+ing' this time, but 'have+en').

127

The verb 'to have' precedes the verb stem, and '-ed' or '-en' follows it, as in, 'They've turned off the water', 'The cat's eaten the goldfish' (but note 'He's dug a hole in the garden.').

The variant forms will make this rather more complicated for the learner, and the problems with the contracted forms will be the same as in the present continuous. Helen uses a plain 'got', in 'Got socks off', but notice the sequence where she says, 'I got tea leaves in that ... I've got tea leaves in it ... got tea leaves in box.' The /'ve/ is used only once, as though she is just beginning to acquire it.

Both the present continuous and the present perfect involve the use of bound morphemes like '-ing' and '-ed'. Another, represented in writing as '-s',* is used with the third person singular of the simple present in such examples as, 'She loves me, she loves me not', 'The sun rises in the east', 'A rolling stone gathers no moss'. In the transcript there is only one example of Helen's using something of the kind: 'Baby like some cornflakes', but it would be pointless to say much about it, for many reasons. First of all, there is only the one example, but that may be because in this situation there was no occasion to use more. Apart from that, there is the usual difficulty of interpretation. Was Helen intending to say what we would convey by saying, 'Baby likes ...', or is it her version of 'Baby would like ...'? Even if we listen to the utterance in context on the tape there is no possible way of being certain. In the same way it would be useless to speculate about Helen's grasp of plurals, also often signalled with '-s'. She says 'socks', 'stairs', 'tea leaves' and 'cornflakes', but there is no evidence within the transcript that these are more than separate items, unconnected with the corresponding singular forms. Incidentally, when we consider that the same morpheme is used to signal not only plurals and the third person singular but also possessives ('Henen's'), we begin to realise how much there is for a child to learn.

We have concentrated on certain aspects of Helen's developing sentence and phrase structure as a basis for comparison in the later commentaries. By so doing we have passed over other areas that could also have been discussed, for example, the growth of certain classes of words, such as pronouns. Before we leave the transcript there are two general points to be made. What should be stressed first of all is that grammar is as much a part of meaning as vocabulary is. In the light of Berry's statement, 'All language works by means of contrasting choices',[2] we can see where the topics discussed in this chapter fit in. Speakers of English contrast 'I go'

* But see follow-up activity a (p. 130).

and 'I'm going' systematically, using them appropriately in various circumstances. The speaker of a non-standard dialect, who might well use expressions that sounded odd to speakers of the standard form, would still be quick to spot some faint nuance of 'un-Englishness' in the usage of even an accomplished foreign speaker of English. We are dealing here with a knowledge of language that goes far beyond the prescriptive niceties of the grammar textbook. We might find difficulty in explaining the difference in meaning between 'go' and 'am going', but we can use them appropriately nevertheless. Just as our vocabulary develops in the ways which were touched upon in chapter 4, so we learn ever more uses for the structures in our repertoire. At two a child may be using '-ing' forms to signal immediately present action, but at twelve the same structures may be used in expressions like, 'We're studying light this term,' and 'No-one's going to make me believe that.' The second point has been half-made already. To talk about Helen's 'grammatical knowledge' is not to credit her with conscious knowledge of what we have been calling 'rules'. We are dealing here with knowledge of, not knowledge about, language – something that no textbook or teacher can teach.

5 Suggestions for further work and discussion
Points for discussion

i. The adult's contribution

   a Collect all the adults' questions in the transcript and see whether the classification of their functions as proposed in the commentary is adequate.

   b Examine all the adult expansions of Helen's utterances and try to work out the 'rules' the adults appear to be following.

   c Find examples of the reverse process – the child reducing an adult utterance – and see if there is a systematic relationship between expansion and **reduction**.

   d An example was given of coaching ('delicious'). Are there others in the transcript?

   e Are there examples of complex sentences addressed to the child?

ii. Helen's use of language

   a Examine the transcript and the tape for more examples of Helen's incomplete mastery of phonemes. Can you see any anomalies (e.g. where she can apparently produce a sound on one occasion and not on another)? Try to account for this and for the other 'errors'.

129

b Do you see any instances where Helen could be practising a structural pattern?

c In the commentary most stress is laid on Halliday's 'imaginative model'. What other models are in evidence in the transcript?

Follow-up activities

Morphemes

a In written English the plural of many nouns is signalled by the use of '-s', and that may give us the wrong impression about what happens in speech. Look at the following examples:

singular	*plural*
horse	horses
cat	cats
dog	dogs
cow	cows

Now listen to the words as you say them aloud. What is printed as '-s' represents three different sounds. What are they? Try to work out the rules that govern which is used when. Next consider the third person singular, as in these examples:

First person	*Third person*
I want	he wants
I dig	he digs
I reach	he reaches
I go	he goes

Are there similar 'rules' for these? Read Jean Berko (1958) to see whether your rules are the same as those she describes.

b Read Roger Brown (1973) on 'Grammatical morphemes and the modulation of meaning' and see how much of what he says you can apply to the Helen transcript.

c Compare this recording with others, preferably made by yourself.

6 References

[1] Halliday, M. A. K. (1969) 'Relevant Models of Language' in A. Wilkinson (ed.) *The State of Language* University of Birmingham School of Education

[2] Berry, M. (1975) *Introduction to Systemic Linguistics* Batsford

11 I can do:
Helen at twenty-six months

---

1 Transcript†

Playing with Tom, a sailor doll; a board with small coloured pegs which can be stuck on in mosaic patterns; a wooden jigsaw puzzle which she calls 'pieces'.

CHRIS Are you going to show Tom how to do that, Helen? (*Stick beads/pegs on the board*)

HELEN Mm. Oh, look at it. (*Laughs, playing with the beads*)

JAN What/what letter are you going to make on there?

HELEN Thank you. Mum, want these off. (*Pulling beads off board*) Likkle knobs.

CHRIS Do you know what colour they are?

HELEN They're red.

CHRIS Are they?

HELEN No t'isn't red. (*It was red*)

CHRIS No, what colour is it?

HELEN Red . . . No don't do that. (*Take the beads out*)

CHRIS I thought you wanted me to do it.

HELEN No . . . want to do it.

CHRIS What are you trying to do?

HELEN Just . . . just . . . getting these out ** somefink.

★　　★　　★　　★

HELEN Tom, Tom, Tom. Tom, Tom, Tom, Tom (*singing tone*). Take these out, take that one out. I want to do it.

† For an explanation of transcription symbols, see p. 21.

JAN I'll lean Tom against there . . . that's right.

HELEN Do it/do it again for me pease. That fell down, silly Mummy.

★   ★   ★   ★

CHRIS Right, what do you want me to make for you?

HELEN These.

CHRIS Right, well get me a red one then.

HELEN This?

JAN Is that red?

HELEN No I want to, those pease. Doan (don't) me.

[CHRIS Don't watch me]

JAN Don't watch you

CHRIS Can Mummy watch you?

HELEN Yes

CHRIS Oh that's kind of you . . . (*12 secs*) . . . Where did we find these Helen? Where were they?

HELEN In toy cupboard.

CHRIS Were they?

HELEN Yes

CHRIS Whereabouts?

JAN What else did you find in the toy cupboard?

CHRIS You mustn't touch that Helen. (*the microphone*)

JAN What else did you find in the toy cupboard?

CHRIS Can you remember where we went to this morning, Helen?

HELEN Went to outside. ?Getting blackberries.

CHRIS Did we? And were there any blackberries?

HELEN No

JAN Oh dear, that means we can't have blackberry-and-apple pie, doesn't it?

HELEN No

JAN Mm

CHRIS What did Aunt Janet do?

HELEN Put some bulbs in *

JAN Put some bulbs in . . .?

CHRIS Put some bulbs in . . .?

HELEN Soil

CHRIS In soil

JAN Yes, how did I put *

HELEN Where's it gone?

JAN How/Here it is? How did I put them in?

HELEN Like this. (Now reverting to showing how the beads peg on to the board)

JAN Show me/tell me how/how did I do it. What did I do? I got a little . . .

HELEN Stab.

JAN A little . . .?

HELEN Stab.

JAN Step did I?

[CHRIS No she thinks you're talking about this now. She says a little stab.]

JAN Oh, a little stab, oh stab it in. Yes, stab it in by all means.

CHRIS No Aunty said to you how did she plant the bulbs?

HELEN Mummy building that up again. Bulla, bulla, bullow. (*Singing*) What's Mummy making . . . a bed! ** What's Mummy maked. (*'ed' not strongly pronounced, but probably present*)

JAN What has Mummy made? (*Sounds of coughing in the background.*)

HELEN What's Mamma doing?

JAN Well what do *you* think Mamma's doing?

HELEN Coughing.

JAN Coughing is she? What else is she doing?

(*Helen tries to play with the microphone*)

JAN No leave that where it is. Now where's that gone?

HELEN I can do

CHRIS Helen, what does Mummy give you when you cough?

HELEN Medicine . . . Can I have

CHRIS Did you like planting bulbs in the garden?

HELEN ?Yes.

CHRIS Did you? Did Aunty get her shoes dirty?

HELEN No

CHRIS Oh I thought that she did? . . . Didn't they get all mud on them?

HELEN No.

CHRIS Mm. What did Grandma/What were Grandma's shoes like when she went out? . . . Grandma had got her . . .?

HELEN Slippers on.

CHRIS She had. Was that naughty?

HELEN No, wasn't

JAN and CHRIS Oh.

JAN When did Grandma go out with her slippers on?

133

HELEN Walking *. I walk in my best shoes.

JAN You walked in your best shoes, did you? When was this? When did you walk in your best shoes? . . . Where did you go in your best shoes? Where did you walk to?

HELEN Blackberries.

CHRIS Blackberries. [She thinks it's cos we were talking about them.]

HELEN *

CHRIS Do you like your best shoes, Helen?

HELEN Nanny put it down. (*The microphone*)

JAN I'm sorry. Is it in Tom's way?

HELEN Yes.

JAN Poor Tom. Where did you find Tom?

HELEN ?Opened cupboard.

JAN In the toy cupboard.

HELEN *Mummy. * Tom, Tom. What's Tommy doing? What Tommy doing?

JAN What *is* he doing?

HELEN (*sings a tune*) * in cupboard for me. (*Brings out a jigsaw*)

JAN Do you like doing pieces? Come on, let me put you on the chair then. Bring it here. Whoops a day. Oh. Do you know we can't get through that crack. Oh, now then.

HELEN ?Wh/What's this?

JAN Take them all out to start with and let's see how it goes.

HELEN No . . . Mummy can do (you) do dese (these). Can do . . . D'yare Mummy . . . D'yare Mummy. D'yare. This is a likkle one, somefin

CHRIS Has it got a picture on?

HELEN Yes

CHRIS What is it?

HELEN Don't know. (*Putting pieces of jigsaw on a box*) S'gone up.

CHRIS Has it jumped up there?

HELEN Yes . . . That's it.

JAN What's it doing?

HELEN Timbing (climbing)

JAN Climbing

HELEN ?Whisking, whisking round.

CHRIS Could you find me a big piece, of jigsaw?

JAN ?Where's there a big piece?

HELEN Dis big piece.

CHRIS And where's the little piece? . . . Thank you very much.

HELEN These are mine Mummy . . . My . . . these mine jigsaws.

HELEN This a big one?

CHRIS Are there any more little ones?

HELEN No.

CHRIS Have a look.

HELEN This a likkle one . . . that a teddy bear, somefin . . . here

CHRIS Which is the tiny one?

HELEN This is tiny ones.

CHRIS Is it very tiny?

HELEN Yes . . . What's this a big piece? What's/what's this Mummy?

CHRIS It's enormous isn't it? . . . Is it enormous?

HELEN Des, Mummy.

CHRIS Is it very enormous?

HELEN Des. What's the/What's the big piece?

JAN What's the picture on that big piece? What's the picture on the piece you've got in your hand?

HELEN Crying . . . crying.

JAN It's crying is it?

HELEN Des.

CHRIS I wonder why? Why is it crying?

HELEN * That's a doggy . . .? What's ? that, Mum?

JAN What is it? What is it?

HELEN * Helen do that piece.

CHRIS You've got a lot of pieces, haven't you? Could you count them for me?

HELEN No

CHRIS Could you *try* to count them? How does Daddy count?

HELEN Oh, oh, oh. (*Rhythm of one, two, three*)

CHRIS What does he start with? He says one

HELEN Want a box Mum.

CHRIS I don't know which box they were in

JAN I think that was the one

HELEN This . . . upside down. *** (*clattering of pieces and laughter*)

CHRIS What's Aunty doing?

HELEN ?Taking me pieces

CHRIS Is she? (*Blowing noises and laughter*)

HELEN No.

HELEN (*Shouts*) ** Lost some pieces . . .? I want some pieces

CHRIS Why?

HELEN Cos I do . . . Where's Tom . . . Tom. Bet det (better get)

Tom hadn't I? Bet det Tom.

[JAN Better get Tom, hadn't I?]

CHRIS Have you found him?

HELEN Yes

CHRIS Has he been a good boy today?

HELEN (*Sings*) Tom, Tom, Tom, *** Tum, Tum, Tum, Tum.

JAN Bring Tom on the table and show him all these pieces *
show him the pieces, tell him what's on the pieces.

HELEN Pictures and *** Looking at his (this – *the microphone*).

JAN Is he looking at it?

HELEN Yes.

CHRIS What can he see?

JAN What can he see?

HELEN ***

JAN Well he's close enough, isn't he?

HELEN Des

CHRIS What's/what's Tom doing?

HELEN (*Screams*) Tom, Tom, Tom. (*Chants*) Tommy, Tommy,
Tommy. D'yare Tom.

8

CHRIS Helen, do you know a little boy called Tom?

HELEN Des

JAN Where/Where does Tom live?

HELEN In Badford (Bradford).

JAN In Bradford, does he?

HELEN Ye . . . in toy cupboard.

JAN In a toy cupboard in Bradford. That's a nice place to live,
isn't it?

HELEN What's that doing? (*Refers to the microphone on the
table*)

JAN And who looks after Tom?

HELEN Mummy.

JAN Oh his Mummy, does she? And what does he do all day?

HELEN D'yare . . . sitting down.

JAN He's sitting down now, is he?

HELEN I've been playing all the day.

[JAN I've been playing all the day.]

CHRIS That's very nice . . . what have I been doing?

JAN What have Mummy and Mamma (*Helen's grandmother*)
been doing all day if Helen's been playing?

HELEN What's this Mummy? What's this Mummy?

CHRIS I think it's a diggery boo. (*Deliberately invented to see if
she picks it up*) What is it?

HELEN ***

CHRIS What is it?

HELEN Tom want to look at it

JAN Well you'd better come and show him then.

HELEN Tom, Tom, Tom want to look at it. Tom, Tom ... s'looking ... s'looking.

JAN He's looking is he?

HELEN D'yare ... he's looked. Hello Tom ... Hello Tom, Tom,
Tom, Tom. D'yare Mummy ... sitting. Sit down, Tom. Sitting
down.

JAN Is he? I think he likes sitting.

HELEN Peanut ... peanut ... I want peanut ... want peanut
pease. (*We were eating peanuts.*)

JAN That's very nice.

CHRIS (*Handing her the tin of peanuts*) What do you say?

HELEN Pease.

CHRIS Good girl ...

[CHRIS That'll shut her up for a bit.]

HELEN Do ? a want one?

JAN Do I want one? Yes please. Thank you, that's very kind of
you.

HELEN Thank you.

CHRIS Have you given one to Tom?

HELEN Mm. **

CHRIS Pardon?

HELEN Given one.

CHRIS *Have* you given one to Tom?

HELEN Des.

JAN Where is Tom?

CHRIS He's here. Oy!

HELEN Had/had a sweetie. Had a sweetie.

JAN He's had one has he?

HELEN Mm

CHRIS Well I think he'd like another one

HELEN (*Gives him one*) Tom ... that's it.

CHRIS Can you give him another one?

HELEN Look at these, Mamma ... look at these.

CHRIS Can you carry that?

HELEN ***

CHRIS Would you like me to carry it?

HELEN No I doing it ... put that in.

JAN Oh

HELEN   Nearly fall down that over (*other*) one.

CHRIS   What did it do?

HELEN   Fall down

CHRIS   Did it?

HELEN   Mm . . . having this Mummy. No don't want to look at it Tom.

[CHRIS   No she doesn't want that.]

HELEN   Bringing toys out cup/cupoard door . . . Mummy doan want these bits . . . what's this one here?

JAN   What is it?

HELEN   **

JAN   Now what've you got?

HELEN   This . . . can build dis one on there . . . no doan want that over one.

CHRIS   Why not?

HELEN   On there Mummy ***. Better put it in to here.

JAN   You better put it in there. Why? . . . What are you going to make?

HELEN   No . . .? dat won't/?dat won't fit in there.

CHRIS   Why not?

JAN   Why won't it fit?

HELEN   No ** That's a big one **

CHRIS   That's a funny little thing, isn't it?

HELEN   Des

CHRIS   What is it?

HELEN   From here, think.

CHRIS   Is it? I don't think it is.

HELEN   Where's it gone? I can't find it.

2   The situation

Once again, Helen is playing – not an unusual activity for a two-year-old child and a convenient opportunity to record her speech – but this time there is palpably much more talk. This could be pure chance, the result of hitting upon a particularly productive stimulus perhaps, but if we look at some of the reasons for the greater length of the transcript, we shall find that some of the factors already discussed are playing a part. True, there are still plenty of questions from the adults, as we shall see when we examine this aspect of the conversation a little later, but we shall also notice that the adults can now ask more complicated questions, and questions of various types. Add to this Helen's own ability to ask more kinds of questions for herself, as well as being able to reply to those that are put to her, and already we can begin to see that it is more likely that the conversation will be sustained.

And this is not all. The capacity that Helen has to resist the adults' direction of the conversation and to initiate topics herself which we noted earlier is here continued and developed. She appears to have more to say, and more skill in saying it: the conversation therefore flows more easily, and her contributions are longer and more complex. At twenty months she was very much confined to the role of respondent and to contemplation of objects, people and events either actually present or in the not very distant environment, and we found it worthy of comment when she used either 'displaced speech' or make-believe. Now, however, she is moving easily from language that is immediately concerned with her present situation ('look at it') to conversations about the past ('What were Grandma's shoes like when she went out?'), and about processes that are habitual in her experience ('Helen, what does Mummy give you when you cough?').

3 Helen's use of language
It is artificial to separate the language forms from the language function, but in this case it will ensure that we look first at what would be our chief preoccupation in the actual situation, namely what the child has to say, and then we can examine the developments in her grammar, in the sense of her control of semantic and syntactic rules. There she is, playing in the presence of, and sometimes with the help of, the adults. Sometimes they speak to her and she needs to be able to reply, sometimes she has some need that only they can fulfil. They are her main source of knowledge, and have, as far as she knows, perfect command of the medium for communicating it; she needs knowledge about both the world and the medium. She wishes to play, to enjoy herself; they are just as concerned that she should enjoy what she is doing and should feel herself part of the group, but they also want to see her develop various skills, one of which is using language. It is therefore hardly surprising if in this situation, as in the 'Lego farm' episode in the next chapter, there are occasions when the interests of child and adult flow together in co-operative dialogue, while at other times the child is so engrossed in what she is doing that the adults' questions are unwanted distraction. This will be particularly obvious when we look at the adults' questions in more detail.

Suppose we start, then, by considering those parts of the conversation in which Helen is making the running. How successful is she in using language to get what she wants? She has acquired that useful formula 'I want' and can ask for objects ('I want peanut'), and for actions to be performed ('Do it again for me, pease'). Where once she used the one word 'No' to great effect, she can now be much more explicit ('don't do that'), and can therefore take a greater share both in the actions and in the accompanying speech. She has, too, learned to temper the naked imperative by adding the polite social formulas that help us to get our own way: she has learned the value of 'please' and 'thank you'. But since there is very much more than objects and helpful action to be supplied by adults, she has also learned to use words to find out information. At twenty months it was Helen who had to deal with 'What's this?', but now the weapon is in her hands and, at this stage at least, she appears to be asking questions for the straightforward purpose of finding the answers. There are other ways, too, in which she is now capable of making her own contribution without prompting. Not only does she tell others what to do, but she can consult them, as for example when she says 'Bet det Tom hadn't I?'

If we examine her responses to other people's remarks, we can see an extension in her repertoire of functions as well as of forms. Now when the adult comments on her actions she can add an explanatory comment ('Just . . . just . . . getting these out'). She can express an opinion ('No, wasn't', she says, when they ask her whether her grandma's action had been naughty). She accompanies some of her actions with speech for her own benefit, directing the activity ('Stab', she says, as she threads the beads), and she can add a comment to someone else's actions ('Silly Mummy', she remarks, as she sees something fall down). At times it is a make-believe world which is being created by her language (as in the account of Tom's imagined activities), or the language sounds themselves are being played with ('Bulla bulla bullow'). There is also an expansion of the things she was able to do before, as, for example, her ability to give answers to a greater variety of questions. We shall discuss these when we examine the development of her syntax.

4 The adults' language
If Helen's contribution to the dialogue has increased, so too has that of the adults. We must stress that there can be no safe generalisations made from such small samples as are presented here, and what is being said now could be quite properly dismissed as subjective or anecdotal. But the feeling that perhaps the adults are unconsciously crediting the child with more understanding can

perhaps be justified. Look back over the earlier transcripts at the adults' utterances and compare them with those in the present one. We have said that adults do not use a modified form of English when talking to children; that their utterances may be simple sentences, but that they do use complete sentences and not 'telegraphese'. But what do we mean by a simple sentence? A short one? One composed of simple words, whatever they are? Here is one suggested criterion. English sentences are composed of clauses, which can be defined as groups of words containing a subject and a verb. (Such a definition has many shortcomings and should be regarded as a purely *ad hoc* one for the purpose of understanding the examples that follow.) Thus, when in an earlier transcript Helen said, 'I'm going in likkle box', she was using a sentence consisting of one clause, the subject being 'I' and the verb ''m going'. Similarly when her mother said to her, 'We'll take a shopping basket,' she was using a one-clause sentence with 'We' as subject and ''ll take' as verb. Look at the first transcripts and see whether the adults usually restrict themselves to these forms, whether knowingly or not. Now look at their utterances in this one. Do you see any differences?

Take, for example, the forms of **question**. Here are some from the conversation in this chapter:

'Do you know what colour they are?'

'Can you remember where we went to this morning?'

It is likely that Helen would previously have been asked the same questions in the following form:

'What colour are they?'

'Where did we go this morning?'

Before, she had one clause to disentangle; now there are two. 'Do you know ‖ what colour they are?', 'Can you remember ‖ where we went to this morning?' This may be pure chance – the more complex forms may have been used on earlier occasions but have gone unrecorded – but it is possible that, as children grow older, we unconsciously modify our language when speaking to them, allowing ourselves to use grammatical structures of greater complexity.

The question forms alone are worth a little more study, but let us broaden the discussion by looking at three things together: the form of the questions, their function (why are the adults asking them?), and the appropriate forms of reply. There are basically four ways of asking questions in English. We can use words that would otherwise signal a statement, but, by changing out intonation, we convert them into a question. This would be the case if, for example, someone said, 'He's left', and we expressed our surprise in the same words with contrasting intonation, 'He's left?' Intonation plays a part in other forms of question when we are speaking, but we also use signals in the grammar. Thus there is the **yes/no question** (so called because those are the words that are used to answer them), where the signal will be a change in the word order, as in 'Is the butcher calling today?' or 'May I take that with me?' In both of these part of the verb is moved to the beginning of the sentence. Then we have the **'wh' question**, so called because it begins with a question word, almost always beginning with 'wh': 'what', 'why', 'when', 'where', 'how'. Finally there is the **tag question**, where a statement is made and then 'tagged' with the question-asking part, as for example in 'That's a pretty colour, isn't it?' or 'You won't be long, will you?' You will notice two things about this kind of question, one about its form and the other about its function. In French, there is a single invariant tag for many different statements: 'N'est-ce pas?' In English, however, there are many different forms of tag, depending on the form of the initial statement. Try adding tags to the following (you will do so without having to think about it, because that's what being a native speaker implies) and then look at what you have added:

'Your father supports Leeds United.'
'I'll send them by rail.'
'The birds aren't hungry.'
'The doctor would be pleased.'

Suppose that you had to write a rule that would guarantee that anyone following it would always produce the appropriate tag. You would find this a much more difficult operation than it sounds.

As for the function of this kind of question, the fact that it begins with a statement offers us a possible clue. Frequently, with other types of question, one is seeking information; with the tag question, it is more a matter of seeking reassurance, confirmation of the truth of what one has just asserted.

Leaving aside the function of the questions for the time being, let us think for a moment about the problems that the different question forms will present to the child. First, the signals will have to be correctly interpreted: what kind of question am I being asked? And eventually there will be the problem of learning the correct form of words for making appropriate replies. Here are some of the questions that Helen meets in this quite ordinary conversation:

'Can Mummy watch you?'
'Is this red?'

'Did you like planting bulbs in the garden?'

'Is it in Tom's way?'

These are all yes/no questions and are dealt with accordingly, as are the rather more confusing elliptical versions which follow Helen's own assertions: 'Are they?', 'Were they?'

But look at the variety of 'wh' questions that come at her thick and fast. Six months ago she was hearing 'What's this?' and could already at that stage supply the appropriate one-word answer. 'What' still prefaces many of the questions but it is not always used in the same way. In the case of 'What's that?' we are often being asked to identify the object that someone is pointing to or has referred to, and a noun is an appropriate response. 'What letter ...?' or 'What colour ...?' are not quite the same: the nouns state categories and invite the child to give instances. 'What are you trying to do?' is even less straightforward; the category this time is indicated by the verb 'do' and the child must identify not an object but a process.

But not all the 'wh' questions are merely 'what' forms. 'Where were they?' is one question, and to the word 'where' the child must learn to associate a word or phrase that signifies location. Even less concrete perhaps is the 'how' question. 'How did I put them in?' must tax Helen's resources at this stage and it's not surprising that her reply is simply 'Like this', and action supplements speech. On the other hand, the question 'Which is the little one?' appears to cause her no difficulty.

But the adults are holding a conversation, not giving a grammar lesson. Why, in the flow of that conversation, are the questions being asked? After all, in most conversations not all the questions are asked purely to obtain information, or for any other single reason, and this conversation is no different. We ask questions to show an interest in other people and their activities. That is the social, conversational purpose of such questions as, 'Can Mummy watch you?', 'Where were they?' 'That means we can't have blackberry-and-apple pie, doesn't it?' Other questions have a much more testing element – such questions as, 'Is that red?', 'Do you know what colour they are?', 'Which is the tiny one?' Specific knowledge of vocabulary items is being checked here, and, of course, the ability to perceive colour and size. Other forms of testing present Helen with greater problems, as, for example, the 'how' and 'why' questions. At least one question seems to be a genuine request for information, when Helen is asked 'What are you trying to do?' as a prelude to the mother's offering help.

How successfully does Helen cope with them all? Look at the questions that have been quoted so far and try to decide the appropriate forms of reply, then examine Helen's replies:

'Is that red?'
'No'

'Are they?'
'No'

No trouble with the yes/no question then.

'What colour is it?'
'Red'

'What do you want me to make for you?'
'These'

'Where were they?'
'In toy cupboard'

'How did I put them in?'
'Like this'

'Who looks after Tom?'
'Mummy'

A variety of 'wh' questions here, needing a variety of different forms to answer them, and once again the child is able both to understand the questions and to use the appropriate form of words in her reply. Where she does not, it is the familiar story of getting by with less than the full repertoire. She says 'These,' and points to, or otherwise physically indicates, what she is talking about rather than using a word; or she demonstrates an action ('Like this') which she cannot yet describe. Failure to reply at all can usually be put down either to boredom with the question because she is too engrossed in what she wants to do, or to the difficulty of the question. Predictably, the 'why' questions do not produce a response, and neither does the 'What have I been doing?' question, which demands a feat of abstraction that is beyond her at the moment. False responses, on the other hand, come when the insistent question 'Are they?' is perhaps taken as an indication that the original identification was wrong, or when the lengthy tag question 'That means we can't have blackberry-and-apple pie, doesn't it?', with its negative in the statement part, throws her off the scent. On the whole, however, one of the reasons that this dialogue moves along so well is that Helen is better equipped to take part in it. People who live in close contact with a young child take such skill for granted for long periods of time and then suddenly realise the strides the child has made.

5 The development of Helen's language

Let us begin our examination of Helen's progress in her production of language by looking at what are called the **contextual types of utterance** that she can produce. In English there are four: the **statement**, the **question**, the **command** and the **response**, and this child can produce all of them. Statements, naturally, abound, and so a single example will be enough: 'They're red.'

There are also many questions. How do these compare with those of the adults? She can use the yes/no question by intonation, as in 'This a big one?', or by inverting word order: 'Mummy, can do do these?' Notice also the number of 'wh' questions. Admittedly, most of them begin with 'what': 'What's Mummy making?', 'What's Mamma doing?', 'What's this?', 'What's this a big piece?', but she is beginning to use different types, and there is at least one starting with 'where': 'Where's it gone?' What is more, she has begun to use the tag question: 'Bet det Tom, hadn't I?'

If we look at the reasons for which the questions are asked we shall find that they are virtually all genuine questions in the sense that she really does want to know the answers.

The third sentence-type, the command, is also represented, as in 'Look at it'.

The response, that form common in dialogue, where the utterance is not a full sentence, also occurs. A typical response in adult English would be 'Saturday' or 'Next week' in reply to the question 'When do you expect to see him, then?' or 'Our doctor' when the question was 'Who's that you were talking about?' In this conversation we have:

'Where does Tom live?'
'In Badford'

'And who looks after Tom?'
'Mummy'

Sentences can not only be of different types, but can also differ in construction. Until now we have been discussing Helen's utterances in terms of the number of elements of which they are composed, but such a measure of development, useful as it can be in the earlier stages, needs to be supported by others as the language becomes more complex. We used one such measure when we considered the language of the adults: we noticed whether their sentences were simple (i.e. consisting of a single clause) or more complex. If a child finds it necessary to use one element and then two, and so on, as she wishes to express ever more elaborate concepts and relationships, it will not be surprising if another stage is the development of sentences consisting of more than a single clause. At twenty-six months it looks as though Helen has not yet begun to do this, although she does string sentences together in longer sequences than before.

But sentences can also become more elaborate in the phrase structure. We saw Helen at twenty-four months beginning to use three elements in a single utterance, having previously been limited to two. For example, she said, 'I'm making some dinner', thus producing a completely normal-sounding sentence, the pattern being subject-verb-object or agent-action-goal. If we split this up into its constituent phrases, we have one word, 'I', as subject, two, ''m making', as verb, and two, 'some dinner', as object. In other words, Helen was beginning to fill out the phrases within her utterances: her phrase-structure was becoming more complex. One would expect to see as the next developments, on the one hand, greater elaboration of the elements already mentioned, and on the other, the introduction of another type of phrase. Helen might have added to her statement a word such as 'now' or 'today', or a phrase such as 'for Dolly' or 'in house'. We call such words and phrases **adjuncts** and they help us to give details of where, how, when, and why events and processes take place. Here are just a few examples. The adjuncts are printed in italic.

1 Try this | *on your neighbour's house.*
2 Everyone makes mistakes | *sometimes.*
3 What's | *in the paper* | *this week?*
4 Are you going grey | *too early?*
5 Come | *to us* | *for your lightweight waterproofs.*

Actually Helen had already begun to use adjuncts at two years, though many of them occurred in responses rather than in her spontaneous remarks. In terms of the increased complexity that we are now considering, they were already fairly elaborate: 'on Mummy's plate' and 'in Aunty Nanny's car'.

At the age of two, what sentence patterns* was Helen producing? She could say such things as:

* Strictly speaking, terms like 'adjunct' apply to constituents of *clauses.* At this stage, however, Helen is using a single-clause sentence, so that 'clause' and 'sentence' are interchangeable.

'I'm making some dinner.'
'Baby's having some.'

all of which exemplify the subject-verb-object pattern, and

'Putting butter on my cornflakes.'

where the pattern is 'verb-object-adjunct'. A third variant is

'I'm going in likkle box.'

This time we have three elements once again, but they are in yet another combination, subject-verb-adjunct. Now we can look out for examples of all four elements within one sentence, or of longer and more elaborately structured elements, or of more than one occurrence of a particular element within a single utterance. Look carefully at the following examples and see whether you think they fall into any of those three categories:
(a) 'Do it again for me, pease.'
(b) 'Mummy building that up again.'
(c) 'I walk in my best shoes.'
(d) 'Better put it into here.'

If we start with (b) we have an example of all four elements used in a single sentence:

```
    S       V       O     A     A
Mummy | building | that | up | again |
```

In (a) there are two adjuncts:

```
 V   O    A       A
Do | it | again | for me
```

and in both (c) and (d) there is a fairly lengthy adjunct incorporated in one of Helen's own sentences:
    in my best shoes
    into here
There is, then, evidence of a kind for saying that the expected development in phrase structure has taken place, but of course no such claim can be made merely on the strength of the small samples of Helen's speech that we have here: it would have to be demonstrated that utterances like (a) – (d) were not being produced at the earlier stage, and, clearly, without recording everything that the child says there is no way of determining that. The most that

147

can be claimed for the examples given here is that they demonstrate one way in which development can be recognised, even if, in the case of this particular child, there can be no question of determining exactly when a particular structure has been acquired.

When showing what is new in a child's language, there is a danger of giving the impression of smooth and logical progression. In fact, it would be easy to set against the examples discussed above, others showing that, side by side with the new forms, there is much that looks like a reversion to an earlier stage. 'Telegraphic' speech would not be an unreasonable description of 'This big piece' or 'This a big one', both examples, incidentally, from a child who can also say 'That's a doggy'. It might be less misleading to consider this simply as evidence of learning still going on. In much the same way, there is the interesting question 'What's this a big piece?' where we could well be seeing Helen beginning to master the class of words that can precede nouns: both 'a' and 'this' fall into this category, but we do not use them both together as she does. This is another example of 'virtuous error' if we assume that it shows that Helen has learned that the two words can be classed together (or have the same 'privileges of occurrence'). (See p. 122.) It would be worth looking at three word-classes – the adjectives of different kinds; the pronouns; and the verbs. It would also be worth looking at the 'rules' that she was beginning to master, such as the 'be + ing' and 'have + en', and at negatives used for denial and not merely rejection ('No, t'isn't').

It may not have escaped the reader's notice that, in spite of the stress laid in previous chapters on the complexity of the process whereby vocabulary is acquired, the emphasis in the commentaries has been very much on syntax. There are several reasons for this. As we have said, meaning is as much a matter of grammar as of the sense of individual words (and of course, the utterance in any case has meaning only in relation to the *situation* in which it is produced). Moreover, many people will find it easier to detect and discuss increases in vocabulary than to observe the kind of development in syntax that we have been examining. Obviously in every sentence which has been quoted because of some grammatical point there could be evidence of Helen's use and understanding of all manner of different words: talk of word-classes is not intended to distract us from the meanings of the words. It would be easy to list dozens of words that, to judge from this one conversation, Helen has begun to use or to understand accurately, and while some of them might appear to fall into the 'label' category that was rejected in chapter 4 as inadequate (see p. 28), (words such as 'knob', 'letter', 'red', for example), many of them will be less concrete (for example, 'again' or 'just'). But there can be pitfalls in assuming that Helen understands a word, just because she appears to react appropriately to one sentence containing it. Can we be sure that she has grasped the meaning of 'remember', for instance, merely because she says, 'Went to outside' when asked 'Can you remember where we went to this morning, Helen?'? For all we know she is responding to the 'where we went to' part of the adult's question. After all, we know that she can understand the 'wh' question which this very much resembles. ('Where did we go this morning?').

We can be sure that she is still enjoying language for its own sake – she plays with the word 'Tom', repeating it and turning it into 'Tum' and 'Tommy'. This is something that she will not lose for a long time, if ever. Long after she has gone into the primary school and learned the kind of lore that the Opies have collected (though some teachers still do not believe it to be current in their own schools), she will very likely continue to be struck from time to time by the happy chance resemblances between words, as were the Junior children doing a cloze procedure exercise* (in which one fills in words that have been left out of passages of prose):

SARAH Come, buy, buy

PAULINE (*Sings*) Cum byar

No question here of being silly or 'playing up'. The chance **collocation** of certain items irresistibly reminded the speaker of the song, just as in the same session when someone proposed 'Buy, buy' she was greeted by the others with 'Good-bye-bye!' There is a good example in the same transcript of the impact of words in particular situations, when for one of the missing words someone suggests 'indescribable', and provokes the plaintive comment 'I thought we were supposed to be finding describing words not undescribing ones'. Children are always delighting us with remarks like that, sometimes because their as yet imperfect grasp of all the senses of a word leads them into usages that strike us as incongruous, and later, of course, because they can begin to make their own jokes. It is instructive to compare the jokes of children at different stages. As has been pointed out by several writers, one needs an increasing degree of grammatical knowledge to understand certain jokes and not just a sophisticated knowledge of

* Transcript of group cloze exercise by courtesy of Mr Parry of Sir Edmund Hillary C.P. School and Mrs V. St John.

the world. For the present, Helen's word play is likely to be confined to the sounds and forms of words, but before long she will also be playing with meanings.

6 Suggestions for further work and discussion

Points for discussion

i. Helen's language
a Little was said in the commentary about Helen's pronunciation. What can be said about developments in phonology since the previous occasion?
b A new sentence pattern is beginning to emerge, judging by such utterances as
    'That's a doggy.'
    'This is tiny ones.'
See how many examples of this structure you can find in the transcript and say what you think is happening in terms of development. Roger Brown (1973) will be helpful here.
c What developments in Helen's phrase structure do you detect? (Look at the present progressive and the present perfect again.)
d Is she using the '-s' morpheme more consistently for plurals and the third person singular?
e Examine the transcript for evidence of development in the formation of different word-classes, e.g. pronouns and adjectives.
f What else would you point to in the development of her language?

ii. The adults' contribution
a Is there any evidence of changes in expansions or prompting?
b What other examples can you find of complex sentences as input?
c You will remember the 'delicious' sequence in the previous transcript. Is there an instance in the present transcript where there is an attempt to teach Helen a word?
d What instances are there of the adult pursuing one line and the child another?

Follow-up activities

i. Record some adult conversation and then listen to the tape for confirmation of what has been said about (a) natural English, and (b) the question-forms which are used in English.
ii. Examine the sentences on page 142, where it was suggested that you should 'tag' them, and try to work out the processes

involved in doing so. Then look at the discussion of tag questions in Brown and Hanlon (1970).

iii. To familiarise yourself with some of the aspects of sentence structure and phrase-structure, read the relevant sections in Berry (1973).

iv. Ask children of different ages to tell (or listen to) a joke and see what differences their linguistic and other knowledge makes to their understanding. (Thus a seven-year-old laughed dutifully at his nine-year-old brother's joke, 'What did the Irishman say when he saw Frankenstein's monster'? – 'Big 'orror!', but later said to his mother, 'Mummy, why is that funny?')

12 Building a Lego farm:
Helen at two years seven months

---

1 Transcript†

Extracts from a play session, building a farm with Lego, plastic animals and a Red Indian figure.

CHRIS Shall we make a farm?

HELEN Mm

CHRIS A Lego farm?

HELEN Mm

CHRIS Mm. What do I have to do then?

HELEN Not put the. Let's just ... we want the pig to go in and out.

CHRIS Do we?

HELEN Mm

CHRIS Why?

HELEN Cos we/ cos we want the/all the amals (*animals*) to go in ... make a Lego f...cos they need a window to look.

CHRIS Do they? Do you have windows in farms?

HELEN Mm

CHRIS I see

JAN And what animals are you going to put in? What's that?

HELEN Horse

JAN Mm, what else?

HELEN A little *. I better leave a space for them

CHRIS What colour's your horse?

HELEN This one?

† For an explanation of transcription symbols, see p. 21.

CHRIS Mm. What colour is it? What colour is your horse?

HELEN Don't know . . . don't want to say the . . .

CHRIS Pardon?

HELEN Don't want to say the . . .

CHRIS You don't want to say the colour

HELEN No.

CHRIS Why, don't you know what it is?

HELEN No. Lets/let they all in . . . leave a little door/door? open . . . leave a likkle space for them? to get out.

CHRIS Now where do you want the window?

HELEN On the side of the farm . . . That one's tucking in look

CHRIS What colour's the horse?

HELEN White like that one? down there

CHRIS Oh I see. How many white horses have you got?

HELEN (*Screams*)

JAN Count how many horses you've got in your farm.

HELEN No

JAN Oh! And what are these animals coming along to walk in? That's a . . .?

HELEN Oh dear, when they got out they can go in.

JAN Isn't there?/ Why can't they go in now?

HELEN No room.

JAN Isn't there?

HELEN I put a lots and lots.

JAN How can you make room for them?

HELEN (*Singing*) Windy windy ? peaka windy windy. He's got good legs hasn't he? (*This refers to the pig. The phrase comes from a story book she reads about a pig*). Don't, do that, daddy cos/cos he possibly wants to go to the other amals. ? Duff he's * look. He's coming up to thoo (*you*) to mend him.

DADDY Thank you very much.

HELEN Mend him with a hank (*invented word*) . . . They can go tuck, tuck, tuck, tuck, tuck, tuck, tuck (*hen noises*). They doing (*going*) to have a nice bekfast (*breakfast*). He's finished his bekfast now, he's going towards his home, look. Now he's going tuck, tuck, with his window . . . going tuck, tuck with his window, look . . . he's got his window now he's tuck-a-tuck, now he's tuck tuck with his . . . now he's tuck tuck home, look . . . (*Sings a rhythmic tune*) Looking at the goose . . . they having a food in there, look . . . They have to get on the window and cimb (*climb*) about . . . and walk about on the window. They have to walk about on the window . . . an . . .

153

they watching what everything's going on ... he's watching
everything going on outside, isn't he? He's watching
everything going ... what's going ... they're laying ... down
... and go to bed ... All fall down and go to bed ... p'raps
mend him with a salad (*invented word*). Oh that's come off
Mum, it's come off, look. (*Reference to the Red Indian's
broken leg*)

CHRIS Is it? Never mind. I think he's all right, he's got the other
leg to stand on. Do *you* think it matters? Does it matter?

HELEN Daddy mend it ... mend it.

CHRIS What can he mend it with?

HELEN That old dog's coming * he can't come in, look.

CHRIS Why not?

HELEN Cos he *

CHRIS Why can't he come in? There's lots of room for
him.

HELEN * That's a ?mare. What's that Mummy?

CHRIS It's a Red Indian.

HELEN Red Indian?

CHRIS Mm.

HELEN An what/ an what does he do? What does the Red Indian
do, Mum?

JAN Well could he be looking after some animals, do you think?
Could he look after the farm yard animals?

HELEN He's doing to get all, I'm, putting them all in, look ...
that's the other doors for the likkle white one to, come ... for
the rough pig to come out (*another phrase from a story book*).

JAN The what pig? What pig?

★ ★ ★ ★ ★

CHRIS Where are you going to take them?

HELEN They're doing to go to anover (*another*) farm.

CHRIS Are they?

HELEN Cos they haven't where to go

JAN Cos they haven't got anywhere to go?

HELEN No

JAN Who's going to look after them at their new farm?

HELEN The Red Indian.

JAN Is he going with them?

HELEN Mm ... He's going with them, look, the Red Indian ...
That's a new farm, they say ... that's a new farm they say ...

that's a new, farm ... they say ... Bye Bye Red Indian (*assumed voice*). (*Sings to herself*) They in a new f/they in a new farm, look ...

CHRIS What do you want, darling?

HELEN Clap handies. Now what could we do ... at this old farm? ... What could we do at this lorry they say? ... What could they do at this lorry, Mum?

CHRIS Well I think perhaps some of those could go to market.

JAN To be sold?

CHRIS Mm, so other farmers can buy them.

JAN Take them to market in the lorry.

HELEN No ... they're not going to market ... Build a new/build a farm called market ...

CHRIS Pardon.

HELEN * Build a farm called market field.

JAN Build a farm called market. Build a farm. Now can you build another farm, Mummy, then we shall have ... how many farms shall we have then? Count how many.

HELEN Market, market, market. These are the likkle beds where they sleep, Mummy.

CHRIS Are they? That's very nice.

HELEN Some can't go in, can they? Some/Oh they can go in, look, Daddy can go in can't he Mum? ... Perhaps he can go ...

CHRIS Do you think animals like to go to sleep?

HELEN Mm ... he can go away ... p'raps he hasn't got a bed ... p'raps he can sleep in that/in that car, can he?

CHRIS Yes, I think he could.

HELEN P'raps/p'raps he can go ... home in that c/car, can he go home in that car? Fink they can go home in that car, can they? It's quite a/it's quite a long way, those ... piggy's in one, that's in one, that's in one ... they pushing the beds/beds back look, where they came from, that/that man'll sleep in that other bed ... these are the ... one, two, three, four, five. Mummy build a market field.

CHRIS A market, right. I bet we could have this as a market, I don't think Aunty Janet ... (*This was the lid of the tape recorder.*)

JAN Oh no, I think that would make a lovely market.

CHRIS Isn't it big?

HELEN Mm.

CHRIS Gosh, that's very big isn't it?

HELEN Gosh . . . Now they're going into market,
>   To market to buy a fat pig,
>   To market to market, to buy a fat pig.
>   What/what could they do when they get in this market?

2 Overall view

It is interesting to note once more how clearly the differing pre-occupations of child and adults come over in this conversation, even though the adults are so obviously concerned to show an interest in what Helen is doing. She concentrates on the immediate situation, on the actual playthings and the possibilities they suggest, especially doors and windows and the processes of passing or looking through them, or on everyday procedures in her own life such as going to bed, assumed as normal also for farm animals. The very tone of her voice on the tape shows how interested she is. Not for her the adult emphasis on naming objects, identifying colours, counting things (all parts of the stock in trade of teachers or parents as teachers). Where the adults' prompting fits in with her own concern, she accepts it; otherwise she is prepared to ignore questions, say 'No', or even scream. Thus there are whole stretches of the transcript in which lines of dialogue alternate (adult/child/adult), contrasted with three significantly longer passages in which Helen 'flies solo', takes over the direction of the talking, loses herself in the imaginary world she is creating, talks at length and without inhibition about something that really interests her. The implications for parents and for teachers of young children are apparent.

3 The adults' role

Although the speakers can be described as two adults and a child, it is important to stress the obvious by saying that they are three people. However concerned parents are to see their children's command of language develop, primarily they respond to a child as a human being in his own right with something to say that is more important than the precise form in which it is said. The veritable fusillade of questions delivered by the adults (two-thirds of their 'input' to Helen) gives more than a tinge of the didactic to their share of the dialogue, but as with the previous transcript, this would be to misunderstand why the questions are being asked. Questions, it was suggested there, are used to start the ball rolling, to show to others that we are interested in them and their opinions. In this particular conversation the questions, however distracting, have a similar function and express a similar concern. At least Helen is being spoken to, not ignored: she can feel that the adults are interested in her and what she has to say; she is building up a model of human interaction which will be of benefit to her when she begins her formal education. When we look more closely at the language used by the adults in this transcript, there will be something to say about the 'teaching techniques' employed and about certain linguistic features, but it is important to stress at this stage that, whatever objections one may have to particular questions, the questions as a whole have the function of initiating and continuing the dialogue. Thus after the initiating 'Shall we . . .?' there are questions which help to maintain the dialogue by encouraging the child to plan ahead ('What do I have to do then?') or by supporting her suggestions ('Do we?'). Sometimes the questioner genuinely seeks to understand what Helen is trying to say ('Why can't they go in now?'), or the aim is to check knowledge or understanding so that, if necessary, this may be supplied ('What's that?'). Yet another use of a question is to invite the child to make a contribution or to look more closely at some aspect of the situation or of life in general ('Could he be . . .?', 'Do you think . . .?'). There is a good deal of teaching technique being employed here that can profitably be continued when Helen goes to school.

It is worth looking at the questions that Helen finds least relevant. Questions such as 'What are these?', 'How many?', 'What colour?' are standard test questions on everyone's list of forms that the child (or second language learner) should know, and Helen shows on at least two occasions that she can deal with them perfectly well. But from the point of view of a child learning language in particular situations and for particular purposes, more interested in the message than in the medium, how confusing it must be to be peppered with questions designed to test mastery of a linguistic form or an item of knowledge when the focus of her attention is elsewhere. It's enough to make anyone scream.

4 What the child is learning
It would be wrong to assume that the transcript shows us what Helen is learning in this particular situation. What she *has* learned previously, perhaps, in similar situations, but certainly not some discernible list of items instantly acquired in the ongoing dialogue. For this reason it would probably be most helpful to look first at the conversation as typical of many others in which Helen has taken part – typical, that is, both in the functions of the language

157

and in the occurrence of certain linguistic forms.

For example, what has Helen come to expect of conversations with others? What is her model of language use? She has learned that adults will show an interest in what she says and does, that activities can be shared and talked about, that it is normal for explanations to be offered and required, that one can think about words (i.e. define them more closely – 'farm' for example), and that one can consider the possible or the hypothetical as well as that which is physically present or previously known. Her uses of 'can', 'p'raps', 'possibly' all bear witness to a background in which it is normal to speculate or to qualify one's statements, every bit as much as her use of 'please' reflects the usual adult concern to teach children the standard forms of politeness. It is interesting to consider the passage from the point of view of Halliday's **'relevant models of language'** ('the image of language internalised as a result of experience').[1] Take the **regulatory model** ('Do as I tell you'), for example. Many a parent has found the 'Shall we?' approach a useful alternative to straight confrontation. This consultative form (cf. the **interactional model** – 'Me and you') still suggests directed activity but on the basis of cooperation rather than imposed authority. Not only will it help adults in the day-long task of guiding the child and keeping her occupied, but it will be teaching her something about the possible ways of interaction, in readiness for the shared tasks of the infant school.

Helen too is controlling others with her repeated 'Look', so typical of the young child, and very often she keeps the interaction going by use of her tag questions ('. . . isn't he?' '. . . can't he?') with their plea for confirmation and reassurance. There is an overlap here with another of Halliday's models, the **heuristic** ('Tell me why'). Considering the number of questions that Helen is exposed to, it would be surprising if she had not begun to use the device herself. You will remember that we discussed this example in chapter 4 (page 33).

HELEN What's that Mummy?

CHRIS It's a Red Indian.

HELEN Red Indian?

CHRIS Mm.

HELEN An what/what does he do? What does the Red Indian do, Mum?

JAN Well could he be looking after some animals, do you think?

First the name is settled, then the function, and to good effect, because a little later we have:

JAN Who's going to look after them at their new farm?

HELEN The Red Indian.

Of course!

As Helen manipulates the objects and talks about them, she is learning through her eyes and her fingers as well as through words, and it might appear that this concentration on physical objects in a here-and-now situation would restrict her talk and her thoughts to the exploration of the matter-of-fact. Instead, as we have seen, on the occasions on which she is able to take over the conversation, it is because the animals have come to life in a world of 'Let's pretend' (the **imaginative model**), where different elements of her experience are blended. The pig is both a toy on the table and a character recollected from a story book. The hen goes 'tuck tuck' because that is what hens do (as parents we seem determined to pass on the repertoire of animal noises), but she also has a home and eats breakfast, and pigs can sleep in cars and even drive them. And, of course, in this make-believe world animals can do more than make noises: they can talk, and Helen's repertoire includes not merely 'tuck tuck' but also an assumed voice, carefully labelled as such with a repeated 'they say'. Just making the 'tuck tuck' noise is pleasurable, like the singing that punctuates the monologue; and language itself is a source of pleasure and amusement, whether it be from the invention of her own words like 'a hank', or from the recollection of whole phrases from a book ('for the rough pig to come out'). Words like 'market' can be repeated and manipulated even before they are understood. Prompted by the adults to examine the concepts represented by words like 'farm', the child can come to use the words with increasing precision: such play will take its part in the process of making sense of the world.

In this brief survey of how Helen is using her language, no mention has been made of the actual resources at her disposal. It has consistently been stressed that children at all stages make good use of whatever resources they have, but our samples of language are so small that generalisations based on them must be limited. This transcript is a single example of only one kind of situation, and one would need samples of speech in many other situations before being able to say what the child can do or (especially) cannot do. There is, too, a danger of looking simply at what Helen says, ignoring what she is able to understand: decoding skills complement those of encoding.

To consider decoding first: the input here is typical in that the child is presented with adult language and not a highly simplified variant, and in that her errors are corrected only rarely, and by offering, without emphasis or reproach, an expanded or modified form of what she has just said (e.g. 'haven't where to go' elicits 'haven't got anywhere to go'.) In general, the child can tell from the adults' reactions whether she is understanding what is being said to her and whether she is making herself clear. The variety of patterns to which Helen is exposed covers a wide range. Examination of a single category – the question form (see chapter 11) – will remind us how soon children learn to understand an array of linguistic forms.

Turning to Helen's own resources, it is easy to classify her 'errors', or more accurately the points at which her language diverges from the adult forms. Easiest of all to pick out as usual are phonological points, where she substitutes a sound of her own for the adult phoneme (as in 'anover'), or omits one element in a consonantal blend (as in 'cimb' or 'bekfast') or a syllable from a word (as in 'amal'). All these can be accounted for fairly simply in terms of difficulties of aural discrimination or of articulation, and to dwell upon them would obscure the fact that such errors are few and trivial compared with what Helen gets right – the tape confirms that she has mastered the patterns of intonation and stress that help to make language meaningful.

In much the same way, we can pick out syntactic 'errors' – such as 'a window to look' or 'I better leave a space for them' or the splendid 'they watching what everything's going on' – and by considering them in conjunction with the many 'correct' utterances, we can illustrate the rules towards which the child is feeling her way. Certainly it is fascinating to follow her progress from transcript to transcript because even from such small samples as these it is possible to see development in particular areas of grammar. Take sentence structure for example. Five months earlier, one-clause sentences were the rule; now Helen is stringing together two or more clauses ('we want the pig ‖ to go in and out' and 'make a Lego f . . . ‖ cos they need a window ‖ to look'). There are thirty-six one-clause sentences and twenty-five consisting of two or more, twenty-three of which can be called **complex** – a significantly high proportion if, as is generally assumed, ability to produce such patterns reflects an ability to relate ideas. Helen shows understanding of cause and effect ('cos when they need a window to look') and of relationship in time ('when they got out they can go in'). Five months ago many of the one-clause sentences were 'telegraphic' ('Just . . . just . . . getting those out . . .', 'Opened cupboard'); now Helen is supplying words like 'I' and 'the'. It is worth thinking about this richness of sentence structure already acquired by the age of two-and-a-half in comparison with the first sentences the five-year-old is likely to meet in a reading scheme.

If we look next at the phrase structure of some of Helen's utterances, it is much the same story. Consider her **verb phrases**, for instance. At two she was using only the simple present tense of lexical verbs ('want' 'get'), but now she can use **modals** ('they *can* go'); a variety of forms of the present continuous (He's *coming*', 'They're *laying*'); the present perfect ('He's *finished*'); and the **infinitive** ('a window *to look*'). She can also differentiate between 'going' as a verb of motion ('he's going towards his home') and 'going' as a marker of future action ('They're doing (going) to have a nice bekfast'). The situation is similar with her noun phrases. At two years a two-element pattern was common ('likkle box'), whereas now Helen can not only modify nouns and other words with several preposed words but she can also postmodify them: in addition to items like '*all* the animals' '*a likkle* space', and '*a nice* bekfast', we have 'a likkle space *for them ?to get out*' and 'white *like that one ?down there*'.

It would not be difficult to look at the development of word-classes such as pronouns or prepositions, and to find similar evidence of progressive differentiation, but such exercises in comparison have their dangers. It is too simple to count words in phrases or clauses in sentences and leave it at that. Always the emphasis should be on the significance of any expansion: what has Helen learned to understand that requires this extension of her syntactic repertoire? The answer is going to be the same in most cases. Just as her vocabulary will grow as she meets new objects and experiences, so her range of syntactic patterns will expand to accommodate her growing awareness of relationships in time, space and causality; her grasp of concepts such as identity, contrast and relative size; and her ability to classify with increasing specificity. There is an overlap here with the semantic area. Helen is constantly learning new words. Or rather, she is learning to make meanings for the words she hears, whether they be the apparently straightforward 'content' words like 'farm' or 'market', or more abstract but equally meaningful items such as 'of' and 'some'. This process is an important element in the conversation on the tape. There is no once-and-for-all learning of the meaning of a word. For example, Helen has met the word 'market' before in the nursery rhyme and in a story book. She can say it. She can use it as a noun. But until she has some direct experience of it, the word remains half-comprehended, its connotations of animals and selling being only a fraction of what she will eventually have built up by the time she fully understands it. 'Farm' is probably further along the road to being comprehended, but even here Helen is still very much tied to the idea of a particular kind of building.

If all this suggests that the process of learning language is an active one rather than one dependent on imitation, the emphasis is deliberate. Of course children do imitate their parents – for example, the echoed 'Gosh!' in this transcript (p. 156) – and the data upon which they depend for their knowledge of the language system is provided for them largely by their parents; but most of the utterances on this tape are patently not merely imitative but are created by the child herself. To see children's language as no better than a more or less successful imitation of an adult model is to undervalue their achievement.

5 The value of play
It was stressed at the outset that what mattered was to see the situation as interaction among human beings in a familiar domestic situation. But it should be borne in mind that it is this normal human reaction to the familiar that makes it difficult to establish what Chomsky calls 'psychic distance'[2] from the subject. It is only when we stand back from the situation and compare two stages in the development of the same child that we realise how much she has achieved. The ordinariness, the obviousness, the predictability of the situation should not blind us to how much is going on. Helen, Chris and Janet are building a Lego farm and talking as they do so. This gives Helen all that is required for a first-class language lesson: her own interest, adult interest, adult guidance and help, objects to talk about, and constant exposure to adult speech. Obviously she has already learned a great deal from other everyday situations such as this one – and not merely about the English language. As far as language is concerned, it has been possible to discuss both the patterns of language that she is learning to control and the uses to which she puts them. Perhaps this is a 'favoured background', and certainly some children will come to school with a more extensive repertoire of words and structures than others, and with a greater experience of their functions. But as teachers we should beware of assuming that any child comes to school with very little language, since most children will be exposed to some adult conversation and will be accustomed to playing, if not with their parents, at least with other children. As parents, on the other

hand, we can happily continue what we already enjoy doing: playing with our children and, deliberately or not, teaching them about language as we do so.

6 Suggestions for further work and discussion

Points for discussion

i. Helen's language
a What does she still appear to have difficulty with in terms of particular phonemes and combinations of phonemes?
b Consider what is missed by having only the transcript available without the tape. Give examples where the printed version is unrevealing.
c Follow up the areas of grammar which we have been looking at in successive transcripts, to see what developments you can find in
  1 use of negatives
  2 be+ing and have + en
  3 'little words': 'a', 'the', and prepositions
  4 pronouns
  5 the construction with 'to be', like 'That is', 'This is', as in 'That's a big one'
  6 phrases like 'in toy cupboard' that tell us where things are.
d Look for examples in the transcript where Helen seems to be playing with particular phrases or constructions.

ii. The adults' contribution
a At one point Jan says 'The what pig?' Discuss the possible effects of such expressions on the child's acquisition of particular structures.
b In all Helen transcripts there have been at least two adults present. Illustrate from this and other transcripts the advantages and disadvantages this could have.
c It is stated in the commentary that Helen is hearing normal adult English. Do you agree?

Follow-up activities

i. To ensure that you have grasped what was said about the structure of sentences, see whether you can divide these sentences into their constituent clauses, like this:
'When they **got** out ‖ they **can go** in.'
Notice that in each clause in the above example there is a verb, shown in bold type.

163

    a They watching what everything's going on.
    b What could they do when they get in this market?
ii. Re-read the transcripts for twenty and twenty-one months and consider what development has taken place since then.
iii. Compare the language in this transcript with that in others, preferably made by yourself with children the same age as Helen.

7 References

1 Halliday, M. A. K. (1969) 'Relevant models of language' in A. Wilkinson (ed.) *The State of Language* University of Birmingham School of Education
2 Chomsky, N. (1968) *Language and Mind* Harcourt, Brace & World

13 Questions in the park:
Matthew at three years five months

---

1 Transcript†

Children present: Matthew – three years five months;
  Daniel – one year nine months.
Adults present: father, mother, aunt.

FATHER What can you see, Daniel?

DANIEL Ducks

FATHER Ducks. My word!

MATTHEW I want to go up there, Daddy.

FATHER Want to go up that way, do you? Right we can go that way, can't we Mummy?

MOTHER Matthew can take us on the walk this morning.

FATHER You tell us where to go, Mat.

MATTHEW Up that road, on that road.

FATHER Which road?

MATTHEW On that road, up there.

FATHER Up this way.

MATTHEW This is a steep road, isn't it?

AUNT Here we are, Matthew ... on the way you want to go, aren't we?

MATTHEW Why are these fir trees broken? Why are these fir trees broken?

AUNT Looks as though it's been rather windy round here.

† For an explanation of transcription symbols, see p. 21.

FATHER They're old, aren't they?

MATTHEW Hey ... where's them branches gone?

FATHER They've been chopped off.

MATTHEW Why have they?

FATHER ?It's near to the road where the motor cars ?are.

MATTHEW Hey! (*Sound of footsteps and bird song*) ... Who's chopped that tree off?

FATHER Council man do you think or is it the National Trust man?

MATTHEW Hey ... what's it lying like that for?

FATHER Shall we go and have a look and see? ... (*8 secs*) ... Well it's just lying like that, isn't it?

MATTHEW Why is it just lying like that?

FATHER Well it's been chopped down, hasn't it? It's very old, Matthew ... (*6 secs*) ... Can you see the cones? Hm?

MATTHEW Look. That tree hasn't got in the way of the road, has it? Who's chopped that off?

AUNT ... Looks as though it's broken off. What kind of tree is is that ?one ?here?

MATTHEW Mmm ...

AUNT Mm?

MATTHEW I don't ... I can't tell.

AUNT Can't you?

MATTHEW I can't.

FATHER Well, let's look at the leaves. What sort of leaves are they?

MATTHEW Mmm. I don't know.

FATHER Don't you know what sort it is? Let Daddy pull some leaves down. Now look at them. What is it?

MATTHEW Er. I don't know.

FATHER Go and have a look then.

(*Footsteps as he does so*)

MATTHEW Mmm. Mmm. A sycamore tree. (*Triumphantly*)

FATHER That's right.

MOTHER Oh you clever boy! That's just what it is.

FATHER ?A sycamore tree. That's right. Come on, sit on, quick, there's a motor car ... (*17 secs*) ... What sort of bush is this?

MATTHEW Mmm. A rhododrendron.

MOTHER Oh you clever boy!

FATHER That's right, and what sort of bush is this?

MATTHEW Mmm ... I don't really know.

[MOTHER They're blackberries.]

FATHER What sort of bush is it?

MATTHEW Mmm . . . I don't know.

FATHER Don't you know that one?

AUNT Blackberries.

FATHER It's a blackberry bush, isn't it? . . . What else can you see, Matthew? . . . Oo, what's these?

MATTHEW What are they?

FATHER Eh?

MATTHEW What are they?

FATHER Looks like a . . . [What is it?]

AUNT Elderberry

FATHER Elderberry

 11

MATTHEW Mmm. Why do you have, what's under sky?

FATHER Pardon?

MATTHEW What's under clouds, Daddy?

FATHER What's under clouds? . . . Air is under clouds, isn't it? What's in clouds?

MATTHEW What's in clouds?

FATHER It's moisture.

MATTHEW Mmm. What's . . . mm . . .

FATHER Spit it out.

MATTHEW Up, up, up, what else is . . . near the sky/near the sky, Daddy?

FATHER What else is near the sky? There's only the sky near the sky, isn't there? . . . The horizon is near the sky, isn't it?

MATTHEW What, Daddy?

FATHER The horizon is near the sky.

MATTHEW What?

FATHER I said the horizon is near the sky.

MATTHEW It isn't.

FATHER Why isn't it?

MATTHEW Because it isn't.

FATHER Why not?

MATTHEW I/I/I don't know why.

FATHER Don't you?

MATTHEW No.

FATHER The sunshine is near the sky, isn't it . . . And the stars and the moon?

MATTHEW Mm. What do moons do?

FATHER They/they shine at night-time, don't they?

MATTHEW Why do they shine at night-time?

FATHER Why do you think they shine at night-time? . . .

167

MATTHEW Why do black clouds at night-time Daddy? . . .

FATHER It's night-time.

(*Traffic noises*)

MATTHEW Why ?do a lot of traffic here?

FATHER There is, isn't there?

MOTHER I think we ought to get off the road.
  Are you tired, Daniel?

DANIEL Mm.

MATTHEW I wonder what's . . . up here?

FATHER What do you think's up here? Sort of tree is that one there?

MATTHEW What?

FATHER This one here.

MATTHEW Mmm, I don't know.

FATHER Well, shall we have a look and see? Eh? What sort is that one?

MATTHEW Ermm, I don't know.

FATHER Have a look.

MATTHEW What sort of leaves has it got? . . . Er . . . it's got a lot of branches, hasn't it?

FATHER It's got a lot of branches on. Yes. What sort of leaf is that . . . Eh? Sort of leaf is that?

MATTHEW Don't know.

FATHER You do.

(*Matthew gives false coughs*)

AUNT Perhaps he can't remember.

FATHER Can't you remember?

MATTHEW Erm. Erm. A chestnut tree.

FATHER That's right. You knew all the time what it was, didn't you?

MATTHEW Why has that tree got a lot of branches?

FATHER Well, it's ?all ?been cut off the trunk and it's all grown again, hasn't it? What sort of chestnut tree do you think it is?

MATTHEW What sort of chestnut tree is it?

FATHER Well who/what . . . you tell us.

MATTHEW You tell me, Daddy.

FATHER Well, have a guess.

MATTHEW I can't have a guess.

FATHER Is it a horse-chestnut tree?

MATTHEW Yes

FATHER Are you sure?

168

MATTHEW Mmmm.

FATHER What other sort of chestnut tree could it be?

MATTHEW Why don't these go over the road these ... mm ... mm ... kick-ups?

FATHER Why are they kick-ups? ... They're part of the road, aren't they? They're creosoted in, they're – tarmaced in.

MATTHEW Why are they tarmaced in?

FATHER So you've got a nice surface for motor cars.

MATTHEW What sort of tree is that?

FATHER Tell me.

MATTHEW I don't know ... Erm ... Will you tell me what sort of tree it is, Daddy?

FATHER No. I'm not telling you what sort it is.

MATTHEW Eh, why are the branches broken off, Daddy?

FATHER Why are they?

MATTHEW I don't know, why are they?

FATHER You tell me what sort of tree it is, and I'll tell you that.

MATTHEW Um ... A cedar tree.

FATHER Yes. You knew all the time, didn't you? You rascal.

MATTHEW Daddy, why are the branches broken off?

FATHER Well, why are they broken off?

MATTHEW Don't know.

FATHER Has the man cut them off with a saw?

MATTHEW This is a nice spot here.

FATHER It is a nice spot, isn't it?

MATTHEW Who's cut this grass?

FATHER It's very short, isn't it?

MATTHEW Why is it? Why is it very short, Daddy?

FATHER I bet the man's been round with the lawn mower, don't you?

MATTHEW Mm ... mm ... There's no mess here.

FATHER There isn't.

MATTHEW Why isn't there?

FATHER It's a nice country spot ...

MATTHEW I don't like this spot being like this.

AUNT Why not?

MATTHEW Because ... I/I ... only when it's not shining.

FATHER Only when it's not what?

MATTHEW Only when it's not shining.

FATHER When it's not shining?

MATTHEW When it's not ... sunshining.

FATHER Oh, when it's not sunshining.

MATTHEW Erm I ... want to go down ... erm ... erm ... where the church is over there.

FATHER Do you? ... Well we'll go down to see the church then, shall we?

MATTHEW Is that the way you go to see the church down there?

FATHER That's the way, yes ... (*15 secs*) ... What's that there then Matthew?

MATTHEW Is that where you go to the church?

FATHER You go down this way to the church ... What's that up there then?

MATTHEW A caravan.

FATHER A caravan.

MATTHEW What?

AUNT They're spending the day out in a caravan.

MATTHEW Mm ... Why do they have curtains in there?

FATHER It's a dormobile, isn't it?

MOTHER People sleep in them.

FATHER Shall we have one to sleep in?

MATTHEW (*Uncertain*) Mm.

FATHER Yes? Where shall we go in it?

MATTHEW Erm ... er ... I want/I want a bed to sleep in.

FATHER Do you?

MATTHEW Mm.

FATHER What, in the dormobile?

MATTHEW Mm.

FATHER What else do you want to do in it?

MATTHEW Erm, and I want some toys to play with.

FATHER Yes. (*Encouragingly*)

MATTHEW And some, some erm, I want mm ... Why do people sleep in dommobiles?

FATHER Because it's cheaper than sleeping in a hotel.

AUNT They sometimes take their dormobiles to the seaside.

FATHER Yes.

AUNT And sleep in them. (*Sounds of coughing*)

MATTHEW What is that? What's that?

AUNT It's a little ... er ... post to keep cars out, isn't it, but Daddy was talking about the bark which was fastened on the silver birch tree, wasn't he?

MATTHEW Mm. It does ... What's that bark for, Daddy?

FATHER Eh?

MATTHEW That bark.

FATHER To protect the tree. To prot/protect the tree.

MATTHEW Why is that cheaper than sleeping in a hotel, Daddy?

FATHER Why you have to pay money to sleep in a hotel, but if you owned a dormobile you don't have to pay anybody do you?

MATTHEW No. Mm ... Why don't you, Daddy?

FATHER Well, because it's yours and there's no money to pay anybody else who owns it, is there? ... What can you see now then, Mat?

MATTHEW ... Christopher hasn't been in countries before, has he?

AUNT What are you talking about?

MATTHEW Erm ... erm ... My house ... over there, isn't it? * What, Daddy? ?What Mummy?

AUNT Your house ?is over there ?isn't it?

FATHER What countries are you talking about with Christopher?

MATTHEW Erm ... That one that we went to. With him ... last week ... that other country.

FATHER What other country?

MATTHEW Er Daddy. Er that country that that tree was bending that I saw like that.

FATHER (*Almost to himself*) Where the tree was bending?

MATTHEW Bending like that, Daddy.

FATHER You mean the countryside. Not/you don't mean England or Wales or Scotland?

MATTHEW Mm ... The countryside.

FATHER The countryside you meant. Ye/Yes.

MATTHEW Er that/That was a tree that was bending like that with Christopher ... we went ... with him last week.

[MOTHER Oh last year yes ... can you remember when we * * Derbyshire?

FATHER * * I see.

MOTHER That was last Christmas.]

FATHER Well what did you do? Can you remember?

MATTHEW I don't know.

MOTHER We went for a picnic with Christopher. Mummy and Daddy and **

MATTHEW Mm.

[MOTHER It was before last Christmas. You know, when we went to Froggatts Edge in Derbyshire. * *]

MATTHEW Er ... How can you get, erm ... over there? ... I want to go ... right down there.

MATTHEW Why do you have towers on cafés?

171

FATHER Towers?

[AUNT He means the clock.]

FATHER So that you can tell what time it is.

MATTHEW Why do you . . . so you can tell what?

FATHER Well, there's a clock on the tower, isn't there?

MATTHEW Why is there?

FATHER So people know what time it is.

MATTHEW I want to go right round there, Daddy.

FATHER Well we haven't got time today, have we?

MATTHEW Why are the/the trees on the river . . . them trees on the river?

AUNT The water's eaten out the bank * *. It's an island now, isn't it?

MATTHEW ?Why is it an island now?

AUNT Because the water's been so strong that it's bitten out all the ground round the trees.

MATTHEW Why has it?

AUNT Because it's so strong.

MATTHEW Eh. What is that tree leaning like that for?

FATHER Which tree do you mean?

MATTHEW That tree.

AUNT What kind of tree is it?

MATTHEW That tree.

FATHER Which tree?

MATTHEW That silver birch.

FATHER Oh . . . The silver birch tree. Well . . . part of its er ground has been sucked away by the water, hasn't it?

MOTHER Are you going to feed birds, Matthew?

FATHER * * bread in?

MOTHER Here you are, look . . . give half to Daniel.

FATHER Are you going to pull little pieces off it . . . and throw it in? Are you throwing some in as well, Daniel?

MATTHEW (*To the ducks*) Here's bread.

FATHER Let's get down there and throw it in. Come on, ducks.

MATTHEW Come on ducks, Ducks, ducks, ducks, ducks.

FATHER Here they come, look.

AUNT They're coming.

FATHER Here come the swans. Here they come, look. They're all swimming over, look.

AUNT Wait till they come
     (*Swan noises*)

FATHER Here they come. Here come/here come the swans, look.

AUNT Don't throw any more in until they get nearer.

FATHER Here come the swans.

MATTHEW Would you like to listen to the/this machine?

FATHER Which machine?

MATTHEW Emm. This machine.

FATHER Well I bet they would . . . yes.

MATTHEW Would you like to listen to this machine?

AUNT He says he likes to listen.

MATTHEW It's bread . . . It's bread.

FATHER Here they come, look. Here they come . . . Here come the swans. (*Swan noises*)

MATTHEW (*Laughter – imitates bird sounds*) They will be big.

AUNT They will won't they, eating all that bread. They must like brown bread.

MATTHEW He eats all that . . . Why haven't ducks/ducks got no eyes?

AUNT They have got eyes on the sides of their head.

MATTHEW (*Laughter*)

AUNT It wasn't quick enough, was it?

FATHER What sort of ducks can you see Matthew?

DANIEL Geese.

FATHER Geese, yes, I can see some geese.

DANIEL Swans.

FATHER Swans, yes.

MATTHEW Throw it right out. Throw it. They will be big, won't they?

AUNT They will . . . What's this little one here? Do you know? It's a mallard, Matthew. Isn't it pretty?

MATTHEW (*Calling duck*) Mallard, Mallard.

AUNT Yes, it's got a lovely green neck, hasn't it and head.

MATTHEW Daddy! (*A swan comes too close*)

FATHER Watch it. He'll have it. He'll have it off you. Don't hold your bread out Matthew.

AUNT Don't hold it out, Matthew.

FATHER Oo, mind that/mind my Daniel, swan. Here you are swan. That's it. All gone.

DANIEL All gone.

FATHER All gone. All gone. (*Swan getting angry*) What a funny noise for a swan to make. Here give me your bread. He is a cheeky little swan, isn't he . . . My word!

MOTHER Now throw your bread to that swan. Throw your bread now.

FATHER My word swan. What's he doing, Daniel?

AUNT He's being naughty, isn't he?

FATHER He is being naughty.

MATTHEW Why/why has he got big feet?

FATHER What sort of feet has he got, Matthew?

MATTHEW What sort?

FATHER He's got webbed feet, hasn't he?

MOTHER Throw your bread and don't torment him Matthew. Let him know it's all gone.

FATHER There are lots of swans and geese, aren't there?

MATTHEW All gone, swan.

MOTHER Oh that rhymed didn't it? All gone, swan.

FATHER That's it.

MATTHEW Eat that big un, you. (*Swan making angry noise*)

MOTHER Oh don't do things like that. [Ian, he's picking stones up.]

FATHER No, he mustn't throw stones at the swan.

MOTHER No, no, that's silly . . . off you go.

FATHER Come on then, let's go. Shall we say 'Bye bye, swans'?

AUNT You mustn't pick stones up, you know. What were you doing that for?

MATTHEW Erm . . . to make them big.

MOTHER Well you can't fool them. They'd know that wasn't bread.

MATTHEW Why would they know that wasn't bread?

MOTHER Well they would . . . and it would be cruelty.

FATHER All gone swans.

MOTHER . . . to throw them a stone instead of bread, wouldn't it, Daddy?

FATHER Yes

AUNT That one's cheeky. It's still standing there.

MATTHEW Is it still standing there?

AUNT It thinks you might have some more in your pocket. Bye bye.

MATTHEW Why does it think I still have some more in my pocket?

AUNT Well they never give up . . . hope.

MATTHEW Eh . . .

[MOTHER We'll be just about right, won't we?]

MATTHEW What are they waiting for now? That/them/them geese now?

FATHER Why do you think they're waiting for? . . . Are they waiting for some more bread?

MATTHEW What are they waiting for? Daddy you shall tell me
what they're waiting for.

FATHER They're waiting for some more things to eat ... some
more goodies for their dinner ...

MATTHEW Why are they w/waiting for some more goodies for
their dinner?

FATHER They like goodies.

AUNT Do you like goodies?

FATHER It makes a change from water fleas.

DANIEL Change ... Cars.

FATHER What's that, Daniel?

DANIEL Cars.

FATHER Cars. Yes there are some cars, aren't there?

MATTHEW Erm, I want to go to the cafe, I do.

FATHER What for?

MATTHEW For a cup of tea.

FATHER Anything else? What else shall we have?

MATTHEW Erm ... Cocoa.

FATHER Cocoa?

MATTHEW Yes.

DANIEL Cocoa.

AUNT Cocoa, Daniel. What else would Daniel like?

DANIEL Cocoa.

AUNT Oh cocoa, yes you can have cocoa, and would you like
anything else besides cocoa?

DANIEL Yes.

AUNT What?

DANIEL Mummy. Who dat?

FATHER Who is it Daniel?

DANIEL Mummy.

FATHER Mummy, yes.

MATTHEW Why do big white ducks peck? (*Matthew has just said
this during the Daniel/Father interchange*)

FATHER What, the swans?

MATTHEW Why do swans peck?

FATHER Because they're hungry. They like what you're giving
them.

MATTHEW Why do they like what you're giving them?

FATHER Because they love brown bread.

MATTHEW Why do they love brown bread?

FATHER Because it tastes nice.

MATTHEW Erm, what sort of beak have they got?

175

FATHER They've got a nice big orange beak haven't they with a black cere . . . That little black knob is called a cere.

MATTHEW Er . . . What do . . . the ducks think?

AUNT About what?

MATTHEW What do the ducks think?

AUNT What about?

MATTHEW The/The ducks . . . ?/said what do the ducks think?

FATHER All they think about is what they're going to eat next. That's all they can think about.

MATTHEW Why is that all they can think about?

FATHER That's all they're concerned about. They haven't got any other worries apart from what they can eat next.

MATTHEW Why do they just have to have bread?

FATHER Well, they can have other things. They can have cream cakes, and Grandma's buns and all sorts . . .

MATTHEW Why do they . . ./why can they have cream cakes and all sorts?

FATHER Because they like anything like that, don't they?

MATTHEW Why do they like anything like that?

FATHER Well, why do you think it tastes nice?

MATTHEW Why do they, Daddy?

FATHER Well, you tell me. Do you like/do you think it tastes nice?

MATTHEW No.

FATHER Don't you? Why don't you think it tastes nice?

MATTHEW I think it's not good for anyone.

FATHER Is that what you think?

MATTHEW Yes.

FATHER Well. Well. Why do you eat cream cakes then?

MATTHEW Erm . . . I don't eat cream cakes.

FATHER Don't you?

MATTHEW Just Grandma Radford's.

FATHER Grandma Radford's what?

MATTHEW Grandma Radford's cream cakes.

FATHER I see. What are you doing, Daniel? Eh? Are you pushing the push chair?

DANIEL Yes.

FATHER You must be quick then . . . you push at the back.

MATTHEW Dander goes like that, doesn't he?

MOTHER Mm.

FATHER Yes, because he's pushing hard, that's why. Isn't he? Oh! Look at him now my word!

MATTHEW Where's he getting it all? What is that for, Daddy?

FATHER Eh?

MATTHEW What is that for?

FATHER That's a motor bike, isn't it?

MATTHEW What are they for? What are them for, Daddy?

FATHER They hold the motor bike up while it's standing, don't they? Eh? . . . They hold the motor bike up while it's standing.

MATTHEW Why do they?

(*Car park attendant arrives*)

FATHER How do you do? Do you want some money? Do you want some money?

ATTENDANT Yes please, if you've got a car.

FATHER I haven't walked/I haven't walked it here, have I?

ATTENDANT Can't see you walking the distance. There's some nice blackberries here behind t' bushes here. If you want a/ fancy an apple and blackberry pie. Have you got a bag? . . . You can come back on this anyway, if you want to.

FATHER Right. Thank you very much.

ATTENDANT It lasts all day. There's quite a few on you know. Backside of these trees on this little footpath.

FATHER Yes.

ATTENDANT I've just walked through and I've seen quite a/a lot.

FATHER Quite a lot.

ATTENDANT Quite a lot of blackberries. Can you get a basin you'll make a couple of pie/blackberry and apple pies.

AUNT Very nice. We've got one for dinner actually.

ATTENDANT What, blackberry and apple? It's nice, isn't it? I like them in a nice bit of cream, you know. Aye . . . they soon slip down. Hello, tiger you look . . .

2 Introduction

Now for a change. Not only a different child, and a boy at that, but a conversation that takes place wholly out of doors, with the father present as well as Matthew's mother and aunt, and another child, his brother Daniel. The conversation will change focus as the walk progresses, giving all the participants the chance to take control from time to time, as this or that object takes their eye, and, although everyone is out to enjoy himself, this is not a play situation in quite the same way as those that we have been examining so far. One interesting difference is that we have the chance to see the interaction between Matthew and his father. On the other hand, there will be many features of this otherwise contrasting transcript

177

which will reinforce conclusions drawn from the discussion of Helen's speech. One feature in particular will almost certainly catch the reader's attention, and that is the number of questions that Matthew asks: of his 150 utterances, no less than 84 are questions, and of those nearly 50 are the question 'Why?' or the closely related 'What for?' If that's what we get on a stroll of a mere hour or so, no wonder that, to some parents of older children, the school holidays must seem to last for ever.

3 Focus of the dialogue

Let us begin by considering the issue of 'focus', the switching of topics as the walk progresses. It's hardly surprising that, on a summer's day in a park, the conversation should centre round the physical environment: trees, the clouds, the choice of route, the swans. Nor should we expect any one person to be always the first to start a topic going, given the fact that everyone can see what is to be seen and has the ability to talk about it. But, in saying that, we are conceding the point that Matthew has this ability. No doubt at an earlier stage he, like Helen, spoke when he was spoken to: the adults put the ball into play and gradually the rallies grew longer. We have seen Helen taking an increasingly active part in starting conversations, and here in Matthew's performance that tendency is developed even further. If we count not merely the broad categories of topic such as the recurrent identification of trees and bushes, but the sub-topics (particular species, ducks' eyes, towers on cafés and so on), and then look to see who started the discussion of them, we find that Matthew is responsible for about four-fifths. What is more, once a conversation begins, he is as good as the next man at keeping it going.

4 Matthew's resources for starting a conversation

Before examining a particular conversation in detail, let us look briefly at how Matthew actually starts one. There are at least six ways, three of them in the form of statements, the others questions. Like the rest of us, he enjoys doing what he chooses and he has learned to use language to help to bring that about. Several times he says 'I want', as in 'I want to go up there, Daddy', 'I . . . want to go down . . . erm . . . erm . . . where the church is over there', and since, on this kind of stroll, the relaxed feeling of not being tied to a route is part of the pleasure, Matthew's wish is allowed to settle the route for the whole party. He has also learnt to express opinions which give rise to further comment from his companions, as, for example, when he says, 'I don't like this spot being like this', 'This is a nice spot here'.

The second statement is reminiscent of the remark which began the whole conversation but is omitted from the transcript because it is indistinct on the tape. His father commented, 'It's a glorious day'. It is the kind of thing that people say when they are enjoying themselves, as though the expression of our enjoyment to others somehow enhances it. The model is there for Matthew, and he appears to have taken good note of it. The shared or sharable nature of the experience is emphasised when Matthew tags his statements, too, 'This is a steep road, isn't it?' Perhaps he is also checking that he has got 'steep' right, but it seems prompted much more by the companionable nature of his relationship with the adults. Another kind of statement simply expresses his curiosity and could almost be considered as another way of saying 'I want', ('I wonder what's ... up here?').

But, of course, it is when we come to the questions that we really see Matthew as initiator. Before we look at them, let us try to put ourselves in his place: if his question 'What do ducks think?' is difficult, so is one that we might just as reasonably put to ourselves: 'What do little boys think?'

As the external observers of the episode at second hand via tape and transcript, we might forget what was stressed in chapter 2: we as adults, seeing the world to some extent through the language system that we have mastered, can easily forget that the child is still learning not only the language but the world itself. It could be that the familiarity of repeated experience and the ability to encapsulate it in words has meant that we pay less attention to things, as though somehow they had been duly labelled and had nothing more to tell us. A familiar view becomes interesting only when something out of pattern appears within it to give it novelty. But a child can find interest in the commonplace. An adult's enjoyment in strolling through a park is mild and predictable, but Matthew's pleasure is intense. Try to think yourself into his situation, first in the simple respect of physical size and hence viewpoint – nearer to the ground, closer to certain objects, dwarfed even more than ourselves by the trees. Then think of the sheer diversity of things to be seen, as yet unclassified, especially if one has learned already that it is possible to subdivide the categories like 'tree' that one has been at pains to acquire. Next, look at some of those questions that were quoted in chapter 4:

'What do moons do?'

'What do the ducks think?'

'What's under clouds?'

and decide what answers you can give, and how you think the knowledge came to you. Consider then to what extent you still ask questions like that. Are there questions to which you feel that you will never know the answers, and others the answers to which you realise you can only take on trust from other people? Does every day of your now established routine bring questions crowding in, not the questions to which you need answers for practical reasons, but those that arouse your intellectual curiosity? Perhaps for Matthew the grass is greener, the tree bark more intricately marked, all his sense-impressions more vivid. And perhaps, though he could not say so himself, one source of pleasure for him may be the feeling that there is so much more to see and to have explained. What is more, at this stage it appears to be so simple: one asks a question and gets an answer. Questions have answers, that's the model that Matthew is working on, and if at times we suspect that his 'Why?' comes as a reflex in the game of keeping the dialogue going, on the whole he really does want to know those answers.

If we look at some of the questions, it becomes apparent that Matthew has seen something which could have produced a simple descriptive statement. Instead, this statement has been made in his head, as it were, and it leads to the demand for an explanation. Thus, instead of 'Look at those broken fir trees', or 'Isn't the grass short?', he says, 'Why are these fir trees broken?', and 'Who's cut this grass?'

This habit of looking for explanations (under his father's constant encouragement) before simply demanding them of others could well stand Matthew in good stead when it comes to reading. Good readers bring to the text not merely their knowledge of the world and knowledge of the language system (both of which are being developed in Matthew) but the habit of questioning what authors put before them. By the time that Matthew goes to school it will be second nature to him to expect and to offer reasons for statements, and he will be able to respond to the promptings of a good teacher but, what is more, to argue with the textbook.

One or two sequences are worth studying in more detail, for example, the 'clouds' passage which suddenly interrupts discussion of the more mundane topic of bushes.

MATTHEW Why do you have, what's under sky?

FATHER Pardon?

MATTHEW What's under clouds, Daddy?

FATHER What's under clouds? . . . Air is under clouds, isn't it?

MATTHEW What's in clouds?

FATHER It's moisture.

MATTHEW Mmm. What's . . . mm . . . up, up, up, what else is . . . near the sky/near the sky, Daddy?

FATHER What else is near the sky? There's only the sky near the sky, isn't there? . . . The horizon is near the sky, isn't it?

MATTHEW What, Daddy?

FATHER The horizon is near the sky.

MATTHEW What?

FATHER I said the horizon is near the sky.

MATTHEW It isn't.

FATHER Why isn't it?

MATTHEW Because it isn't.

FATHER Why not?

MATTHEW I/I/I don't know why.

FATHER Don't you?

MATTHEW No.

FATHER The sunshine is near the sky, isn't it? . . . And the stars and the moon?

MATTHEW Mm. What do moons do?

There is no denying that it is Matthew who starts the dialogue. Up to this point the adults have been trying to persuade him to say what kind of bush they are looking at, but his attention moves on to something of his own choosing. He registers that it is clouds that he is looking at and, characteristically, passes on to the more interesting question of how they stay up. We can, of course, only guess that that is what is behind his question, because obviously we cannot know for sure what Matthew is thinking, and he would find it hard to tell us, even if we asked. Perhaps he has thought about this before, he has seen the great bulk of clouds resting apparently on nothing, and asked first himself, and now his father, how this comes to be. Or perhaps the question is posed for the first time to both. Whatever the case, here we have a human being in a world which will continually pose questions, whether he wants it to or not, and here, he believes for the time being at least, there are means at hand for finding out the answers. Look at the father's reply: first a repetition of the question, to give him time to think about it, and then an explanation with the 'isn't it?' tag. Matthew is fortunate in that not only does his father listen to him and give him a helpful answer, but the form of the answer also suggests a kind of participation in the supplying of it: this is the consultative style of

181

sympathetic parents and teachers, and it will ensure that the child asks questions again and tries to think of answers. Apparently it satisfies him, for he switches from 'under' to 'in'. We cannot decide whether or not he has understood the reply without knowing a great deal more about previous conversations and whether or not air had been discussed before. The same would apply to the next answer, although it seems likely that Matthew has previously heard the word 'moisture'. So far the pattern has been: question-answer next question-answer and so on, and this is continued, interrupted only by his inability to formulate the question. His father is willing to wait during this momentary hiatus, because he is really interested in what Matthew is saying and more than ready to help him to develop the skill to say it.

The fumblings are instructive in themselves. Prepositions have served the boy well so far and he tries 'up' – another word to do with location – before settling for 'near'. But what a question! 'What else is near the sky?' Are we to take it that the 'else' refers to the clouds as being near the sky? In any case, we do not think of the sky as something that other things can be near to. Is the summit of Everest any nearer the sky than the top of Nelson's column? This is the typically naive question that makes us realise that we can know what we mean by something, without being absolutely certain we know all that it means. No wonder Daddy again repeats the question, then gives the less than confident answer, 'There's only the sky near the sky, isn't there?' before settling for the enterprising, 'The horizon is near the sky, isn't it?' We can perhaps think of what we would have said given warning and the time to ponder, but Matthew's father has neither. Until now father and child have kept the dialogue going smoothly, but now we have the first real obstacle when the uncomprehended 'horizon' proves too much for Matthew. First of all, he tries to puzzle out what the word is, as though he may be mishearing a word he has met before:

MATTHEW What, Daddy?

FATHER The horizon is near the sky.

MATTHEW What?

but when his father's second repetition of the word still leaves him baffled, he opts out of the discussion, rejecting the whole of his father's statement because of the single impenetrable element:

FATHER I said the horizon is near the sky.

MATTHEW It isn't.

FATHER Why isn't it?

MATTHEW Because it isn't.

182

FATHER Why not?

MATTHEW I/I/I don't know why.

What he does know is that he cannot make sense of his father's statement: as far as he is concerned, there is nothing that he can see near the sky that he can associate with this 'horizon' thing, and in that sense the statement is untrue. Given that initial incomprehension, the subsequent 'why' and 'why not' questions must be even more baffling, as the father is quick to sense, so he replaces 'horizon' with more familiar things such as 'sunshine' and 'stars and the moon'. Now that Matthew finds himself with words he does know, immediately the whole process begins again with 'What do moons do?' – a question which not only starts the next interchange, but incidentally demonstrates an ability which Helen was beginning to develop: using the simple present tense to express a general or habitual action, attitude or function, as Matthew also does when he says 'I don't eat cream cakes'.

For our second sequence we could take the following:

MATTHEW What sort of tree is that?

FATHER Tell me.

MATTHEW I don't know ... Erm ... will you tell me what sort of tree it is, Daddy?

FATHER No. I'm not telling you what sort it is.

MATTHEW Eh, why are the branches broken off, Daddy?

FATHER Why are they?

MATTHEW I don't know, why are they?

FATHER You tell me what sort of tree it is and I'll tell you that.

MATTHEW Um ... A cedar tree.

FATHER Yes. You knew all the time, didn't you? You rascal.

MATTHEW Daddy why are the branches broken off?

FATHER Well why are they broken off?

MATTHEW Don't know.

FATHER Has the man cut them off with a saw?

MATTHEW This is a nice spot here.

The sequence begins with Matthew asking what appears to be a question genuinely seeking information but the father's reply suggests that this is not so, particularly when he refuses the information a second time. It's as though a game is being played in which the two sides are determined not to give in: Matthew knows already the information he professes to be seeking, his Daddy knows that he knows, and he knows that his Daddy knows. The next move, therefore, is a change of question: 'Eh, why are the branches broken off Daddy?' It may well be that he does want to know this and may have made this his next question anyway, but Daddy suspects that once again this is a question intended to keep the adult busy rather than to seek information, and so he turns it back on Matthew, who in turn turns it back to his father. So sure is his father that Matthew's first question was unnecessary that he is prepared to barter one piece of information for another: 'You tell me what sort of tree it is, and I'll tell you that.' Pat comes the answer and Daddy is vindicated, while the detected 'rascal', unabashed, works away at the next question. When Daddy begins to use the same tactics again, but this time with the extra device of offering Matthew a clue or a solution to be considered, Matthew appears to lose interest and switches to the next topic, or perhaps the proffered explanation is accepted without further question and the switch of topic comes with a change of locality.

Matthew's 'why' questions appear, then, to fall into two simple categories: those springing from the insatiable curiosity of any child of this age, and those which are merely used to keep the adult on the hop. Similarly we have noticed that Matthew's father is more than equal to Matthew's tactics, and treats the questions accordingly, answering some of them without demur, but on other occasions volleying them straight back with a 'Why do you think?' Before considering this further, however, let us quickly complete what we were saying about the ways in which Matthew initiates a topic by asking a question. One kind of question, when explanation is being sought, is obviously 'Why?' or 'What for?' Then there is the simpler 'What?' or 'What kind?', and finally the tag question where some kind of reassuring assent is being demanded. By ringing the changes on these, Matthew can keep the adults constantly alert to his succession of not always related questions.

We spoke earlier of the relationship between Matthew and his father which comes out so clearly in the transcript, and already in the examination of these two sequences we have seen something of its nature. The fluency and the eager expectation of rational replies throughout Matthew's conversation reveal a background in which answers are forthcoming. And it is not only his father who responds to Matthew's questions. He is sometimes given answers by at least two adults, and thus the chance to consider alternatives. For example, when he asks, 'Why are these fir trees broken?' he is offered, 'Looks as though it's been rather windy round here', and 'They're old, aren't they?' In one case the external force is identified, in the other the vulnerability of the old, frail trees.

5 The question 'Why?'

Question and answer, then, appears to be a feature of the transcript that can bear even more scrutiny. It is suggested above that not all the questions Matthew asks are genuine requests for information; possibly some are almost a reflex, a habit, an excuse to have something to say without being particularly concerned about the answer. To investigate this further, let us contrast some of the 'Why' questions that Matthew asks. We have already suggested that, when he sees something, he sometimes omits the intermediate stage of describing it or commenting upon it, and immediately asks the question 'Why?' For example, 'Hey ... what's it lying like that for?', and 'Why don't these go over the road these ... mm ... mm ... kick-ups?' Here his eyes alight on something and the questions almost ask themselves. On other occasions we cannot be so sure. Take, for example, this from the 'swans' sequence:

MATTHEW Why do swans peck?

FATHER Because they're hungry. They like what you're giving them.

MATTHEW Why do they like what you're giving them?

FATHER Because they love brown bread.

MATTHEW Why do they love brown bread?

One could be forgiven for thinking that this is the familiar game in which whatever one person says is immediately countered with a formula which keeps him at a disadvantage. On the other hand, the Matthew who is capable of asking such penetrating questions could well be rejecting some of the answers he is getting because they do not really explain what he wants to know. After all, to be told that swans like something because they love it does not advance his understanding very much. But what is an adult to reply to questions which at times come close to the virtually unanswerable 'why are things the way they are?'

6 Answering Matthew's questions

Notice that there is no question, genuine or otherwise, that goes unanswered, and, more than that, there is no deadening stonewalling or unimaginative sameness about the answers themselves. Sometimes the information which has been asked for is supplied directly:

MATTHEW What's that bark for, Daddy?

FATHER Eh?

MATTHEW That bark

FATHER To protect the tree. To prot/protect the tree.

185

Sometimes alternatives are offered, tagged with 'do you think?',
inviting the child to consider the reply as a possibility rather than
an authoritative pronouncement:

> MATTHEW Hey! . . . Who's chopped that tree off?
> FATHER Council man, do you think, or is it the National Trust
> man?

Another tactic is to invite Matthew not just to speculate but to
examine the evidence more closely:

> MATTHEW Hey . . . what's it lying like that for?
> FATHER Shall we go and have a look and see?

At other times the question is treated as a statement:

> MATTHEW Why ?do a lot of traffic here?
> FATHER There is, isn't there?

But by far the most characteristic technique, and the most productive from the point of view of encouraging the boy to think for
himself, is what was earlier referred to as 'volleying' the question
back. By refusing to move like a puppet as the string is pulled, the
father ensures that, if the question is genuine, the child makes some
attempt to think first of his own answer, and, if the information
sought is already known, that it is not repeated by the adult
gratuitously. Here are some examples:

> a MATTHEW Why do they shine at night-time?
> FATHER Why do you think they shine at night-time?
> b MATTHEW What sort of tree is that?
> FATHER Tell me.
> c MATTHEW I wonder what's . . . up here?
> FATHER What do you think's up here?

There is one little sequence in which the techniques are combined in
such a way as to encourage Matthew to chance his arm with what
he thinks he already knows:

> MATTHEW What sort of chestnut tree is it?
> FATHER Well who/what . . . you tell us.
> MATTHEW You tell me, Daddy.
> FATHER Well, have a guess.
> MATTHEW I can't have a guess.
> FATHER Is it a horse-chestnut tree?
> MATTHEW Yes.

Honour satisfied on both sides presumably, and a fragment of
knowledge consolidated for Matthew.

In assuming that, even occasionally, Matthew's questions are not
much more than a conversational device, we may well have done
him an injustice. Let us look more closely at a sequence where the

first answer to a 'why' question immediately evokes a second question.

> MATTHEW Why are the/the trees on the river ... them trees on the river?
>
> AUNT The water's eaten out the bank * *. It's an island now, isn't it?
>
> MATTHEW ?Why is it an island now?
>
> AUNT Because the water's been so strong that it's bitten out all the ground round the trees.
>
> MATTHEW Why has it?
>
> AUNT Because it's so strong.

The aunt's first reply is reasonable enough: if we accept Matthew's unstated premise that trees don't normally grow on rivers, then it is helpful to explain what has happened to create this apparent exception. However the introduction of 'island' has perhaps confused him, so his next question too may well be more than mechanical. In trying to cope with the perennial and perennially difficult question 'why', the aunt goes back to the eating, biting water, the island-maker. From simply contemplating cause and effect (what happened to produce this tree-island), he is now directed to another possible question: What is there about water that should lead it to do such a thing? Possibly the anthropomorphic 'eaten' and 'bitten' have bewildered him.

In the later part of the 'swans' passage we see Matthew keeping up the stream of 'why's, and may again wonder how much of it is curiosity and how much cussedness, when suddenly we get this:

> MATTHEW What are they waiting for now? That/them/them geese now?
>
> FATHER Why do you think they're waiting for? ... Are they waiting for more bread?
>
> MATTHEW What are they waiting for? Daddy you shall tell me what they're waiting for.

There, surely, speaks overriding curiosity and not mere wilfulness. Father believes so and ends the rally with a straight answer.

7 Coping with the grown-ups' questions

How does Matthew fare when it is the adults' turn to ask questions? Let us look at two examples. In the first it is plain sailing, because it is a straightforward matter of identifying a tree, which he has obviously been encouraged to do on other occasions. In the second he starts the topic himself and the adults have no idea what he is talking about, so that there is the problem of getting on to the same wavelength. Here is the first:

FATHER Which tree do you mean?

MATTHEW That tree.

AUNT What kind of tree is it?

MATTHEW That tree.

FATHER Which tree?

MATTHEW That silver birch.

First he points with his finger, and leaves room for doubt as to which particular tree is intended, appears to do the same again in spite of his aunt's prompting, but then is able to use his perhaps previously inert knowledge of trees and of language to 'point' with greater precision.

The other example gives greater difficulty, and provides another example of learning actually taking place. 'Country' is the word that causes the trouble. As we suggested in chapter 4, no word exists in isolation: words have meaning in relation to situations and to other words. Part of the meaning of 'country' is its contrast with 'town': we talk of 'living in the country'. But we can also talk of 'leaving the country', whether we live in a town or a village, because of that other sense which we understand when we talk about the different countries of Europe, or the Common Market countries. For us there is no difficulty, because we have learned the different uses of this word. Put yourself in the place of Matthew, who knows that he sometimes goes for a walk in the country, but may well believe that each piece of what we call 'the countryside' is 'a country'. Given his restricted knowledge on the one hand and the more extended knowledge of the adults on the other, we are all set for confusion:

MATTHEW Christopher hasn't been in countries before, has he?

AUNT What are you talking about?

Later his father starts the process of disentangling his meaning, with that necessary and almost always justified faith in there being one to disentangle:

FATHER What countries are you talking about with Christopher?

MATTHEW Erm. That one that we went to. With im ... last week ... that other country.

Another confusing factor has come into play here: a child's sense of time past. The adults know that Matthew has never been abroad, and they are even more puzzled if he was allegedly there last week. But Matthew has done his best to be precise with his, 'That other country', and Daddy's 'What other country?' must seem rather perverse. Matthew shows the beginnings of impatience with the

188

'Daddy' that prefaces his next attempt:

> MATTHEW Er, Daddy. Er, that country that that tree was bending that I saw like that.

His syntax is strained to breaking point as he tries to convey what is so clear to him and yet so inexplicably incomprehensible to these people with whom he knows he shared the experience to which he is referring. Daddy is getting warmer now, as the bending tree provides a clue and so the first confusion is resolved: 'You mean the countryside. Not/you don't mean England or Wales or Scotland?'

Not only does he supply the right word, but he gives instances, within Matthew's experience, of the now discarded alternative. Notice Matthew's reaction. He repeats the word, trying it out, before the conversation continues along the path he had chosen. Now that they all know what occasion is being referred to, it is easy to put right the other misapprehension when he again says 'last week', and the conversation moves on to what time of year it was and what was done. The only remaining uncertainty of the original statement is whether or not Christopher has in fact been 'in countries before'. Once again the child has been helped in learning how to express meaning by adults with the patience to listen to him and give him credit for knowing what he wants to say, just as they are quick to praise him when he shows that he has learned something as a result of direct teaching:

> MATTHEW Mmm ... Mmm ... A sycamore tree.
>
> FATHER That's right.
>
> MOTHER Oh you clever boy! That's just what it is.

8 Matthew's language development

The emphasis in this section has been on the questions of both child and adults, since questions clearly play such an important part in helping the child to come to grips with the world, especially when he is fortunate enough, as Matthew is, to have parents who appreciate what is going on. In terms of language development, Matthew's ability to produce and deal with so many questions is, of course, also evidence of increasing language skill. Notice, too, the greater specificity of his replies – when he was talking about the birch tree, for example, or in this kind of statement: 'On that road, up there.'

There is also a complexity of sentence structure of the kind that the two-year-old Helen was beginning to develop: 'I want to go down ... erm ... erm ... where the church is over there', 'Is that the way you go to see the church down there?', each of which consists of three clauses which are not simply strung together with 'and's and 'then's. A moment earlier he had said, 'I don't like this spot being like this', a deceptively simple-looking utterance that combines the two statements, 'This spot is like this', and, 'I don't like that fact', in a way that not all three-year-old children will have learned. As well as producing complex structures he can also understand more complicated sentences. It was suggested in chapter 10 that adults unconsciously allow themselves to use the full range of their syntax as the child's ability grows. In this transcript one can pick out examples in which the adult apparently feels no qualms about using quite complicated sentences in explanation of points that puzzle the child: 'Why you have to pay money to sleep in a hotel, but if you owned a dormobile you don't have to pay anybody, do you?' and 'Well, because it's yours and there's no money to pay anybody else who owns it, is there?'

But all this is to labour the point that in general this dialogue is fluent, partly because there is always something to talk about, partly because the adults are sympathetic to what the child wishes to say, and partly because everyone, not forgetting Daniel, whose few remarks the reader may wish to compare with those of Helen at a similar stage, has some skill in talking. As we have seen, there are times when the flow is momentarily halted until one person has cleared up what another is talking about. At other times we have seen learning actually taking place, as in the 'kick-ups' sequence, where there is the characteristic use of the home-made word substituting until the adult vocabulary is introduced; and the use of 'mallard', called to the duck like a name. On the whole, however, it is the perpetual motion of the dialogue that is most striking. 'Where's he getting it all . . .?' Matthew asks his Daddy, referring to Daniel's energy, and we might well ask the same of his own irrepressible curiosity.

9 Suggestions for further work and discussion

Points for discussion

i. Daniel

Although nothing was said in the commentary about the other child on the tape, it would be useful for readers to examine what is said to, by, and in the presence of, Daniel, for comparison with some of the remarks made in chapter 3 and in the earlier Helen commentaries.

a What examples can you find of Daniel beginning to build up the same question-and-answer model as his brother? Look at his questions, his answers, and the parents' reactions to his answers.

b Examine some of the 'input' to him. Consider the swans episode, for example, and the repetition of vocabulary and structures, in context, as the swans approach.

c Does the use of 'all gone' in this transcript throw any light on why many children appear to use this phrase as a so-called 'pivot' word?

d Would you regard his 'Who dat?' as a two-word sentence?

ii. Matthew

a It has been suggested that the input to children in terms of the speech they hear is often 'deviant' (i.e. ungrammatical or elliptical). To what extent does this transcript support the argument?

b What other examples can you find, apart from those given in the commentary, of complexity of structure and difficult vocabulary in the adults' speech?

c There are several occasions in the transcript when the parents respond to the truth value of a statement by the child and ignore errors in grammar or pronunciation. See if you can find them.

d Examine any of Matthew's mispronunciations and try to decide their probable cause.

e What examples can you find of any of the following:
Matthew showing an appreciation of causality?
Matthew paraphrasing instead of using the adult term?
Matthew returning to a theme after it had apparently ceased to interest him?
Direct imitation?

f It was suggested in the commentary that for the most part we could assume that Matthew's 'Why?' questions were genuinely seeking information. Listen to the tape to see whether there are any clues (perhaps, for example, the 'Mm' beginning to some of his utterances) which might be the sign of a kind of game with his father.

g What would you say that Matthew learned in the course of his walk about (1) himself, (2) the world, (3) the English language?

Follow-up activities
i. Listen to, and record if possible, a parent–child interaction in an appropriate situation (e.g. at home, or on a visit to a park, zoo, children's playground etc.) and then compare it with the

    Matthew recording in respect of the child's questions and the adult replies.

ii. Read some of the dialogues in *Focus on Meaning* by Joan Tough (1973) and look for further points of comparison.

iii. Listen to some child–child conversation to see whether any of the adult strategies encountered in the transcript are used by children themselves.

iv. With the permission of a sympathetic head teacher, try to record the questions asked by reception or nursery-class children in the course of a single session (morning or afternoon) and the kind of answers that they receive. There is a useful article by Pit Corder on 'The Teaching of Meaning' in Fraser and O'Donnell (1969).

14 Tailpiece to part two

Throughout the commentaries in this section we have tried to keep to the spirit of the fourth chapter by directing attention to the functions of the children's language as well as to its form. True, we have looked at such things as sentence structure and phrase structure, developments in phonology, and the learning of new words. But all the time there has been an emphasis on the many purposes for which language was being used by Helen and Matthew, on the 'models of language' that they were building up. There has also been much to say about the part played by the adults as the children learned to talk and learned through talk: the language they addressed to the children, and the teaching and encouragement that they provided.

The transcripts are, of course, limited. Child does not talk to child, for example, and the range of situation and age of child is limited. In the preoccupation with the language of the children in the transcripts, perhaps too little has emerged about them as people; and because of the concentration on syntax there has been less time to speak of semantic and cognitive development. Though there has been an attempt to present enough facts about language to make points about what the children are learning, we have not tried to teach any model in detail, and the reader should be aware that it is possible to be less eclectic in approach and to concentrate on one particular model of grammar. The sample has been small, and generalisation from it correspondingly tentative.

But after all that has been said, we hope that the reader will have at least a hint of what it is possible to observe in the everyday speech of a child. We hope that these transcripts have given readers some basis for considering the traditional assertions about the speed with which children learn to talk, the active part they play in the process, the role of their parents, and above all the magnitude of their achievement. With that accomplishment behind them or at least well-begun, children can move on to the stage illustrated in part three which takes place in the classroom where, according to Bloom (1975), the most important development is: 'the child's increasing ability to use the linguistic code, both to speak and understand messages, independently of eliciting states or conditions or of the circumstances in which speech occurs'.[1] Children of four and five may have learned to talk, but they have not yet 'learned the language'.

Reference

[1] Bloom, L. (1975) 'Language Development Review' in Horowitz *et al.* (eds) *Review of Child Development Research* Vol. IV University of Chicago Press

PART THREE
Talking to learn

15 Introduction to part three:
Classroom interaction

In parts one and two our aim was to show how a human being, growing up in a community, learnt the language patterns which enabled him to communicate with the people around him, and how this gradually developing command of language enabled him to fulfil personal needs, and to interact with other human beings.

This is a very general summary of pre-school language development, and in practice we have to recognise the wide diversity of experience children bring to school. It is a mistake to assume that the linguistically deprived child is necessarily a socially deprived child. The Norwich Feasibility Study found when visiting families with a first child of about a year old that there were examples of potential linguistic deficiency in all socio-economic groups. But through the home visits of specially trained teachers there was a real growth of parental awareness of the place of language in learning, and a keenness to find out how the home could prepare children for school. The child who has a good start at school is one who has had a wide range of experiences out of which his language has grown, encouraged by concerned and loving adults.

Before a child comes to school, he follows his curiosity in all directions, asking questions, receiving answers, talking about the answers he gets, the things he sees and the things he does. By means of his own talk he is able to relate the new to what is already familiar to him. Until he has made that relationship he has not yet discovered. The discovery comes in seeing the meaning of what is new in terms of what is familiar; in his talk he creates for the new a personal context, nobody else can do it for him because it has got to be in relation to his own experience. And he does that, above all, in his talk.[1]

It is the teacher in the classroom who has to assess the widely differing experiences and language which each child brings to school, and then to plan activities which build on those foundations, whatever they may be.

In part three we want to consider the ways in which the developing command of language for a variety of functions continues through the primary school, and how pupils use language in their learning. Our traditional view of school, and perhaps our own experiences, may lead us to think of school in terms of a place where the teacher who 'knows' hands on information to the pupils who do not. Attempts to investigate the processes of learning in the individual classroom have been viewed with distrust, perhaps because of fears that the autonomy of the individual teacher might be threatened. In the past, methods of recording what happened in the individual classroom were inadequate, but now, with efficient tape recorders and video tape viewers, it is possible to listen and watch in an attempt to find out about the learning process and the part played by language in this process. Particularly at the primary stage, open-plan classrooms and team-teaching situations have gradually helped individual teachers to overcome their suspicions and fears, and to share their work with colleagues and parents.

It will perhaps be helpful at this point to review the work which has already been carried out on classroom interaction, drawing attention to the limitations of its methods and approaches, as well as to the insights which it can offer into the learning process. We offer only a brief summary of the work in this very complex area. It is neither easy nor desirable to make comparisons between the findings of different investigators who have each begun with different areas of study in mind. We hope, however, that this will serve as a guide to further reading for the interested reader.

Much of the existing work has its origins in America, where Ned Flanders, among others, has been working for a number of years, initially with the aim of evaluating the effectiveness of the teacher, and in devising more efficient teaching methods. Flanders proposes ten categories under which the activities in the classroom can be coded at three-second intervals by an observer practised in using the code. Seven of these categories are concerned with the language of the teacher in the classroom, and include asking questions, giving lectures or giving commands. Two of the categories are devoted to the forms of pupil response, and the last category records silence or confusion.[2] By totalling the codings under each category at the end of the lesson, it is possible to form an overall impression of the lesson, showing the relative percentages of pupil and teacher talk, and the broad nature of that talk, such as whether statements, questions, or other forms of language interaction predominate. The concentration here is on the teacher's role in the classroom, and what might loosely be called the teacher's 'style' of teaching. Though this system concentrates on spoken language, it cannot be a complete record of the language used because of the sampling at three-second intervals. It makes no attempt to examine non-verbal communication such as gesture or facial expression. Pupils cannot be identified, and one cannot concentrate on the learning process of an individual pupil. The observer must make swift decisions about the categorisation of the ongoing speech, and no permanent record of the language exists on tape to be referred to in retrospect. The categories as they stand are very broad. When, for instance, we compare Flanders's category 4, 'Asks questions', with Barnes's thorough analysis of teacher/pupil questions (discussed on pp. 201–2), it is easy to see that Flanders may over-simplify the picture. There is no provision for recording the diagram on the board, or the piece of apparatus which may supplement the verbal element of the lesson. The context in which language occurs plays a vital part in shaping learning, and it cannot be discounted in any study of classroom interaction.

A further American system, that of Bellack, is concerned with the structuring of the lesson as a whole, attempting to show how, through verbal means, teachers indicate the different stages of the lesson, how they evoke and reward pupil responses, and how pupils in turn react to teachers, and know when to respond to teachers' questions. Bellack divides the stages of the lesson into the following categories:[3]

1 *Structuring* The method by which the teacher may initiate the lesson. E.g. 'Now, we're going to learn about the wheatlands of the prairie.' Here, words such as 'Now' and 'Right' indicate to pupils the opening of a new sequence.

2 *Soliciting* The way in which the teacher elicits various responses from pupils – by questions, for instance, e.g. 'Who can tell me the names of the principal towns of the Canadian wheat belt?'

3 *Responding* The various ways in which pupils answer the soliciting move of the teacher.
   Pupil 1 'I don't know, sir.'
   Pupil 2 (Silence)
   Pupil 3 'Saskatchewan', etc.

4 *Reacting* The ways in which the teacher reacts to the responding move of the pupil.
   Teacher to Pupil 1 'Haven't you been listening?'
   Teacher to Pupil 2 'See me at the end of the lesson.'
   Teacher to Pupil 3 'Very good, Brown. Team point.'

Bellack's system has several major advantages over that of Flanders. It is designed to record a complete sequence of interaction, so that the connection between the verbal strategies of the teacher and the learning outcome for the pupils is made clear.

Bellack's ideas form the basis of work carried out at Birmingham University between 1970 and 1972.[4] This research, under the direction of Professor J. Sinclair, used a method of analysis similar to Bellack's and attempted to find answers to a series of questions important in the classroom situation:

1 How are successive utterances related?
2 Who controls the discourse?
3 How does he do it?
4 How, if at all, do other participants take control?
5 How do the roles of listener and speaker pass from one participant to another?
6 How are new topics introduced and old ones ended?
7 What linguistic evidence is there for a discourse unit larger than the utterance?

This system was not designed to handle pupil/pupil interaction in project work, small discussion groups or situations outside the classroom, although it is obvious that each of these situations has its own structure, and that some of the questions above apply to them, too. Sinclair *et al.* have been able to show that both teachers and pupils recognise the different stages of the lesson by linguistic markers which simplify interaction procedures by signalling meanings accepted by both groups.

> The teaching situation is one in which the dominant participant is anxious that his structuring should be as clear and obvious as possible to the other participants. If he is leading a class through a series of steps towards a conclusion he wants them to recognise each step as a discrete unit.[5]

Using their method of analysis, each lesson might be broken into a series of exchanges between teachers and pupils, each exchange consisting of a number of different kinds of acts, each signalled by certain linguistic markers, tacitly accepted by teachers and pupils.

Acts
a Boundary Acts
Framing – by which the teacher indicates he is ready to start a new sequence, signalled by a linguistic marker such as 'Right', 'Now', etc.
Focusing – in which the teacher directs pupils' attention to the area of work he wishes to cover by a focusing statement, e.g. 'Today, I thought we'd . . .'
Each of these boundary acts can be used to signal the beginning of

a new exchange.

b Teaching Acts

Opening – in which the teacher may question, direct, or inform pupils.

Answering – in which pupils acknowledge the teacher by replying, reacting or commenting, as appropriate.

Follow-up – in which the teacher responds to the pupil's answer by accepting, evaluating, or commenting upon it.

A typical piece of classroom dialogue might be analysed in the following way using this approach.

TEACHER Now, right (*Framing Act which indicates that the teacher is beginning a new sequence*).

TEACHER Today we're going to learn about the wheatlands of Canada. (*Focusing Act. A brief introductory summary of the material to follow, which helps pupils focus their attention*).

After an opening informative statement the teacher may move on to a questioning sequence, in which he seeks to elicit responses from pupils, and himself gives an evaluative feedback.

TEACHER And why do the prairies constitute such a good wheat growing area? (*Opening Act signalled by a question.*)

PUPIL Because the soil is rich, sir, and the climate is right. (*Answering Act, in which the pupil replies.*)

TEACHER Very good, Smith. (*Evaluative Act in which the teacher accepts and comments upon the pupil's reply.*)

The pattern of interaction here is not simply Teacher/Pupil, but Teacher/Pupil/Teacher when the pupil's response to the teacher is followed by a further remark from the teacher which acts as an evaluative feedback to the pupil, indicating to him whether his answer is acceptable to the teacher. The absence of evaluative feedback can indicate to the pupil that his answer is not acceptable. In the same way, a hesitant 'Yes' with an upward intonation indicates a partial acceptance, and both responses enable the teacher to avoid the outright verbal rejection 'No'. It is the teacher who chooses the topic of the lesson, and decides which pupil will speak. Sometimes the teacher may ask for 'bids' from the pupils.

TEACHER Who knows the answer? Hands up.

He may remind pupils of the correct way in which to bid.

TEACHER Now don't shout out.

Pupils do, on occasion, initiate exchanges, but this is rare (and Barnes's work supports this view). In most cases their initiations are not concerned with lesson content, but with procedural matters.

PUPIL What heading shall we put, sir?

The verbal pattern of a class lesson, indicated above, is a common one, so common in fact that a failure to obey its rules, either by teacher or pupils, may result in chaos. It may be that some of those teachers who experience difficulties in classroom control are not giving the verbal signals pupils are accustomed to. The researchers themselves note that an important area for research is an investigation of the ways in which pupils in nursery and infant schools are initiated into the ways of verbal behaviour which play an important part in the interaction of teacher and class. It may be that with changing methods in the infant school, this common pattern is no longer being perpetuated, and in this instance it would be interesting to find out what new patterns are developing, and whether these are being recognised in the later stages of education.

One of the most helpful pieces of work investigating the verbal interaction of the classroom was carried out by D. Barnes, and reported in *Language, the Learner and the School*.[6] Here the emphasis was on the individual verbal exchanges of teachers and pupils rather than on the overall structure of the lesson. This research was based on a study of lessons taken by eleven-year-olds during their first term in the secondary school, and was designed to investigate the relationship between the language experiences and expectations children brought from home and the primary school, and the linguistic demands made by teachers in the secondary school. The aim was to examine the whole language environment of the children during lesson time by means of tape recordings of the lesson, supported by the notes of an observer who recorded seating arrangements, the use of apparatus and visual aids, and collected any diagrams or notes used during the lesson. This was an attempt to widen the focus of language studies in the classroom, taking in not only the language of the teacher, but also the language arising from interchanges between teacher and pupils, and pupils and pupils, examining in detail the way in which language and learning were interdependent. The tape-recorded data, supported by the observer's additional notes, were analysed under the following main headings:

1 Teacher's questions
  i factual
  ii reasoning – 'open'
          – 'closed'
  iii 'open' questions not calling for reasoning
  iv social questions, e.g. 'Will you open a window, please?'

2 Pupils' participation
   i in response to the teacher
   ii unsolicited comments
   iii proportion of pupils contributing to the lesson
   iv proportion of time taken by pupils' contributions
3 The language of instruction
   i register specific to a subject
   ii the language of secondary education
   iii the use made of this language in the learning process by
       pupils and teachers
4 Social relationships and the ways in which these are
   manifested through language
5 Language and other media, such as pictures and diagrams,
   and language and non-verbal tasks such as experiments.

Barnes's analysis framework should be studied in detail in order to appreciate the ways in which it extends the categories used in previous analyses of verbal interaction. A comparison of Flanders's broad category *'Teacher:* Asks questions', and Barnes's breakdown of this area indicates the latter's concern with the *meaning* of the interaction for teachers and pupils as well as with its *form,* and with the different demands made on pupils by the various types of questions. He focuses also on the language particular to different subjects, and acknowledges that language in the classroom has a social as well as informational function. The findings of Barnes from his analysis of a number of lessons supported previous work in showing that classrooms were dominated by teachers, and that pupil-initiated sequences were rare. The Bullock Report emphasises this finding by noting that 'the teacher talks for three-quarters of the time in the usual teacher–class situation', and that 'in a 45-minute period the amount of time left for a class of 30 to contribute is an average of some 20 seconds per pupil'.[7] Barnes's examination of teachers' questions showed that teachers were predominantly concerned with the factual nature of the subject and with enabling pupils to recall and verbalise previously taught sequences. There were very few opportunities for pupils to develop the higher reasoning skills, or to think through a sequence 'on their feet'. Many teachers had preconceptions about the answers to their questions, so that an apparently open question such as 'What can you tell me about a bunsen burner, Alan?' depended not on the pupil's reasoning but on his recall of a very specific statement from a previous lesson – viz. 'A luminous and non-luminous flame'. As Sinclair's work showed, the traditional class lesson is a very tightly structured unit in which the teacher manipulates the class and works towards the answers he has envisaged, shaping the knowledge of the pupils according to his own views of the subject. But the rapid question and answer technique leaves pupils no opportunity for the tentative or hesitant offering, which is rarely supported by a favourable evaluative comment from the teacher.

The Bullock Report notes:

It has also become clear what difficulties face the teacher if he is to encourage genuine exploration and learning on the part of the pupils, and not simply a game of guessing what he has in mind. What the teacher has in mind may well be the desirable destination of a thinking process; but a learner needs to trace the steps from the familiar to the new, from the fact or idea he possesses to that which he is to acquire. In other words the listener has to make a journey in thought for himself. The kind of class lesson we are describing has therefore to be supported by others in which the pupils' own exploratory talk has much more scope. Where it builds upon such talk the class lesson can be an important way of encouraging the final steps by which a new piece of learning is securely reached. But it can achieve this only if the teacher-directed discussion takes up and uses the contributions of the pupils, for these indicate the stages at which pupils' thinking now stands, and they point the steps by which the distinction can be reached. 'Guessing what the teacher has in mind' becomes only too easily a substitute for this more arduous process.[8]

Barnes found that many teachers seemed more concerned with getting pupils to use the specialist subject register, than ensuring that they understood the processes described by the language. A biology lesson on respiration seemed concerned solely with pupils' recall and use of technical vocabulary, such as 'trachea' and 'bronchii'.[9] It was clear that many pupils were excluded from an active participation in lessons because they were unable to understand the language used by the teacher, and did not feel able, themselves, to use the language with confidence, although it was made clear to them in many cases that the teacher regarded the language as a necessary part of the subject. *relate to TP.*

So far the systems of analysis described have all been concerned with the formal class situation in which the teacher works with, maybe, thirty or more pupils, but it is evident that the constraints of that situation, or 'orchestrating the exchange' to produce a single

203

tune, distort normal social relationships and verbal interaction.[10] Outside schools and other institutions we do not normally hold conversations in groups of thirty or more, and our conversations do not follow the question and brief answer pattern. For most of us, the one-to-one situation, or participation in a small group, is much more representative of our real-life encounters with people.

A piece of research which recognises this factor and is aimed at finding out more about the language of children as it is used in small groups in the learning situation, is the SSRC project *Communication and Learning in Small Groups*, undertaken by Douglas Barnes and Frankie Todd. Working with pupils aged thirteen, of average ability, grouped in threes and fours, the intention was to 'examine the relationship between short-term, small-scale aspects of the social interaction of small groups and the cognitive strategies generated in the course of this interaction'.[11] The groups of children were given problem-like tasks linked closely to the subject matter of their current lessons, which they were invited to discuss. The particular lessons chosen included the humanities, literature, and science. The tasks drew on children's everyday experiences and ranged from the use of apparatus and a discussion of the implications of particular experiments, to others connected with the literature they were reading, or a consideration of environmental problems such as the siting of National Parks and the provision of leisure amenities. The children were taped outside the classroom, largely because of the technical problems of recording in a busy, noisy environment, and an observer was not present during the discussions. Once the material had been collected, the chief problem lay in devising a category system which would help in the analysis of talk arising from an informal situation. As Sinclair *et al.* showed, teacher/pupil talk in the classroom is relatively well-structured in patterns accepted by both teachers and pupils, whereas in the informal setting, unguided by a teacher, each group creates its own structure and method of working, and as yet we know very little about talk produced in these circumstances. It would take too long to summarise the papers arising from this report which include, in addition to the final report, a manual for teachers, *Monitoring Small Groups*, giving practical advice on equipment and locations recording, and *Making Sense Together* which is a descriptive guide for teachers, taking them through the recorded conversations, and setting up a framework within which they can analyse the talk they record from pupils in similar circumstances. The framework covers four main areas:

1 collaboration of pupils
2 social skills
3 cognitive strategies
4 reflexivity – i.e. the pupils' awareness of the processes they themselves employ in such discussion, and their appreciation of the contributions and strategies of other members of the group.

This paper also examines the failures and limitations of some groups, and suggests positive ways in which teachers can promote the skills necessary for children to work productively in the small group.

In contrast to the 'public' nature of teacher/pupil talk in the classroom with its emphasis on short 'correct' answers, the emphasis in the research was on the 'exploratory' talk described by the Bullock Report, arising out of an intimate group where hesitations, tentativeness, and a willingness to put forward hypotheses, to modify one's views and to accept the validity of other views might be expected to play a far greater part than it would in teacher/pupil interaction in the structured lesson.

Douglas Barnes describes the work for the SSRC project in greater detail in *From Communication to Curriculum*. He does, however, take the implications of his findings further when he suggests that the traditional methods of question and answer techniques are a result not only of particular educational philosophies, but of political and social factors outside the control of the teachers in the classroom, and are a result of the way we, as a society, value school knowledge and select children for particular roles in that society.

What I have called communication is not just a matter of the classroom, nor does it involve only teachers and pupils. I might have included (were I qualified to do so) a chapter on how a head teacher can arrange the patterns of communication in his school to see to it that not only the pupils are encouraged to assume wider responsibility, but parents and teachers too. Some head teachers argue persuasively that this is where change in communication must begin. We could go further and consider the communication system between teachers and local authority officials to discover why it is that most teachers will attend courses given by authoritative figures but few will take part in self-directed working parties outside the confines of the school. Each communication system is embedded in other larger ones, so that in writing about communication I find myself indulging in vague gestures towards larger things.[12]

Douglas Barnes is not alone in tracing an intimate relationship between schools and the values of the society in which they flourish. Basil Bernstein in much of his work has been concerned to suggest that the failure or success of some pupils in school is largely a result of the values and attitudes of the particular socio-economic group to which they belong. That we have not discussed Bernstein's views at length is a result principally of lack of space to do justice to his often controversial but highly influential ideas, which have undergone considerable modification since he first began writing. It would be a mistake to perpetuate his over-simplistic division of language into 'restricted' or 'elaborated' by any brief summary of our own. Suffice it to say that enough damage has already been done by a misunderstanding and garbling of his ideas, which, on occasions, he himself has failed to present clearly. Nothing at all can be achieved by labelling children as either 'restricted' or 'elaborated' code users. Such labels serve as blinkers which prevent us assessing what children *can* do with language. A very much fuller analysis of some of the methods of describing classroom interaction discussed in this chapter, is to be found in *Language in Culture and Class*, A. D. Edwards (1976).

No book which discusses teachers, children, and language, can be altogether devoid of an educational philosophy of some kind, or fail to make some points concerning the educational implications of changing attitudes to language. However, our aim in writing this book is not to suggest that certain methods or techniques are 'correct' or that there should be only one form of language interaction between teachers and pupils. Our concern is primarily practical, in that we feel more access is needed to examples of children talking both with their peers and teachers, so that readers can themselves assess what children are capable of, and explore the linguistic implications of different kinds of interaction. We are also concerned to find ways of looking at language which can be made available to parents and teachers, because we are aware that the complexities of systems such as those of Flanders and Bellack render them impractical outside the controlled research situation in which they could be used by observers fully conversant with their methods of analysis.

The material in part three of this book is, therefore, designed to enable the reader to study, at first hand, pupils and teachers talking outside the classroom situation. The following tapes and transcripts are of a variety of situations:

1 a teacher talking to Michael, aged 5, on his own, during break

2 Elaine and Stuart, aged 6+, talking about a tank of snails which had been sent up to the classroom. For part of the time the teacher and a visitor are present, but for the majority of the time Elaine and Stuart work on their own

3 a teacher with four eleven-year-old pupils, two boys and two girls, talking about the poem 'Timothy Winters' by Charles Causley

4 a transcript of the same teacher and group of pupils discussing the opening paragraph of 'Cider with Rosie' by Laurie Lee. This transcript is prefaced by suggestions for lines of enquiry.

In all instances, except 'Cider with Rosie' the following information is given:

1 a full transcript of the discussion

2 taped extracts which we hope will give the 'flavour' of each occasion and of the individual speakers

3 a commentary on each transcript which gives background details about the setting, information about the speakers, and an indication of the major points to note about the language of the interaction.

All the recordings were made by practising teachers with some knowledge and experience of the workings of tape recorders, but with no claims to be skilled research workers. Both the transcripts and the commentaries were made with the help of the teachers involved, and all agreed that the opportunity to stand back as observers was a valuable one from which they were normally precluded by the demands of a busy classroom. It is possible to replay the discussions and to consider carefully what strategies children use as they approach different tasks. We can evaluate their understanding of material covered in the classroom situation, and their ability to apply this learning to new situations. It is also possible to learn a great deal about the structuring of small groups, the most effective methods of presenting tasks and materials, and the nature of our own participation as teachers in such groups in the most constructive way.

We are not suggesting that group discussion with or without the teacher is the only method of teaching, but it is increasingly recognised that it calls for very different skills from both teachers and pupils, and it is a necessary adjunct to the class lesson with its public approach to learning. While inevitably what is said has implications for teaching methods, this book is not primarily about methods, but about learning to listen to children talking.

We have no fully developed methods of analysis to offer for use on the material; indeed, as yet, one has not been designed. Our ideas and methods owe most to the work of Douglas Barnes, but we can say from experience that it is easiest to work on material which one has collected oneself, because then the context of the situation is fully known. The way to begin any analysis is to transcribe the material and then to listen, and listen again, to the tape. One develops a feel for the key points in discussion which are likely to be worth studying, using whatever framework seems appropriate, whether it is an analysis of questions or an examination of social skills, collaborative effort, exploratory talk or cognitive strategies.

References

[1] Britton, J. 'Speech in the School' in *NATE* 2 no. 2, Summer 1965

[2] Flanders, N. (1970) *Analysing Teaching Behaviour* Addison-Wesley

[3] Bellack, A. A., Kliebard, H. M., Hyman, R. T. and Smith, F. I. (1967) *The Language of the Classroom* Teachers' College Press

[4] Sinclair, J. McH. and Coulthard, R. M. (1975) *Towards an Analysis of Discourse; The English used by Teachers and Pupils* OUP

[5] Coulthard, M. 'Approaches to the Analysis of Classroom Interaction' in B. Wade (ed.) *Functions of Language* University of Birmingham vol. 26 no. 3, June 1974

[6] Barnes, D. (1969) *Language, the Learner and the School* Penguin

[7] Bullock, A. (1975) *A Language for Life* Report of the Committee of Enquiry appointed by the Secretary of State for Education and Science, HMSO, 10.4

[8] Bullock, A. *op. cit.* 10.2

[9] Barnes, D. *op. cit.* p. 49.

[10] Bullock, A. *op. cit.* 10.2

[11] Barnes, D. and Todd, F. (1975) *Communication and Learning in Small Groups* SSRC project, University of Leeds, p. 1, now published (1977) as *Communication and Learning in Small Groups* Routledge

[12] Barnes, D. (1975) *From Communication to Curriculum* Penguin, p. 184

Further reading

Barnes, D. (1973) *Language in the Classroom* Language & Learning E. 262 Block 4 Open University

208

Barnes, D. (1971) 'Classroom Contexts for Language and Learning' in *Educational Review* **23**, no. 3

Britton, J. (1970) *Language and Learning* Allen Lane

Cashdan, A., and Grugeon, E. (1972) *Language in Education* Open University, section 4

Creber, P. (1972) *Lost for Words* Penguin (particularly appendix 1)

Lewis, R. 'Language and Learning in the Primary School' in *NATE* **9** no. 2, Summer 1975

Mills, R. D. 'Small Group Discussions' in *NATE* **8** no. 2, Summer 1974

Martin, N., *et al.* (1976) *Understanding Children Talking* Penguin

Rosen, C. and H. (1973) *Language in the Primary School* Penguin

Stratta, L., Dixon, J. and Wilkinson, A. (1973) *Patterns of Language* Heinemann

Taylor, M. T. and Sharp, R. M. 'Classroom Analysis' in *Education for Teaching* ATCDE, Autumn 1971

Williams, P. 'Talk and Discussion' in *NATE* **5** no. 2, Summer 1971

Wragg, E. C. 'Interaction Analysis as a Feedback System for Student Teachers' in *Education for Teaching* ATCDE, Spring 1970

16 Mrs Parkin and Michael

---

1 Transcript†

A conversation between Michael, aged 5, and his teacher, Mrs Parkin. Throughout this tape background noise of children in the playground.

MICHAEL Pep/Dinky/Pepoe's at Dinky's chocolate again and/ and Pepoe's ate Dink/Pep/Dinky's again ... and Dinky's ate Pepoe's ... and the babies 'ave ... you know what the babies have done is they've/they've bin in their nappies ... oh! ... I've bought a toilet seat for them except they never use/use it!

TEACHER What do they do then?

MICHAEL They do it in their nappy!

TEACHER What do you do?

MICHAEL I smack them ... mm, and/and do you know I/I bought a new tape/tape-recorder for me, you know and I made a/a se/security-box for it, and/and do you know those babies have bin in the secur/security-box and they've/they've had that tape-recorder on and broken it ... and I/I had it new! ... mm, I, and they are a naughty fam/family really ... oooh! just hark at that noise and we've got the classroom door shut except the/the ... and we can/we can hear it *right* through.

TEACHER Mm

MICHAEL Mm ... It's rather a noise, I think they/they shou/ they make a bit too much noise ... yes ...

† For an explanation of transcription symbols, see p. 21.

TEACHER Do your babies make a noise?

MICHAEL They do, they squeal and screa/and oh dear ... mm and/and I told them to be quiet, except they don't take any notice ... eh I've got paint on me hands. Whe/when I went to put my bottle away ... I's the last one finishing milk. (*Laughs*)

TEACHER Were you?

MICHAEL Yes ...

TEACHER Why was that?

MICHAEL ... Well ... mm ... well, I/I won with, I won ... yesterday ... I won some people yesterday except I'm/I'm last today ... d'y know ... I say ... I've bin wondering where *this* had got to, I thought it had got lost 'cos we haven't had it for such a long time. (*Michael is referring to the tape-recorder*)

TEACHER No ... I took it home at the holidays.

MICHAEL ... Oh, h'I see and you/and you only just brought it back today.

TEACHER Yes.

MICHAEL Or did you keep it in the cupboard for a bit?

TEACHER Yes, it was in the cupboard for a little bit.

MICHAEL ... Oh ... and then and then y/you c/came and got it out of the cupboard ... didn't you?

TEACHER Yes.

MICHAEL Oh, I wish, I coul/I wasn't so frightened to go.

TEACHER You wish you weren't frightened to go?

MICHAEL Yes, but I, but there's too much *noise* isn't there?

TEACHER Yes, and what else frightens you?

MICHAEL ... Well, the noise in the playground when I go out and and motor-bikes frighten me when I'm going down street on my bike in Dove Road in case they're coming down 'ere ... oh dear ... 'cept Dove Road isn't a very busy road, is it?

TEACHER No.

MICHAEL No, we don't have much cars come down only Gales, they've got a lot, they've got a motor-bike and one car and a van.

TEACHER And do they make a noise?

MICHAEL They do and it frightens me in case they are van, when it's a noisy car or bus or lorry ...

TEACHER And what else frightens you besides noise?

MICHAEL Well/well ... banging (TEACHER Mm.) still that's/that's something to do with the noise isn't it? (*Laughing*)

TEACHER Yes, it is.

MICHAEL (*Laughs*) ... mm ... hm ... well ... y'know what

frightens me h'is . . . y'know . . . when there's a crowd of cars and/and/and water running when I'm walking near it in case I fall in it.

TEACHER Oh dear.

MICHAEL . . . I'm frightened of a lot of things.

TEACHER Yes, we all are.

MICHAEL Still, my Richard h'is/is even fright/frightened of a horse. (*Laughs*)

TEACHER Is he?

MICHAEL (*Laughing*) Yes . . . (*Laughs and giggles in amusement*)

TEACHER And are you frightened of a horse?

MICHAEL I'm not! *I'm* not frightened of it. (*Laughs*)

TEACHER No.

MICHAEL . . . One/one time when we were playing outside a horse came/ca down my road and Richard/and Richard went running in going . . . (*Loud screams to demonstrate. Then Michael laughs at this.*)

TEACHER Screaming?

MICHAEL Yes (*Laughs*) . . . y'know if he ev/ever has a horse he says 'ooh dat 'orse will bite me' . . . (*Confidentially*) D'y'know how he talks, he says 'b' for 'bus' . . . and/and he used to say 'da' for 'car' . . . but I cou/could talk . . . say 'Daddy's car' when I was even none . . . Richard was saying . . . (*Gibberish – Michael demonstrates this beautifully*) and he says when/when he was none he said 'Mu, Mu, Mummy' and he think he was talking properly . . . he can say 'car' now, Richard can . . . and/and he says 'ooh dat 'ouse' and he says 'me' instead of 'my' . . . he said, 'mm/mm oh' he said 'mm,' and when we play and Richard says 'me pooh in my clean naa'. (*Laughs*)

TEACHER He says what?

MICHAEL Me pooh in my clean naa!

TEACHER And what does that mean?

MICHAEL I've poo/poohed in my clean nappy.

TEACHER Oh dear! (*And both burst out laughing*)

2 Introduction

This first tape was made by a teacher talking to a five-year-old boy during the lunch hour. The school, of about 300 pupils, is situated on the outskirts of a semi-industrial town. The building is old, and classroom conditions cramped, but it is generally a lively and happy place.

212

Michael began school in September 1970, and the tape was made one month before his fifth birthday, February 1971. He was in a class of 42 children (frightening in its educational implications) all of whom started with him in September 1970, working with a young and exceptionally skilful teacher. Michael lived close to the school, and went home for his dinner, but he very much liked to stay behind until all the dinner children had gone in, and talk to the teacher. At home he had a younger brother, Richard, aged two. He was very fond of his grandparents and spent a considerable amount of time with them. Pepoe and Dinky are two of the dolls he plays with at home.

As you listen to the tape we suggest that you bear in mind several questions.

1 What is the role of the teacher in this conversation?
2 What do you learn about Michael on a personal level?
   What kind of games does he play on his own?
   What aspects of school has he found difficult to adjust to?
3 What evidence is there of his capacity to think through ideas and to generalise about experiences?
4 What conclusions can you form about his ability to get on with
   (a) adults?
   (b) other children?

3 The role of the teacher as a sympathetic and tactful listener

A quick initial glance at the transcript of the tape reveals a very important feature of this conversation – that Michael does by far the most talking, and generally he develops his utterances at length, while his teacher makes short comments or asks questions. In many classroom situations the teacher is the dominant speaker, the one who chooses the topic of conversation, decides which pupils are to speak and for how long. Here the teacher is a sympathetic listener who gives him room to develop his ideas. This does not mean she is merely a passive listener. She is ready to prompt him with a tactful question which might help him to explore his ideas: 'Yes, and what else frightens you?'; to offer support where it is needed: 'I'm frightened of a lot of things.' 'Yes, we all are.'; to share a joke with him: 'And what does that mean?' 'I've poo/poohed in my clean nappy.' 'Oh dear.' (*And both burst out laughing.*)

Her concept of the role of teacher does not, in this instance, mean correcting his expression. There are a number of places where Michael uses non-standard forms of English. In 'Pepoe's ate

213

Dinky's chocolate again' he uses the past tense of the irregular verb with the auxiliary ''s', instead of the past participle, 'eaten'. 'I's bought a new tape-recorder for me' and 'I's the last one finishing milk' have the contracted form of 'is' instead of 'have' and 'am', and the non-reflexive 'me', instead of 'myself'. It might be thought the duty of a teacher to correct these errors, but at this stage interruptions might divert Michael and ultimately his desire to communicate could be over-ridden by what he would see as the teacher's demands for conformity to adult standards. There can be no hard and fast rule about when the teacher should intervene on these occasions. Many children entering the infant school still use the relics of immature forms, both syntatic and phonological, or non-standard forms, but in many cases they correct these themselves as they listen to other children and adults. One seven-year-old, listening to herself on the tape recorder, commented, 'I say "wiz" and not "with", don't I?', and never again used the immature form. This was an instance of a habit having remained long after the adult phonological patterns had been developed in the rest of her speech and which she was able to correct herself. The teacher must judge when to intervene, and in most cases this can be done in a quiet aside, not as a public rebuke which eventually inhibits the speaker.

The teacher was fully aware of the problems created by the size of this class, and recognised that there were occasions on which as she walked round the class it was all too easy to toss out encouraging but superficial comments such as, 'I like that painting', without really engaging with pupils at a much more vital level. She said herself, after we had listened to this tape and discussed it as a group, 'The tape recording has taught me to be a better listener, and to make time to listen, no matter how pressed I may be'. She came increasingly to recognise the value of informal moments during break and lunch hour like this one with Michael, when time and opportunity are available for getting to know each child. She had found some pupils in this reception class who were happy to go away quietly during the day and 'speak' to the tape, in the knowledge that their teacher would listen to what they had to say during the evening, and talk to them about it the next day. This does point to the need of children to be listened to, and ancillary help and the visits of parents would seem of utmost importance in a class of this size.

4 Michael's use of expressive language

As adults, we are probably surprised by the frankness and honesty with which Michael admits his fears and fantasies, and the fact that he feels able to speak so freely is a measure of the confidence he has in his teacher, although he has not known her for long.

Throughout the conversation Michael's language is strongly expressive of himself as a person. We might say that his concern is not only to convey to his teacher his observations on the kinds of vehicles in Dove Road, or to seek information about the tape-recorder, but also to express his own feelings in relationship to the things he is speaking of. James Britton sees language fulfilling certain functions for the user ranging from the 'transactional' which is concerned with the giving and seeking of information; through the 'expressive', in which the speaker feels free to express the attitudes and opinions which reflect his innermost feelings and concerns; to the 'poetic', in which the speaker is concerned more with the shape and form of the utterance. This is to represent, rather crudely, ideas which James Britton has worked out in great detail in a number of books and articles[1]. We need to remember when we use his ideas that he is describing a functional continuum. It is never possible to chop spoken language into units, and label each one with a single function, because so often when we speak our intentions at any given moment are multifarious. Providing we bear this in mind when using either Britton's or Halliday's classification of functions, both can be helpful in enabling us to look closely at the apparently inchoate language which arises in a conversation such as that between Michael and his teacher, and to make some sense of the intentions of speakers and listeners.

Michael's language is accurately summed up by James Britton's definition of expressive speech as 'language close to the speaker: what engages his attention is freely verbalised, and as he presents his view of things, his loaded commentary upon the world, so he also presents himself. Thus, it is above all in expressive speech that we get to know one another, each offering his unique identity and (at our best) offering and accepting both what is common and what differentiates us'[2].

This is language offered in intimate circumstances in which the speaker does not plan carefully beforehand what he is going to say, or offer what he says as a coherent and carefully organised utterance. Often there are sudden shifts of topic and attention by the speaker: 'I told them to be quiet, except they don't take any notice ... eh I've got paint on me hands.' There is no obvious

215

logical connection between seemingly disparate topics, which are not made explicit by the speaker unless the listener questions the relationship specifically.

Various preoccupations do surface through Michael's conversation like the top of the iceberg above the sea, whose depths conceal its origin. He is overwhelmed by the noise of the busy playground, and acknowledges his fear of going outside; similar sudden loud noises, the motor bikes in Dove Road, also frighten him, even though he recognises that Dove Road is comparatively quiet.

Another preoccupation his teacher commented on was his dislike of dirt, and this probably underlies his remark about the paint on his hands. Halliday speaks of the child who through interaction with others is 'enabled to offer someone else that which is unique to himself, to make public his own individuality [which] in turn reinforces and creates this individuality'.[3] It is the use of language in the personal model which Michael is primarily engaged in here.

His imaginative world is still a powerful creation, peopled by the 'babies' Pepoe and Dinky who constantly threaten his control – 'they've bin in their nappies'; 'they've had that tape-recorder on and broken it . . . and I/I had it new! . . . mm, I, and they are a naughty fam/family really.' Perhaps these are the things Michael himself would like to do, or perhaps what he fears he *might* do. In imaginative play, still a very important feature of the infant classroom, he is trying out adult roles as he himself experiences them. Just as he has experienced language in the 'regulatory' model as his parents have controlled him, so he is trying out language in the same mode in controlling his dolls, and will later use it in attempts to influence his classmates and perhaps his brother, Richard.

As adults we have learnt to be deceptive in presenting ourselves, often concealing what we are and deliberately creating for the world a picture of the person we should like to be. In a later tape, 'Timothy Winters', we can see Mark creating an image of himself as a 'tough guy', aided by the myth his listeners invent. Michael, in his own way attempts this, as with laughing bravado he says, 'I'm not frightened of it' (the horse), or remarks that he finished his milk first the previous day. But he is as yet ingenuous enough to reveal his inner fears, although slightly shame-facedly, in a way which he is unlikely to do so openly when he is older. Social convention in our culture inhibits the revelation of very personal feelings. In connection with this, Barnes (1969) in *Language, the Learner and the School*, notes the way in which pupils in the first term of the secondary school, cease to refer to personal anecdotes when speaking to their teachers. It is partly our view of education as concerned with 'subjects' and handing on information which inhibits references to events outside the classroom, but it is also the neglect in education of the affective domain. Benjamin Bloom in *The Taxonomy of Educational Objectives*, book 2, describes the affective domain as 'the human reaction or response to the content, subject matter, problems, or areas of human experience.'[4] We tend to think of language in the classroom as concerning chiefly the cognitive area for the recall of knowledge, for thinking, and for problem solving, but we do a great disservice to the child as a developing human personality if we neglect that language with which he is struggling to realise himself as a feeling individual.

Fortunately for Michael, he is in contact with a teacher who welcomes his expression of those concerns which are close to himself. Perhaps it is easier for him to confide in a comparative stranger than in his own parents. We have all perhaps been recipients of intimate confidences from strangers on trains, or have felt the relief of unburdening ourselves to strangers in similar circumstances. Suffice it to say that in this classroom there is no great divide between the subject matter of education, and the feelings of the learner. Michael is being encouraged to come to terms with the new skills of reading and writing, but he is also being encouraged to come to terms with himself. These two aspects of the developing personality should go hand in hand; we cannot, and should not, attempt to educate half the person, but all too often, particularly in secondary education, the development of the affective domain is considered rather a time-wasting exercise by the teacher, and the 'facts' are thought more important. This is a short-sighted view, because an ability to come to terms with the self may affect the whole personality, which is bound in turn to affect educational progress.

5 Michael's use of language for cognitive functions: the heuristic model

In this conversation between Michael and his teacher language is, however, serving other purposes, besides the expressive, for the boy. His unprompted realisation that 'banging' is another example of his general concept 'noise' shows his ability to use language to reason about a difficult concept. He uses language to make acute observations about his brother's speech in a delightful and perceptive way: 'y'know how he talks, he says "b" for "bus" . . . and/and he used to say "da" for "car" . . . But I cou/could talk . . . say

217

"Daddy's car" when I was even none', and even goes on to reproduce the babbling noises made by Richard. Another aspect of learning is revealed by his ability to ask questions of his teacher, and in doing so to find out what has happened to the tape-recorder. Halliday calls this the heuristic model of language: 'When he is questioning he is seeking not merely facts but explanations of facts, the generalisations about reality that language makes it possible to explore.'[5] The child's awareness of this particular language function is closely connected with the parent–child communication in the home setting. There are parents whose answer to children's questions is to tell them to 'Shut up'. I heard recently from the teacher of a reception class of a small boy who at first didn't understand or make any attempt to answer her questions, and simply repeated them after her. She discovered that he had spent a large part of his early years with a child-minder, who looked after ten children a day, and it was unlikely that she would have had time to deal with his questions in the way that, for example, Matthew's father did with Matthew. It is not that the child cannot use the form of the question; more fundamentally, he does not understand the purpose of questions as a means of finding out, because he has not experienced them in this function. When we realise that a large part of education is conducted through teacher/pupil question and answer, then the handicap under which such children suffer becomes obvious, as they are gradually alienated from the whole process of education.

6 The move from home to school

In choosing this tape as the first example of language in the classroom, we quite deliberately selected an example which was not concerned with any of the usual subjects on the curriculum. Michael at 5, in the new, and, as he makes clear, sometimes bewildering and frightening surroundings of school, is still coming to terms with the need to move out from his home. His concerns are still to some degree with the family and the world he leaves behind each day, and his teacher recognises his need to talk about such matters, as she also recognises that he needs time to adjust to a new routine and activities. When she listened to the tape, she herself asked, 'Do we as adults always give children time to talk and explore their surroundings? Do we listen to them when they do talk?' In some classrooms Michael's conversation might have been steered by the teacher into what she considered matters of more relevance to school life and work, and had this been the case we should never have known what it was that concerned Michael as a person, not just as another pupil in a very large class.

7 Suggestions for further work and discussion

a. You might listen to a group of pupils at play in a Wendy House. What are the subjects which preoccupy them? What models of language do they show themselves able to use?

b. If possible, talk and listen to one pupil. You might use a model he had made, a painting, or a book as your starting point, but let the child do the talking. Again, note the topics of conversation and the models of language used. You need to bear in mind that Michael and his teacher had established a good relationship; on your first meeting with a pupil do not be disappointed if you are unable to achieve the same degree of confidence in each other.

8 References

[1] Britton, J. (1970) *Language and Learning* Allen Lane

[2] Wilkinson, A. (1975) *Language in Education* OUP, p. 176

[3] Wilkinson, A. *op. cit.*, p. 171

[4] Bloom, B. (1964) *Taxonomy of Educational Objectives* book 2: *The Affective Domain* Longman, p. 3

[5] Wilkinson, A. *op. cit 2*, p. 171

17 Snails

1 Transcript†

Two infants, Elaine and Stuart, 6+, discussing the snails in a glass-sided container in the classroom — part of a science project involving an older group of children. Initially the tape includes the teacher, who is acting head, and a visitor to the school, who occasionally joins in the conversation. This made transcription difficult on the earlier part of the tape. The complete tape lasts for approximately 35 minutes.

ELAINE They're snails aren't they? I think they're snails.

TEACHER Well what are they?

STUART Snails.

TEACHER Are you sure?

STUART Yes.

TEACHER Positive?

STUART Yes.

TEACHER How many do you think there are?

STUART Mm, all on 'ems got lines. Coloured . . . coloured.

ELAINE *

STUART You can see it clearly through there.

ELAINE *

STUART *

ELAINE That's because you know/you know they leave a trail
wherever they/well you know, slime

STUART Slime, yes . . .

† For an explanation of transcription symbols, see p. 21.

220

ELAINE * I bet they're baby snails.

STUART They is a lot of baby snails, one there . . .

ELAINE *

STUART That's to make 'em wet, that's to make em wet. Look, they go on there then that glass makes 'em wet, then they slide down there . . . Ugh. * Just look like . . . er . . . coloured mushrooms, don't they? They just look like coloured mushrooms, don't they? . . . Somebody's/somebody's been digging here. They've been digging, haven't they? Can you see? Can you see?

ELAINE Some of 'em are bigger than other . . .

TEACHER You can take the top off if you like. You take the top off and have a look.

STUART I don't fancy/I don't f/I don't fancy looking at 'em.

VISITOR Are you going to have those, you know, toasted or between a slice of/slice of bread?

ELAINE This one's stuck to side, this one's stuck.

TEACHER I don't know. We had some bread made yesterday, didn't we, in the juniors, had lots of bread made.

STUART They won't bite.

ELAINE I know.

STUART Elaine thinks they'll bite her.

TEACHER Well, have you decided what they are yet?

ELAINE Snails.

TEACHER Snails . . .

STUART Just like like mushrooms.

VISITOR (*Surprised tone*) Mushrooms.

ELAINE AND STUART Yes. (*Laughing*)

VISITOR Do they? Why do they look like mushrooms?

STUART That one does.

ELAINE I think they look a bit more like seashells.

VISITOR Aye (*tone of agreement*). They do look like seashells, don't they? Do you mean they're the same shape as mushrooms, is that what you mean?

STUART Mm, yes.

VISITOR I see.

TEACHER Is that one asleep?

STUART Yes.

TEACHER What makes you think they're asleep?

ELAINE They're not moving.

TEACHER They're not moving. Can you find any that are moving?

221

STUART No.

ELAINE I don't think so.

STUART If this one moves, I'm going to put t'lid on again.

TEACHER You're going to put the lid on again?

STUART Yes, in case it bites me.

TEACHER I don't think it'll bite you.

ELAINE What will it do?

TEACHER See if you can count how many there are and have a look ever so closely 'cos I'm sure there's some that are hiding . . . I mean I can see one that's moving.

STUART There's a/there's a/there's a hole here. Someone/there/somebody's been digging . . . one moving. Ugh, I just heard some'at move . . . Watch out, Elaine. Ugh.

ELAINE Eh, I can see one moving look, down there look.

TEACHER That's it, I can see them as well, look.

ELAINE AND STUART ('Ugh' and other sounds of distaste)

STUART You know them er

TEACHER Shall we have him out?

STUART You know/you know them big things that's sticking up

TEACHER Mm.

STUART Well they their eyes, aren't they?

TEACHER Yes, that's right . . . let's have him out.

VISITOR He probably, er, knows it's nearly dinner time, d'you think?

TEACHER Do you think he does? Look at him.

STUART Does he want summat?

TEACHER You look at him. How many things has he got sticking up, Stuart?

ELAINE AND STUART Four.

TEACHER Four.

STUART He's got four eyes.

TEACHER D'you think he *has* got four eyes? You have a look ever so closely on it.

ELAINE He looks a bit more like a baby slug.

TEACHER Baby slug?

ELAINE Yes.

TEACHER How different is it to a slug?

ELAINE Well

STUART Can they come out o' shells?

TEACHER I don't know. You'll have to watch. D'you think if you pulled hard they would? . . . D'you think the shell would come away?

? No.

TEACHER No.

STUART No! No!

TEACHER Why not?

STUART 'Cos every time they move, that shell moves with them.

TEACHER It does, doesn't it? I think it's grown on. You have a look at the tentacles, that's the name for the things that . . .

STUART I can see little black things in them eyes.

TEACHER Yes, can you see little black things on the ones/the small ones at the bottom?

(*Noise of other children moving about the school*)

STUART Can't even see in front on 'em.

ELAINE *

TEACHER Can you, Elaine? Can you see any little black eyes in the bottom ones?

ELAINE Can't see really . . . a bit hard, without magnifying gl(ass).

TEACHER Let's put him down, see what he does. See if you can see him then, and I'll try and find another one that's moving.

STUART Shall I put t'lid on?

TEACHER Mm, if you want. Let's try and wake this one . . . I bet he doesn't like it, you know.

STUART Ugh! Ugh! He might bite you . . .

TEACHER There he is look. Let's see if he moves or if he goes to sleep again.

STUART Yes, they have got/they have got that thing, I've just seen

TEACHER The top ones have. Have the bottom ones?

STUART Yes.

TEACHER Are you sure?

STUART Yes.

TEACHER You have a look.

ELAINE AND STUART * (*to each other*)

TEACHER They're hard to see, aren't they, Elaine?

ELAINE Yes . . . I think they have

VISITOR P'raps you need a magnifying glass, don't you?

STUART This one's moving.

TEACHER Have you got a magnifying glass in your room, or have you taken it back?

ELAINE AND STUART Yes.

TEACHER Go and get it then. You go and ask Mrs Vintner. D'you know which her class is? For a magnifying glass. J 4.

Just round the corner and through the door. She's got one,
she borrowed it from me.

(*Teacher and visitor engage in a lengthy private chat. Elaine
must have returned silently, as she joins in, and it seems as if
Stuart is focusing the glass on the snail*)

STUART Can you see or am I blinding you? Look at it! Look at
it!

ELAINE I know, have you noticed tail of that one? Can you see
the tail now?

STUART Mine's moving.

ELAINE Mine's is.

STUART Mine's moving to your'n . . .

ELAINE * I know there's some at t'top . . . (*4 secs*) . . .

STUART They've got black things underneath, haven't they?

ELAINE I think they've got some . . .

STUART I do.

? *

ELAINE Mine's moving round in a ring and I can't see . . .

STUART Mine's not. (*Proudly*) Mine's turning to me.

ELAINE Eh I think/I think mine's gone to sleep.

STUART *

ELAINE *

STUART When he's looking at me I'm not going to look at him.

ELAINE I know it's the light what I think . . . that . . .

STUART He's turning to me . . .

ELAINE Mine's not . . . Oh gosh.

STUART Is your'n going in? Elaine's is going in . . . Mine's not
even gone in . . .

ELAINE No he's not, I don't think, is he?

STUART He's just turning round . . . Is that/is that the shell
broke? Is it broke, that top of t'shell? Is it broke?

? *

STUART . . . It's moving/it's moving to there.

ELAINE *

STUART Ugh! Ugh!

ELAINE I think they have got eyes up there, I think.

STUART Look at this ones. Look at this! Look at it . . . Oh, he's
going over (the edge of the tank).

ELAINE I think he'd better get away from it.

STUART Get away! Get away! Get off! You're not going any
more further . . .

ELAINE Can you see it's beginning to dry up the . . . slime?

STUART Ugh.

ELAINE I think it's because

STUART It's leaving wet behind, isn't it?

ELAINE I know, but it's beginning to dry up there . . .

STUART (*Excitedly*) Look at this one! I can see this eye! You (*to the snail*) stay there while I . . . look (*to Elaine*) come here, here, just come round here . . . See that eye.

ELAINE Yes, is it a bottom one? It's got a black spot in (*At this point the head and visitor move out of the room*)

STUART Top . . . Come on

ELAINE It's alive!

STUART I know it is, if I do that to it, it'll/it'll, blind it . . . You/ You'll blind it . . .

ELAINE You will.

STUART Look at this one! (*Excitedly*)

ELAINE Shall I pick it up and get it off?

STUART You daren't.

ELAINE I dare.

STUART Go on then.

ELAINE I'm having a job, it won't. It's a bit sticky . . . I'll try and move this one. (*Sound of an effort being made*) I might pull t'shell off if I pull it any further 'cos it slides.

STUART Oh, this one's going off, hooray. (*In conspirational whisper*) Mr Godfrey's not here.

ELAINE Eh shall I pick one, shall I try and get one off? Shall I?

STUART *

ELAINE Eh, shall I touch this, shall I touch it in here?

STUART Eh look at this baby 'un. Look at this baby eye . . . Come and have a look at this . . . Elaine . . . Bloody hell where's that one going to?

ELAINE I'm trying to stop it moving.

STUART I'm trying to stop this one moving. How can I stop this one moving? It'll tumble over t'edge. Can I just borrow this? . . . And now I'll get you. Now see if you can get over there . . . He's getting over there. I can't believe it.

ELAINE Eh, I think I'm gonna move this.

STUART No leave it, it'll tumble over t'edge.

ELAINE *

STUART Yes, I'm gonna move it up here. Ugh! Ugh! Bloody hell look what he's doing now!

ELAINE I don't think bottom one's

STUART That's giving him a lift to get on there.

ELAINE Hey, I think this is a tape recorder. (*As a snail approaches the recorder*)

STUART 'Tis . . .

ELAINE I thought it was.

STUART When that/eh up, can you notice anything on this? It's got a long neck. (*Excitedly*)

ELAINE Well I didn't notice anything on mine.

STUART Leave it, it'll/it'll/when there's/ugh . . . look at it, it's not not slipping down, it's just climbing up. Better go and find Mr Godfrey before it breaks the recorder . . . Yvonne (*to a child who enters the room*) have you seen Mr Godfrey?

YVONNE Yes, he's out on the yard.

ELAINE (*Shouting as if to the disappearing Stuart*) I'm gonna watch it . . . it's climbing on tape recorder . . . (*8 secs*) . . . (*Stuart comes back, running*)

STUART Where is it? Where is it?

ELAINE (*Shrieking*) Stuart, mine's turning round again.

STUART (*Equally excited*) Look at mine though.

ELAINE I know. (*Laughing*) I shouldn't go . . . Look light'll blind it, if I just light it, it might come down. Shall I shift it?

STUART Mm, shift it.

ELAINE Shall I?

STUART Yes . . . Go on.

ELAINE Well wait a bit. What shall I shift it with?

STUART That (*We don't know what this is*). You can pick it up in that.

ELAINE Mm, of course I can, if it'll just climb on it, it'll be better. (*Laughs*) Eh, this is gonna be funny . . . whoops.

STUART Leave it! Now pull it off! Now put it in t'middle of table . . .

ELAINE Saved it, didn't I?

STUART See, I'm brilliant.

? (*Probably another child who has entered the room – next referred to as 'child'*) Come and have a look at these slugs.

STUART They're not slugs, they're snails.

ELAINE (*In a very gentle voice, as if to younger child*) Look at the snails.

STUART Look, see them big ey/See them big things well they the eyes. Look, some at bottom, look in there . . . Eh up, have a guess what, that one climbed right up there . . .

ELAINE Yes, an I've shifted it down.

STUART Eh up.

ELAINE (*In a warning voice to the other child*) Look you can't pick 'em up.

CHILD I know.

ELAINE * slimy, cos you might *

STUART (*To the snail*) Go on home, go on, 'cos you might get in trouble. Here pick it up and put it with that one . . . (*6 secs*) . . .

ELAINE Get down please, that way . . .

STUART I mean together. Do 'em together . . . Go on then . . .

ELAINE Don't slide 'em else you'll wear the feet out if they've got any. (*Laughs*)

STUART How do you think I can wear the feet out when they're slippery. (*Rather scornfully*)

ELAINE Well, we've got to describe 'em. Well the shells . . . Kind of a browny colour, aren't they?

STUART Look at that shell moving.

ELAINE They make all slime behind 'em and I think . . . and I don't think they've got four eyes (*This is a continuation of her previous description*)

STUART I don't think

ELAINE Well we'll have to have a close up . . . look.

STUART Have a close look. (*A deliberately gruff voice, as he bends very close to the tank*)

ELAINE Eh, shall I pick one up with this ?thingy and have a look then. Well it's very hard to see at the bottom. Look if that would just climb up

STUART Have a look in t'bottom. Go on just . . . yes pick it up, now pick it up more . . . look under t'bottom, see all them . . . thingies (*Sound of distaste in his voice*). Put it down it's gonna . . . bite you, it's gonna bite you. (*Nervous laughter*)

ELAINE No, they've only got two eyes. I say they've only got two.

STUART I say they've only got four . . .

ELAINE I say they've got two . . .

STUART Well/well them big 'uns must be the eyes

ELAINE Well, we'll ask Mr Godfrey.

STUART Them big 'uns/them big 'uns must be the eyes . . . No them big 'uns/them big 'uns must be the eyes, (*shouts to make himself heard*) them little 'uns must be the tabs (*ears*), or them little 'uns must be the eyes and them

ELAINE (*Finally getting a word in edgeways*) Look I/look don't let's argue, now I know that those big 'uns are the eyes, and I don't think the bottom ones are because I can't see nothink,

227

believe me Stuart I can't see no dots in the others.

STUART I can't. (*Screams*) Get a magnifying glass. Wo, wo, wo (*a sort of rhythmic singing*).

ELAINE * (*Laughs*) I touched it, I touched its tail.

STUART Wo, wo, wo, wo, wo. (*Laughter from both*)

ELAINE Oh dear (*not of weariness, but of amusement*).

STUART That one's going in, i'n't it. (*Elaine screams*) Eh up, pick it up and put it where that one is.

ELAINE (*In an excited whisper*) Eh, wait a minute Stuart, you ought to see. I think it's the cheeks come right out like this. (*Demonstrates*)

STUART A what? A what?

ELAINE You ought to have a look, look. Watch, watch at the cheeks, look, come out. Look you can see, look? Is that the mouth? Mouth! I can see the mouth, look. (*Very excited*)

STUART (*Equally excited*) Mouth!

ELAINE And they're like gluey.

STUART That's *glue* that they're leaving behind, i'n't it?

ELAINE No it can't be because (*Interrupting each other in excitement*)

STUART Bloody hell, it is.

ELAINE It's drying up again.

STUART It is, it's glue.

ELAINE Are you sure?

STUART It's glue.

ELAINE (*Shrieking with excitement*) Look at that one, it's trying to climb on t'other one

STUART It's glue or it's

ELAINE Look, they're playing follow my leader. (*Laughing*) Learn to climb on, piggy back. Piggy, piggy, piggy, piggy, piggy. Now look, see

STUART See them wobbly things, well they the legs, I think ... Wobble, wobble, wobble (*Both laughing*). Eh up, *that* is glue (*Very positively*) or it is water, or it is ... that's water or it's glue ... or it's (*trails off rather lamely*)

ELAINE Eh, what's that it's left behind?

STUART Just a piece of grass out of there ... Eh up, I don't know

ELAINE Eh look at this, look at this Stuart, you'll never believe it look, look, have a look at this and you see how it looks. Gosh a giant snail. (*Squeals of excitement*) You want/Look through this glass, look through this glass. No this way, look, can you see?

STUART Giant . . . This is gianter than your'n.

ELAINE Gosh it's not. Eh, I say, when I bring it close to my eyes it's ever so small. Whoop, whoop, whoop (*a sort of swooping sound to herself*).

STUART Pick it up! pick it up! It might drop. We don't want that to happen.

ELAINE (*Challengingly*) Why daren't you pick it up? . . . I dare pick it up with its bottom.

STUART Go on then.

ELAINE What, do you mean underneath?

STUART Mm . . . It might bite you (*In a warning tone*)

ELAINE Bite me? Snails don't bite, do they? . . . Snails don't, do they? (*Rather doubtfully*)

STUART Did you just hear summat. It just went summat squeaky.

ELAINE (*Makes high pitched squeaky noises*)

STUART Yes, like that.

ELAINE Not so loud though, was it?

STUART (*Makes more subdued squeaky noises*)

ELAINE Look now, if I put this to their eyes they're supposed to turn round . . . Watch, I told you they'll turn round . . . If they touch that glass they'll turn round.

STUART Eh watch when their eyes go down. Look, you can see it coming up, can't you?

ELAINE Look now you should see whether they've got eyes or not.

STUART I know but now you can see whether they've got eyes or not now, can't you? The bottom things they haven't got eyes have they?

ELAINE Look, but look how it looks . . . Look can you see whether they've got eyes at t'bottom or not now, Stuart?

STUART See that, like a star, well (*Interrupted by Elaine*)

ELAINE Well have they got eyes at t'bottom now, 'cos I can't see? (*Laughter*)

STUART Eh up, you won't be able to see through it.

ELAINE What?

STUART Take it off. (*The snail has climbed onto the glass on the recorder*)

ELAINE I can't.

STUART (*Laughing*) Take it off, come on.

ELAINE I daren't I might break its shell. Honest, I couldn't get it off.

229

STUART You can. Get it off, and then

ELAINE If I break the shell, don't tell Mr Godfrey *I* did it . . . (*Tries to take it off*)

STUART Go on, it's coming off.

ELAINE Oh gosh.

STUART Come on. (*Elaine laughs*) This one's going in.

ELAINE You'll have to have a try, Stuart, I can't/I daren't get it off. P'raps it'll get over here, I hope it does . . . I'll give it a little help. I told you didn't I, Stuart?

STUART Eh up, I know . . . Put it on that/put it on there. NO! On there.

ELAINE Where?

STUART On this wood * see if it'll slide. No, on that wood. Yes, see if it'll slide down . . . Pick it up. (*Elaine laughs*)

ELAINE Take it.

STUART What?

ELAINE Take that rubber

STUART *

ELAINE I've got to make it tip back this way so as I can get it . . .

STUART Yvonne, Yvonne . . . Come and have a look at these snails.

ELAINE (*Excitedly*) I'm trying to get a piece of wood out

STUART (*Shouting*) Look at this one! That one's/that one's gone underneath. Leave 'em! They're Mr Godfrey's.

YVONNE I know they are.

ELAINE I can't get that piece of wood off.

STUART We've got to see what's different.

YVONNE Where?

STUART (*To other child who has come into the room*) Boney, we've got to mess about with it.

BONEY What you got to do to it?

STUART If Mr Godfrey sees you

ELAINE We've got a tape recorder on.

STUART We've got a tape/you know that one it climbed right up there.

YVONNE What you got to do with t'tape recorder?

ELAINE Well we've got to describe it. Oh gosh

YVONNE Well shush. Is it on?

ELAINE AND STUART Yes.

YVONNE Well you can hear all * everything. (*In a conspirational whisper*)

STUART You can hear what?

230

YVONNE All what they've saying. (*General laughter*)

ELAINE You can, it'll play back all that they're saying. (*Laughter*) And all that *you're* saying (*to Stuart*).

STUART (*Loudly as if for the benefit of the tape*) Eh up snail, can I see you? Move your shell for me.

ELAINE Eh mine's going in.

STUART Go on, put 'em back in. Put 'em back in.
(*The tape is forgotten and they revert to their previous voices. The other children seem to go out of the room*)

ELAINE * watch it's coming out again.

STUART * No I know, get one of these cloths, put them two in and get one, get one, put one in. There's one here moving.

ELAINE Where?

STUART A great big 'un. Look! There! Pick it up ... Put that one back ... Put both on 'em back ...

ELAINE Got to make sure it don't go to sleep ...

STUART He'll come out.

ELAINE I'll pop it on table then it won't. Mine's out.

STUART Yes, but, get this baby 'un out.

ELAINE Which one?

STUART That one.

ELAINE Which one?

STUART That one.

ELAINE What, this one?

STUART Mm.

ELAINE That one?

STUART Mm.

ELAINE That one? Well is it?

STUART It don't do owt (anything).

ELAINE Well is it awake?

STUART Leave it.

ELAINE It's not awake, it's stuck with glue.

STUART T'isn't.

ELAINE 'Tis ... (*Laughing*) Oh now he's glued my magnifying glass up.

STUART Let's have a look.

ELAINE I can't see very well ... too good frough (through) it now, it's a bit spotty

STUART A bit giant.

ELAINE Eh watch this look ... Boing, Boing (*Laughs*). Eh look, I magnify everything ... Well let's get on with the describing er ... em ... well it's kind of spotty i'n't it? ... Kind of dif-

231

ferent colours ... they're like one of the seashells at the sea-side ...

STUART Look they leave a trail behind 'em. Look at that one, that one's gone to bloody sleep.

ELAINE (*Laughs*) Look now, that tape'll record what you just said.

STUART (*Shouts for the tape*) Get off that paper. (*Elaine laughs*) Get off that paper. We've got to write about *them* you know.

ELAINE (*Laughing*) I know we have, I can't get it off me flippin' paper. Oh just too bad ... gonna make a slime on that paper.

STUART Pick it up.

ELAINE I can't.

STUART We'll have to/we'll have to get another paper then, won't we?

ELAINE I'm just seeing if it's gonna make a trail 'cos I'm gonna tip it upside down if it don't.

STUART It's making a trail.

ELAINE It's all greeny stuff.

STUART Better keep both on it.

ELAINE Come on.

STUART No, leave 'em. Can easily get another piece of paper.

ELAINE One's gone to sleep ... Now out he comes.

STUART Look, piece of paper for me ... two pieces of paper for me ... Look picture, writing, picture ... writing ... no, writing on that side, writing on that side ... picture on that side and picture on that side then

ELAINE Then writing on that side and writing on that side, picture on that side, picture on that side

STUART No, you'll have to get another one.

ELAINE I know. Eh, I say

STUART You dare *

ELAINE Oh, dear

STUART (*To the dinner lady who comes into the room*) D'you know how to get these off of there? We durst pick 'em up but

DINNER LADY Is that for your dinner?

STUART No.

CARETAKER (*To some visitors*) Up school yard. You go through there. He's (Mr Godfrey) up school yard. (*Noise of every-one talking together*)

STUART Me and Elaine's got to have them for us dinner.

DINNER LADY I think so an all. My goodness

ELAINE No we haven't. (*Laughing*)

DINNER LADY Blooming 'eck.

STUART There's little spots in there.

ELAINE We can't get 'em off of page, and we need that paper, it's Mr Godfrey's.

(*Voice of Mr Godfrey in the background*)

STUART Mr Godfrey, they're climbing on this paper.

ELAINE They're climbing on your paper.

TEACHER Pardon?

STUART They've climbed on there, now they're going on there.

TEACHER Have they?

STUART We'll have to get a new paper . . . for there.

TEACHER A new paper . . . Have you noticed anything about what they're leaving behind them when

STUART Yes, a trail of something

DINNER LADY It's like slime or something, i'n't it?

STUART We can't even get these off.

ELAINE *** (*Noise of preparations for dinner*)

STUART **

ELAINE Wait a bit, I'm going to magnify this one.

DINNER LADY Oh, that poor snail.

2 Introduction

'Snails' was recorded in a Derbyshire primary school where the teacher had set up a glass tank of snails in an open work area as part of a science project he was organising for a class of top juniors. The tape recorder was set up with the microphone hanging over the coat pegs ready to record pupils' responses. This is a clear recording considering background conditions, and this may be partly due to the coats hanging up absorbing the sound. Two younger pupils Elaine and Stuart (aged 6–7), were looking at the tank when a visitor arrived and the teacher was engaged in conversation.

3 The initial questions of teacher and visitor

The teacher's initial questions are concerned with the relatively straightforward matters of identification – 'Well what are they?' – and number – 'And how many are there?' These are, perhaps, the kinds of questions that teachers feel they ought to ask, particularly in a science lesson. As in the tape of 'Building a Lego farm', the adult questions do not reflect the preoccupations of the children, and serve as an unwelcome distraction. Much more interesting are the concerns of Elaine and Stuart revealed in their comments.

Initially they express their feelings, as well as making factual observations. They do begin to count at the teacher's prompting,

233

but Stuart's fear of handling the snails interrupts this activity – 'I hope/I hope we don't have to pick one up.' His sounds of distaste 'Ugh, ugh' convey his strong feelings of revulsion, and he gets round the problem by directing Elaine to handle them! His reassurance about their not biting seems as much for his own benefit as hers. This tape is particularly revealing about the ways in which children think and learn in the infant classroom. The comments they make *are* about snails – about their mushroom-like appearance and slimy wet trails – but they are also strongly expressive of Elaine's and Stuart's feelings. We learn something of them as people, of their excitement conveyed in the tone of their voices as they discover new and puzzling facts about the snails. It is easy to forget that effective learning has both a cognitive and affective element. Just as Michael was reasoning out what had happened to the tape-recorder, while at the same time experiencing fears that it might be broken, so Elaine and Stuart observe and comment, but at the same time reveal their feelings and interests.

Their initial observations on the shiny trail left behind, and Stuart's imaginative simile likening the snails to coloured mushrooms, go far beyond the teacher's demand for identification and number, which he returns to on a number of occasions. It is possible to limit pupils' thinking by the banality of our questions. The visitor, while commenting, remains detached from the learning situation, and his comments, like those of the dinner lady later, are facetious ones about eating snails (which the children do not understand or respond to), or dismissively scornful and sceptical, 'mushrooms'.

It is Stuart who makes the first tentative suggestion about the eyes – 'them big things that's sticking up ... Well they their eyes, aren't they?' It is the visitor who suggests using a magnifying glass and the teacher who takes up the point by asking Elaine to fetch one from another classroom. Stuart is interested in whether the shells are part of the snails (shells are rather baffling, being so obviously unlike skin or fur). The teacher, with a question, 'D'you think if you pulled hard they would? ... D'you think the shell would come away?' encourages Stuart to reason this out for himself, and the boy offers quite a sensible reason for his conclusion that the shell is part of the snail, ' 'Cos every time they move, that shell moves with them'.

4 Elaine and Stuart alone with the snails

As the head and his visitor become more and more absorbed in their own conversation, Elaine and Stuart refer increasingly to each other for help, asking questions of each other, 'They've got black things underneath, haven't they?' and telling each other to 'Look'. This tape shows clearly the social interaction and cooperation which play such an important part in the learning process. Each classroom has its own social structure, involving both teachers and pupils, and it is the nature of this social microcosm which makes it possible for learning to become a shared process. As teachers we are often so concerned with the content of the lesson and the handing over of information that we tend to ignore the social consequences of our language. Nor do we recognise social interaction between pupils in the classroom as a valuable activity. As long ago as 1965 Andrew Wilkinson put the matter forcefully in *Spoken English*:

And it has been left to the Newsom Report, *Half Our Future*, 1963, to recognise the development of powers in the spoken language as one of the central concerns of education (para. 36) and to relate it unequivocally to the human condition:

'There is no gift like the gift of speech; and the level at which people have learned to use it determines the level of their companionship and the level at which their life is lived' (para. 330)

'This matter of communication affects all aspects of social and intellectual growth. There is a gulf between those who have, and the many who have not, sufficient command of words to be able to listen and discuss rationally; to express ideas and feelings clearly; and even to have any ideas at all. We simply do not know how many people are frustrated in their lives by inability ever to express themselves adequately; or how many never develop intellectually because they lack the words with which to think and reason. This is a matter as important to economic life as it is to personal living; industrial relations as well as marriages come to grief on failures in communication.' (para. 43)

This is the view of speech taken in this book; that it is a central factor in the development of the personality and closely related to human happiness and well-being.[1]

While we may talk about socialisation as an important factor in the educative process, it is seldom that we have the chance to see the ways in which participants talk themselves into sociability, or to realise so forcibly how the ability to interact does contribute to what is learnt.

5 The nature of the learning taking place

This tape has been played to many students and teachers, and while they argued about the nature and quality of the learning taking place, there has always been agreement on one point, and that is the involvement of Elaine and Stuart in the experience, conveyed by their excited voices, and tones of wonder at what is happening in front of their eyes. As teachers planning such a lesson we might well have doubted the ability of pupils at this age to concentrate for forty minutes on this topic. We might, beforehand, have produced a structured lesson plan setting out the orderly progression of the learning experience, and there is always the danger that because we dominate the classroom, we may impose this plan on pupils. It would not have included notes on the excitement of learning, on the childlike identification with the snails – 'mine' and 'your'n', and the way in which they attempt to outdo each other with bigger and better snails. For them the individual snails are anthropomorphised and assume personalities almost – Stuart: 'When he's looking at me I'm not going to look at him', and they begin to address remarks directly to the snails – 'Eh up snail, can I see you? Move your shell for me.' It is easy to see how close the world of imagination is to them at this age, as if at any moment they might slip into a fantasy peopled by snails, and in doing so find out all about their puzzling aspects.

Social interaction between the children themselves is very important, too. They both have a grasp of the linguistic structures which facilitate interaction and we can see that they have both experienced the use of language in this function. They address each other by name – so much better than the impersonal 'you' that we often use in class. 'Come and have a look at this . . . Elaine.' 'Look at this Stuart, you'll never believe it, look . . .' Both have a command of tag questions which serve to draw the other person into the activity – 'That's *glue* they're leaving behind, i'n't it?' Elaine: 'No, it can't be because . . .' – to confirm their findings. Sometimes the imperatives 'Look', and 'Come here', serve to emphasise the urgency with which they seek each other's support. Left alone they are united in conspiracy – Stuart: 'Mr Godfrey's not here.' Elaine: 'Eh shall I pick one, shall I try and get one off?'

They begin to make explicit, in statements to each other, their views on the number of eyes the snails possess, and then jointly attempt to work out logically the placing of the eyes – 'No they've only got two eyes . . . believe me Stuart I can't see no dots in the others'. Working in a larger group there might not have been the opportunity for them to speculate in this way, and at the other extreme, working alone there could not have been an audience – that external pressure to formulate a hypothesis. A difficult moment arises when it almost seems that a quarrel might break out, but Elaine has the language and experience to settle it amicably and decisively, surely an echo from home – 'Look don't let's argue'. On another occasion she may not have such a compliant partner, and further language strategies will be required of her.

Their conversation on the nature of the slimy trail, whether it is glue or water shows a similar co-operative effort – 'That's *glue* that they're leaving behind, i'n't it? . . . It's glue' – and it is significant that this conversation of ideas tossed backwards and forwards enables Stuart to reach the point of using linguistic structures to set up an hypothesis – '*That*'s glue, or it is water, or it is (and he tries a rephrasing) that's water or it's glue . . . or it's', although he hasn't yet the knowledge to design an experiment to test his ideas. What *is* important is that by a joint effort they are able to frame the questions which they are seeking answers to. It is part of the teacher's role (of which we shall say more later) to help them find the answers to these questions. It seems that their joint activity gives them confidence which places them in the teacher's role of having information which they can give others, in this case another child. And surely it is by providing an audience that we can give purpose to the activity of organising experience and making it explicit. Too often in both written and spoken language we set tasks which pupils undertake in a vacuum which gives them no guidance as to context or audience. It is seldom that the classroom provides a realistic learning situation, because the majority of questions asked by the teacher are those to which he already has answers. (See introduction to part three.) Here is a situation in which the children, being knowledgeable because of their observations, can supply the answers to the genuine questions of another pupil.

Towards the end of the tape, Stuart begins to organise their experiences, moving towards a written record and pictures. Elaine on two occasions is certain that they need to describe the snails, and the image of the shells is evoked. Their efforts in this direction must, to some extent, be shaped by previous teaching and what they have absorbed of teacher expectations, but this desire to record their experiences is in no sense an imposed task; they plan with enthusiasm because of their interest and excitement. Here interaction is a vital part of the learning process, and Douglas Barnes points out that using language successfully to cooperate with others is connected with learning, for 'it is impossible to make a sharp distinction between the verbal strategies adopted by pupils in learning and the manner in which they negotiate relations with one another'.[2]

This question of successful interaction is, of course, also bound up with classroom organisation. There are situations in the primary classroom which, if taken to extremes, may prevent pupils from working together. One is the type of individualised programmes which operate in some schools, where, at the beginning of the week, children are given tasks to be accomplished by the end of the week. In some primary schools it is very difficult to draw pupils together even to share a story! When a method is carried to these lengths it is easy to see where children might lose out, although ostensibly they have timetables structured to suit their individual needs. A second cause for concern is the move to base more learning on work cards; children cannot communicate with them, they cannot ask them questions or answer back. Many teachers and students will have had bitter experiences of trying to construct work cards whose language (very often specialist language) is within the comprehension of pupils. Elaine and Stuart can talk, and learn, in language which is at the appropriate level for both of them.

Another important part of the learning process – exemplified by Halliday's 'heuristic' model – is to ask questions of ourselves and of each other. For adults much of the questioning has become an internal dialogue; we have learnt to ask questions in our heads, as it were, and no longer always need the prompting of another voice. But is is unlikely that we shall learn to frame questions for ourselves without first going through a process where we make them explicit for other people, and in so doing formulate the problems we encounter, as Elaine and Stuart do:

ELAINE Don't slide 'em else you'll wear the feet out, if they've got any.

STUART How do you think y' can wear the feet out when they're slippery.

In referring and responding to each other Elaine and Stuart are not only cooperating but learning *how* to learn. When a teacher is present, as the source of authority to whom children turn, a large number of questions asked by pupils are concerned with administration and procedure, 'Shall I rule a margin?', and less often with subject-matter or reasoning. Elaine and Stuart are not always capable of providing answers to the questions they raise (e.g. the whole question of movement, of feet and wobbly legs isn't sorted out). But the point is, surely, that in educational terms we need to know *what* we need to know before we can begin searching for answers, and one of the skills required in higher education is the ability to question, rather than passively to accept ready-made answers. In these exchanges, the questions Elaine and Stuart ask themselves and each other are purposeful, motivated by the task in hand, unlike many teacher-directed questions which may be quite irrelevant to pupil needs. Large classes and pressure of time can cause teachers to 'offer' pupils so much information that they are quite unable to assimilate it and make it part of their own knowledge. Elaine and Stuart show that they are quite capable of formulating important questions. What they lack at this point is a way of finding out, and this is where the teacher's role becomes a vital one.

Many teacher-directed questions are not only irrelevant to the concerns of pupils at a given moment, but also involve the use of the technical vocabulary of a specific subject. This may be not only beyond the understanding of the pupils, but also beyond their ability to use, thus making them reluctant to answer and participate in the lesson. Elaine and Stuart have an advantage over secondary pupils, for instance, in that they are not bound by expectations about the nature of vocabulary required in science. (Compare here Barnes's chemistry lesson in *Language, the Learner and the School*.) Their imagination is unrestricted by subject labels and the 'correct' words, so they are at liberty to use language in an almost poetic way, seeking to capture the essence of the snails in successive images – 'They just look like coloured mushrooms, don't they?', 'I think they look a bit more like seashells', and later, 'See that, like a star'. Elaine describes the snails imaginatively when she says, 'Look, they're playing follow my leader', and later in a piece of writing she used the phrase 'They're following their captain'. There are other ways of learning than listing facts – ways which are not always given enough attention.

On this tape there is a freedom in the use of language, in that Elaine and Stuart play with language and exploit it in a way which most adults have forgotten. Stuart's snail is 'gianter' than Elaine's, and how much more effectively than the more usual 'larger' does his use of that comparative suggest the frightening sight of the enlarged snails. His 'Bloody hell' would probably not have been used in his teacher's presence at this age (although it may well be used by older pupils quite intentionally to shock). Children learn surprisingly early what language is appropriate to a particular

239

situation. What is clear here is that Stuart has no intention of shocking. His tone of voice suggests his wonder as he looks at the snails – 'Can this really be as it seems?'

Both Elaine and Stuart find pleasure in the sounds of the language – in the repeated 'piggy, piggy, piggy' and 'wobble, wobble, wobble' – which adults might classify under 'poetic' use of language. Here it plays a part in describing the movements of the snails, and is akin to the rhythmic and repetitive sounds with which Helen accompanies activity.

There may have been one word quite unfamiliar to some listeners, and this is the dialect word 'tabs' meaning 'ears'. In the shared intimate context it is understood by Elaine and Stuart, but its use outside this particular situation might create difficulties in understanding. It is certain that Stuart does know the standard form 'ears'. The sensitive teacher will ensure that there are more public situations in which Stuart is given the opportunity to use it – perhaps when he is talking to a small group of pupils about what he has seen.

6 The role of the teacher

Clearly it is not possible to comment on this tape and transcript as if it were a lesson, because the arrival of the visitor disrupts the intended organisation of the classroom. We can, however, notice the various preoccupations of teacher, visitor and pupils to see what, if anything, they tell us about learning patterns.

The teacher's questions seem concerned with drawing on pupils' previous factual knowledge: 'Well what are they?', 'How many do you think there are?' This is repeated later as 'Can you count them?' We have already noted how Elaine and Stuart's questions have gone beyond the matter of identification. The teacher's next question seems to be an 'open' reasoning one: 'Is that one asleep?' Barnes defines 'open' questions as those where a number of different answers would be acceptable. In the light of his next quick question, however, 'What makes you think they're asleep', one wonders whether his first question is as open as it seems, and whether he had in fact hoped for the answer 'asleep'. The visitor, after his surprised tone at Stuart's simile of the mushrooms, does go on to try and find out what Stuart had in mind. 'Why do they look like mushrooms?' Understandably he gets no direct answer to this question. Too often we press for clarification of a sudden flash of insight, when we should know from our own adult experience that we cannot always immediately find reasons for what is a sudden inspiration, but need to think later about exactly why ideas come to mind as they do. Elaine's simile of the seashells is acceptable, possibly because the shell connection is a much more obvious one, but not necessarily more accurate. The visitor presses Stuart for reasons and eventually supplies a suggested answer himself: 'Do you mean they're the same shape as mushrooms, is that what you mean?' Faced with this particular question structure demanding an affirmative answer, it would be an exceptional child who would say: 'No I don't mean that'. The question of the number of eyes, raised by Stuart, is left as an open one by the teacher, 'Do you think he *has* got four eyes? You have a look ever so closely on it', and this is one of the problems that Elaine and Stuart pursue during their later talk. Stuart, with the aid of the teacher, reasons through another of his questions, 'Can they come out o' shells?' He also notices the 'little black things' on the tentacles and confirms that he has seen them; his teacher encourages him to look more closely with a supplementary question 'The top ones have. Have the bottom ones?'

This tape raises the questions of how far, and at what level, the teacher should direct the lesson by his questions. Initially, it is *his* interests which are pursued, restricting Elaine and Stuart to what could be superficial tasks. Later, however, he takes up pupil pre-occupations in a responsive, sensitive way, and leaves the children with certain dominant questions which effectively preoccupy them, until the ongoing movement and behaviour of the snails sets them off on other trails. From the comments of Elaine and Stuart while the teacher is present we can see the easy relationship which was part of the school's atmosphere and of this particular teacher's attitude.

In the primary classroom it is possible to have a snail tank available for a longer period of time, so that pupils can study it over several days. In the average secondary school this could prove virtually impossible as a result of lesson timetables and room changes, and many teachers would feel that a firmly directed lesson of one-and-half hours would be the only way to cover the work. We are not denying that there is a place for the teacher's direction and focusing, but there is surely a preliminary stage of making random observations before experience is organised in either spoken or written terms. The need for 'tentative, discursive inexplicit talk' which is the 'natural outcome of an encounter with unfamiliar ideas and materials', is fully discussed in the Bullock Report 10:12. The teacher's role in the initial stage is only partly to raise questions himself; it is also to listen to and note the pupils' questions, and then help them to find the answers, by suggesting ways of designing experiments, or referring them to suitable books which will help them to discover, for example, whether in fact snails have two or four eyes, how they move, and what is the nature of the slimy trails.

The 'Snails' tape confronts us with a problem that many teachers of all subjects are becoming increasingly aware of and that is the use of the specialist language of a subject. Barnes (1969) in *Language, the Learner and the School* shows countless examples of teachers whose insistence on the use of specialist vocabulary by pupils had overridden lesson content and the understanding of complex processes. Some pupils made an effort to participate in the lesson on the teacher's terms, making brave efforts to use unfamiliar words, but many pupils felt inadequate and simply opted out. Geoffrey Thornton in *Language, Experience and School* makes the following comment, 'It is very easy for a subject specialist, immersed in it as he is, to believe that the language of his own subject is part of what he imagines to be a "common language", the kind of language that everyone has, or should have, in common.'[3] Both Barnes and Thornton are discussing the use of specialist language at secondary level, but the tape makes us aware that it can be an issue in primary schools.

It is Stuart who first looks at the snail and asks if 'them big things that's sticking up' are the eyes. Probably most of us apart from the biologist would have equal difficulty in knowing what in fact 'them big things' are, and how to refer to them. Mammals have eyes, but do molluscs? There is a problem here of terminology *and* of function, and until we know something about function it is difficult to attach names. Stuart, working on an analogy with human beings, later wonders if the other two 'big things' might be 'tabs'. But do snails have ears? The teacher here accepts Stuart's term, and shows he values the contribution by a further question, using Stuart's vocabulary: 'How many things has he got sticking up, Stuart?' A few sentences later he introduces a technical term: 'You have a look at the tentacles, that's the name for the things that . . .' and he gets no further as an excited Stuart points out something else he has noticed. The availability of a technical term would be an advantage here, because, as Stuart and Elaine later find, identification between 'them big 'uns' and 'them little 'uns' is not an easy matter. They have the snails to point to, but if in fact they had been describing the snails for an audience, perhaps in another class, they would have needed more accurate references than 'big uns' and 'little 'uns'. There is the seed of this situation in the description to Yvonne, when they are pointing out what they have already observed. Elaine's written work, already referred to, was a public utterance, for readers who did not have the snails in front of them, and this too requires the accurate references, if it is to be clear as a description. Introducing the technical vocabulary, which serves to clarify ideas, requires a sensitive and responsive teacher who is aware of the time when pupils are ready to use the vocabulary to help them sort out their own ideas. No doubt the teacher, had he remained, would have helped them to observe the way in which one pair of tentacles operates by feeling, and in fact bears no relationship to ears.

A similar situation arises when Elaine and Stuart comment on the snails' 'feet', if, as Elaine says, 'they have any'. Here the use of the word 'feet' does raise for user and listener an image of a particular kind of movement, which does nothing to convey the totally different movement achieved by the snails' muscular strength. Here, too, the teacher would need to help the children observe, to compare snails, humans, and snakes, in order to help them see how the snail progresses. The teacher's concern at both primary and secondary level should not be to insist that children achieving accurate 'labelling', without understanding the process behind the label, and certainly not to insist on the use of specialist vocabulary in written work before children can use it confidently in spoken language.

The Bullock Report emphasises the need to accept and assess the nature of the linguistic resources the child brings with him to school from his previous experience – as Geoffrey Thornton says, 'starting where the pupil is in terms of his own language'.[4] 'Snails', if it does nothing else, must convince us that, young though Elaine and Stuart are, they have linguistic resources which enable them to learn about snails, and to frame together some of the questions about snails they want to ask. This is a valuable educational experience, whatever our criteria.

7 Some facts about snails for the non-specialist

The snail has two sets of tentacles. The top pair with projecting black spots are sensitive to light, but are not 'eyes' in the sense we understand them; snails do not see 'pictures' in the way that human beings do. The lower pair, the shorter ones, touch the ground over which the snail moves, so that the snail has a chemical/sensory approach to the environment.

The snail moves on its one elongated 'foot', actually a large muscle in about ten segments, by muscular waves passing from the back to the front. Mucus glands in the head secrete mucus which drops under the foot, so that the snail moves over a carpet of mucus. The snail's entire body secretes mucus which prevents the snail from drying out. This mucus is acidic and protects the exposed head and foot of the snail from predators. In very dry spells or hot sun the snail withdraws its head and seals the opening of the shell with mucus as protection.

The snail is born from the egg with a tiny shell, which gradually develops harder layers. The snail is attached to the shell by a special muscle from the centre spiral, which enables it to pull itself into the shell in adverse conditions.

The large tongue, or 'radula', which rasps over food has about 15,000 teeth, renewed all the time.

8 Suggestions for further work and discussion

a. Compare the use of specialist vocabulary in 'Snails' by pupils and teacher with that in the Chemistry and Biology lessons discussed in *Language, the Learner and the School*, D. Barnes (1969), pp. 46-56.

b. Make a list of the questions asked by the teacher and visitor about the snails. Compare this with a list of questions asked by Elaine and Stuart about the snails. Are teachers and pupils concerned with finding out the same things?

c. What linguistic devices do Elaine and Stuart use in interacting with each other, with other pupils, with their teacher, and the visitor?

d. What do Elaine and Stuart learn about each other?

e. What do they learn about the snails?

f. What do they learn about language?

g. It might be possible to make your own tape of a small group of pupils working together at a task with a piece of apparatus and to examine the language they use.

h. The language used by the pupils in g. could be compared with that of pupils working together during a task of a non-practical nature. *From Communication to Curriculum*, D. Barnes (1975), chapters 1 and 2, gives some useful ideas about work in small groups.

i. Reference has been made in this chapter to the problems of language raised by the use of workcards, and the section in *From Communication to Curriculum*, pp. 134-8 discusses a number of these problems. It is interesting to look at a set of commercially produced workcards, and perhaps a set you have produced yourself. What problems concerned with language are likely to arise for pupils using these cards?

9 References

[1] Wilkinson, A. (1965) *Spoken English* University of Birmingham Press, p. 12

[2] Barnes, D. (1976) *From Communication to Curriculum* Penguin, p. 38

[3] Thornton, G. (1974) *Language, Experience and School* Edward Arnold, p. 53

[4] *ibid.*, p. 15

18 Timothy Winters

Timothy Winters

Timothy Winters comes to school
With eyes as wide as a football-pool,
Ears like bombs and teeth like splinters:
A blitz of a boy is Timothy Winters.

His belly is white, his neck is dark,
And his hair is an exclamation-mark.
His clothes are enough to scare a crow
And through his britches the blue winds blow.

When teacher talks he won't hear a word
And he shoots down dead the arithmetic-bird,
He licks the patterns off his plate
And he's not even heard of the Welfare State.

Timothy Winters has bloody feet
And he lives in a house on Suez Street,
He sleeps in a sack on the kitchen floor
And they say there aren't boys like him any more.

Old Man Winters likes his beer
And his missus ran off with a bombardier,
Grandma sits in the grate with a gin
And Timothy's dosed with an aspirin.

The Welfare Worker lies awake
But the law's as tricky as a ten-foot snake,
So Timothy Winters drinks his cup
And slowly goes on growing up.

prays At Morning Prayers the Master helves
For children less fortunate than ourselves,
And the loudest response in the room is when
Timothy Winters roars 'Amen!'

So come one angel, come on ten;
Timothy Winters says 'Amen
Amen amen amen amen.'
Timothy Winters, Lord.
Amen.

CHARLES CAUSLEY

1 Transcript†

A discussion among Mark, Andrew, Judith and Julie. During this session the group had read and discussed other poems, before the teacher handed out 'Timothy Winters'.

MARK Somebody can read ... er somebody can read the first verse, and then somebody second, then somebody third

ANDREW I'll read second one.

MARK Then somebody third

? I'll be second

? I'll be first.

MARK Somebody fourth. I bags first.

JUDITH Hard luck.

MARK And er

TEACHER Look could you do that while I go to my car and get something?

MARK First, second, third, fourth. (*Pointing to indicate speakers for each verse*)

TEACHER Can you carry on until (*Babble of planning, which is untranscribable, silenced by Mark beginning the reading*)

MARK 'Timothy Winters comes to school
With eyes as wide as foot/as a football pool.
(*Read with a questioning tone as if he doesn't understand the meaning*)
Ears like bombs and teeth like splinters

† For an explanation of transcription symbols, see p. 21.

247

And blitz/a blitz

JUDITH A blitz

MARK ... of a boy is Timothy Winters'.

ANDREW (*Slowly and laboriously*)

'His belly is white, his neck is dark

And 'is 'air is an exclamation mark (*Judith helps him with the pronunciation of exclamation*).

'Is clothes are enough to scare a crow

And though (*should be 'through'*) 'is britches the blue winds blow'.

JUDITH 'When teacher talks he won't hear a word

And he shoots down his head (*should be 'down dead'*) the arithmetic-bird,

He licks the patterns off his plate

And he's not even heard of Welfare State.'

JULIE (*Read with increasing laughter*)

'Timothy Winters has/has bloody feet,

He lives in a house on Suez Street'.

MARK (*Laughing, corrects her pronunciation*) Sooz Street

JULIE Suez

MARK Sooz

JULIE 'Street,

He sleeps in a sack on the kitchen floor,

And they say there aren't boys like 'im any more.'

CHORUS (*Dominated by Mark who mispronounces 'missus' and 'bombardier' and is corrected by Judith, and also produces his own garbled reading of several lines*)

'Old Man Winters likes his beer

And his missus ran off with a bombardier,

Grandma sits in the grate with a gin

Timothy dozes with an aspirin.'

(*Laughter from Julie. Verse 6 is omitted*)

MARK (*Reads the glossed word 'prays' on the sheet, as part of the poem*)

'Prays. At the morning prayers the master helves'

CHORUS 'For children less fortunate than ourselves,

The loudest response in the room is when

Timothy Winters roars "Amen!"

So come one angel, come on ten

Timothy Winters says "Amen

Amen, amen, amen, amen"

Timothy Winters, Lord.'

MARK 'Amen.' (*Rushes to say this before the rest finish*) 'Charles
   Causley.'
ANDREW I like that one (*pointing to the verse with 'bloody' in it*).
JUDITH Go on, read it out then.
ANDREW (*Laughing*) 'Timothy Winters has bloody feet'
? Shush (*Laughter from all*)
   (*The teacher returns at this point*)
MARK Miss, we've read it.
TEACHER You've read it, have you?
MARK 'Amen'.
TEACHER What about talking about it?
ANDREW Can we read it again? It's good.
? (*Laughter*)
TEACHER Yes.
CHORUS (*Untranscribable*)
MARK 'Timothy Winters comes to school
   Wiv 'is eyes as wide as a football-pool,
   'Is ears like bombs, 'is teeth like splinters
   A blitz of a boy is Timothy Winters.'
JULIE ''Is belly is white, 'is neck is dark
   And 'is hair is an exc/exclamation-mark,
   His clothes are enough to scare a crow
   And though (*through*) his britches the blue winds blow.'
JUDITH (*Read with expression*)
   'When teacher talks he won't hear a word
   And he shoots down dead the arithmetic-bird,
   He licks the patterns off his plate
   And he's not even heard of the Welfare State.'
ANDREW (*Read in a halting way*)
   'Timothy Winters 'as bloody feet
   And 'e lives in a 'ouse on . . . Sooz (*Suez*) Street,
   He sleeps in a sack on the kitchen floor
   And they say . . . there aren't boys like him any more.'
TEACHER Yes, are we going

MARK 'Old Man Winters likes his beer,
   And 'is mussus (*Judith corrects to 'missus'*) muss/missus
   Ran off with a bombarder (*bombardier*)
   Grandpa sits . . . in the grate wiv a grin
   Timothy's dozed off wiv an aspirin.'
JULIE 'The Welfare Worker lies awake
   But the law's as tricky as a ten-foot snake,
   So Timothy Winters drinks his cup

Slowly goes on growing up.'

JUDITH 'At morning prayers the master heaves/helves
For children less fortunate than themselves,
And the loudest response in the room is when
Timothy Winters roars "Amen!" '

ANDREW 'So come on (one) angel, come on ten
Timothy Winters says "Amen
Amen, amen, amen, amen."
Timothy Winters, Lord.
(*Joined by Mark*) Amen.'

MARK 'Charles Causley' (*Claps*)

TEACHER You said you liked this poem. (*To Andrew*) You said it's good.

MARK Oh I don't like it as much as 'The rooks are alive in the tops of the trees'. (*Resigned laughter from the rest, as he had mentioned this in the previous discussion*)

ANDREW 'Cos it rhymes

MARK And that doesn't rhyme very much.
(*Babble of voices, untranscribable*)

TEACHER Well let Andrew tell us why he likes this poem.

MARK (*Scornfully*) Go on, Andrew, explain it. Come on then.

ANDREW Well I can't really explain it. It's just one of them

? Funny ones.

ANDREW Old blokes, like

MARK Well, 'What the weather does' is nice. (*Speaking of a poem*)

TEACHER Em, is it an old man?

MARK 'My dog Spot's' nice (*Speaking of a poem*)

TEACHER Actually?

JULIE Well it's a boy first then it grows up into a . . . a man, isn't it?

MARK It doesn't.

? Well look

MARK It tells you about his old grandpa

JULIE 'And slowly goes on growing up.' See.

MARK Yes but, 'Prayers. The morning prayers the master *halves*.' He wouldn't have a master if he was grown up

CHORUS Helves.

MARK Halves.

CHORUS Helves.

MARK Helves.

TEACHER Er, it means 'prays', the master prays. So . . . em . . . is he growing up, do you think?

MARK No.

JUDITH Slowly growing up

TEACHER Mm.

ANDREW Slowly.

TEACHER Mm.

JULIE Same as Mark is.

TEACHER Well, what sort of boy is he?

? Horrible

? A rough 'un.

JULIE Like Mark.

MARK He's like Timothy.

JUDITH Like you.

MARK Like Judith.

TEACHER Mm.

JUDITH I'm not a boy.

TEACHER You said that

MARK You could have fooled me.

JUDITH Ooh er.

TEACHER You said rough, didn't you?

MARK Yes, I'm not rough. I haven't had a fight this term.

TEACHER What makes you think he's rough?
    (*Growling noises*)

JUDITH Ran after my brother. (*Sounds of protest from Mark*)

JUDITH You hit him with a stick.

MARK I never, not this term, it were last term.

? Well . . . when he throws

MARK And I didn't hit him with a stick

ANDREW 'He sleeps'

MARK He started fighting me.

 ANDREW Belt up! 'He sleeps in a sack on the kitchen floor'

TEACHER (*Aside to Mark who is going to take his belt off*) No, I
    don't think I should, actually. Just/let's listen. Now, Andrew,
    what were you going to say?

ANDREW 'He sleeps in a sack on the kitchen floor.'
    You don't really do that, do you? . . . I mean

MARK Tramps do, and slummers, people who live in slums . . .

TEACHER Mm, they do don't they?

MARK Mm, usually.

TEACHER Em, anything else that makes you think . . . you said he
    was rough.

MARK Oh I know, 'Timothy Winters'

251

JUDITH When it says 'Old Man Winters'

MARK 'Timothy Winters ... er ... teeth like splinters, a blitz of a boy is Timothy Winters.'

TEACHER Mm, what do you think that means? You like verse don't you?

MARK He's a bully.

TEACHER Yes. What/what makes you think perhaps he's a bully?

MARK A blitz of a boy

JUDITH Teeth like splinters

TEACHER Mm.

MARK (*Growling noises*)

TEACHER Yes, his teeth are sharp and pointed, aren't they?

MARK Dracula.

TEACHER 'Eyes as wide as a football pool. Em, ears like bombs.' What's/what's that mean?

? He can hear everything. (*Mumbling in the background*)

MARK You say it then, I'm not, I don't like it.

ANDREW I don't.

MARK 'Timothy Winters has *bloody feet* (*said slowly and with emphasis*) and lives in a house in Sooz Street.'

ANDREW That's a colour, isn't it?

MARK What's Sooz Street?

TEACHER Suez, is the name of the place

MARK It says So-o-oz

TEACHER Well you pronounce it Suez. Em

MARK 'He sleeps in a sack on the kitchen floor
And says/say there/they say there aren't any ... boys like that any more.'
Well there isn't any hooligans like that any more. But there is

JUDITH There is, there is. You

MARK Ooh er. I haven't got blitz ... blitz of teeth, no ... er ... splint/splinters.

TEACHER It says/it says he's got bloody feet and Andrew says well that's a colour, isn't it? Em ... what do you think it would mean there? You said
(*Chorus of voices untranscribable*)

JUDITH Bluish red, bluish red.

ANDREW (*Scornfully*) Bluish red. It's a rough colour

MARK It's er ... when you've got blood on you ... covered in blood all over. Uh. (*Distaste*)
(*Pause*)

MARK 'The Welfare Worker lies awake'

ANDREW Yes I wondered about that

MARK 'But the law's as tricky as a ten-foot snake.'
I don't get that . . . I don't, and that says 'Prays. At the morning prayer the master halves'

JUDITH Prayers, prayers.

TEACHER Helves. The word 'prays' is put in because 'helves' means 'prays'. Em . . . you didn't understand the verse about the Welfare Worker, did you?

MARK Oh, I understand about a Welfare Worker but I didn't. (*Reads back*) 'Old Man Winters . . . Er . . . Welfare Worker lies awake but the laws are tricky as a ten-foot snake.'

TEACHER Mm.

MARK A ten-foot snake isn't as tricky as a one-foot snake

JUDITH What's the law got to do with it?

TEACHER Well what

JUDITH (*To someone in the group*) Don't ask me. I've got no idea.

TEACHER Anybody got any idea?

MARK I don't like this one as much as 'The Rooks are alive'.

ANDREW The law's after him, 'cos he's so tricky that it's trying to/trying to get him.

TEACHER Yes, is it trying to get him or do you think it might be/ the law might be trying to catch someone else? Is it him or

MARK They're after him, he's an escaped convict . . . might be.

TEACHER Andrew, is it after him?

ANDREW Well . . . well poem's about him and then it gets on to law doesn't it, so I presume (*this word said self-consciously*) it is

MARK You presume. That's a new word. I've never heard you/ he's never said that before.

JUDITH He's learnt it, 'asn't he?

MARK When did you learn it?

ANDREW (*Crossly*) Oh, I don't know.

TEACHER Em, you say you presume it is, Andrew. Em . . . the poem's about him. Might it be about the people who look after him? What does it tell us about the people who look after him?

JUDITH Hardly anything.

MARK They aren't/they're not very good for him.

JUDITH They're not bothered about him.

MARK His mother goes out with a Jerry.

253

TEACHER With a bombardier. It means a soldier
MARK A bombarder.
TEACHER You pronounce it bombardier, it's a soldier
MARK Well I say bombarder, and bombarder's the enemy.
TEACHER Oh, well, it's rather like that, yes, bombardier. Em, yes, you say they aren't very good they don't look after him. Can you tell us a bit more about that?
MARK They make him sleep on the floor.
TEACHER Mm . . . what/what
ANDREW He takes drugs. He takes aspirins.
TEACHER Does he *take* them do you think?
JUDITH Yes . . . he's forced to.
MARK 'And Timothy dozes off with an aspirin.'
ANDREW He might get a headache from being shouted at every day.
MARK It isn't sound that gives you the headache
JULIE 'He licks the patterns off his plate.'
JUDITH He's hungry, he doesn't get much food.
ANDREW So he starts biting the plate. (*Laughter from the group*) That's solved that bit . . . (*4 secs*) . . .
MARK I don't like this one much, though.
TEACHER Don't you.
ANDREW Eh, that's that colour. (*Pointing to a red spot on his jersey*)
TEACHER Yes, it is rather, isn't it?
MARK How did you get that on?
    (*Chorus, untranscribable*)
TEACHER Julie, Julie, em you were saying you looked at the verse 'He licks'/we said that he doesn't get enough to eat because he licks his plate very clean, doesn't he, every scrap
MARK Licks patterns off
TEACHER Em, in that verse what else does it tell us about him? Can you have a look?
JULIE 'And he shoots down dead the arithmetic-bird.'
TEACHER Anybody got any ideas on that?
JUDITH He doesn't like arithmetic.
ANDREW No it's . . . I don't.
18 MARK Welfare/'He's not even heard of Welfare State.'
ANDREW State
MARK I've never heard of Welfare State
JUDITH I've not
MARK I didn't know there was a state called Welfare.

TEACHER Mm.

MARK Did you? (*To Julie*)

JULIE No.

TEACHER Nobody's heard of the Welfare State?

ANDREW I have

MARK I haven't heard of a state called Welfare

ANDREW You have, Andrew?

ANDREW It's er

MARK I know there's er/there's er fifty states, but I didn't know that was one of them.

ANDREW It's er ... they look after children. It's a Welfare ... er Children's Welfare.

TEACHER Mm.

ANDREW It's not a sort of ... a drinking place, it's where people stay when they're not wanted.

TEACHER Mm. Em, it really means the way in which we look after people, as you say, who can't take care of themselves, like the old age pensioners. In a way Britain is a Welfare State because we look after the people who can't look after themselves, don't we?

ANDREW China is.

TEACHER Pardon

ANDREW China's a lot better 'n England.

MARK It isn't.

ANDREW Old folk it is

MARK Comm/ooh er, the youths are always protesting, smashing windows, and they expect

ANDREW Yes, but I mean for looking after children

MARK *We* are. We're the best state in the world for looking after us old people.

ANDREW Well it didn't say so on

MARK An Americans just * stupid people

ANDREW It said that on *People of Other Lands*, didn't it?

MARK Japan.

ANDREW Japan, that's it.

MARK In Japan, it's terrible, it's the worst, it's good for industry but terrible for its old people.

JULIE They live a lot older than English do.

MARK Yes but they don't look after them unless they

JULIE They do

ANDREW They do, a lot better, don't they?

(*Chorus of voices, untranscribable*)

MARK The families look after them better but they haven't got many Welfares.

ANDREW * got a Welfare

MARK Not that sort ... Er Children's Welfare like that ... Welfare Homes ... which/do you know any poems Andrew?

JUDITH You do, 'The rooks in the ...'

(*Laughter from the group*)

MARK 'The rooks are alive in the tops of the trees'. Do you know one?

JUDITH No.

(*Chorus of voices, untranscribable*)

TEACHER Why don't you ... em could you go and fetch us this poem so you can read it to us?

(*Chorus of voices*)

MARK I know it

ANDREW He knows it

TEACHER Say it for us then if you like it.

CHORUS Go on *

MARK 'The rooks are alive in the tops of the trees
They look like a hive of jolly black bees,
They squawk together and loud is the squawking
It must be the weather that sets them talking.'

ANDREW Miss shall I go and get a

? I know a book of a thousand poems

TEACHER Em, well, have you got a poem that you'd like to read?

CHORUS I know one.

JUDITH Miss, I've got a nice one

MARK Miss, I know where there's a poem I'd like to read.

TEACHER Look Mark, just tell us, why do you like that poem? What is it about it?

MARK It rhymes and it's ... er about nature. I like 'My Dog Spot' as well.

? Go on

MARK I can't remember it.

TEACHER Oh, em ... Have you seen any rooks in the tops of trees?

MARK Yes, we've got a rookery in our wood.

TEACHER Have you? Do you think the poem describes the rookery well? What/how did it describe them?

MARK Er, 'They look like er ... load of jolly black bees and loud is the squawking'

TEACHER 'Bees', dear, or 'beads'?

MARK 'Bees'

TEACHER 'Bees'. I thought you

MARK 'And loud is the squawking'.

TEACHER Mm. (*An aside by the teacher to someone at this point*) Yes, all right.

TEACHER Do they squawk?

MARK Yes, they're always gabbling.

? Miss may I fetch a poem?

(*Chorus suggesting poems, and asking if they can fetch things*)

TEACHER No, I don't think we've got time 'cos it's twenty to, we'll just

JULIE The bell goes at quarter to

(*Chorus of voices, untranscribable*)

MARK They're all old-fashioned poems like this

JUDITH I know one, I know one

TEACHER Do you think 'Timothy Winters' is an old-fashioned poem, then?

MARK Yes. Miss, I reckon it tells yer, it says er 'And they say there aren't boys like that any more', so it must be fairly old.

ANDREW Miss, I'll read you this one in a minute.

(*Chorus of voices, untranscribable*)

TEACHER 'They *say* there aren't boys like him any more', but really there are, there could be

MARK Not one with splintered teeth very often and blitz and eyes like bathing pools.

JUDITH Well what's/er Jane, er . . . Jane —— got big eyes.

MARK Yes, but she hasn't got splintered teeth.

JUDITH Well they're not all that straight. Me mam's got splintered teeth

MARK I have

JUDITH Two down the front.

JULIE Well, he couldn't help that, could he?

TEACHER Em, when/when the poem says 'They *say* there aren't boys like him any more', well what are they saying about him? Like what?

JUDITH Unusual.

TEACHER Only unusual, or do you feel sorry for him at all? Judith?

MARK Stephen, Stephen

JUDITH A bit.

TEACHER Why?

JUDITH Doesn't sound as if he's looked after too much.

TEACHER No, it doesn't, does it?

JUDITH He doesn't have all the things he wants, kind of

ANDREW Well, do you?

MARK Miss, that little book of poems I mean, Miss, it's got all modern poems and bits like that.

TEACHER Has it, and you like that do you?

MARK Miss, yes.

TEACHER And you don't think 'Timothy Winters' is about any boy em ... about any kind of person who might be walking round today?

MARK Yes

TEACHER You don't know anybody in this school who might

MARK Yes, I do

JUDITH Yes, yes, I do

MARK I do, Michael ——

JULIE Mark ——.

MARK Michael ——/I haven't got splintered teeth

ANDREW Oh shut up 'cos Michael ——'s an orphan

MARK Well? He isn't an orphan. He's still got one of his parents

JULIE He hasn't

MARK He has, he's got his mother

ANDREW His mother's still alive.

JUDITH Oh still alive (*meaning 'alive' but 'uncaring'*). She doesn't look after him, does she?

ANDREW Oh, it's not very nice though, is it?

MARK No she abandons

ANDREW Let's not talk about

MARK He lives at his Aunty Madge's. Anyway, I know other people who are like that

JUDITH Who?

MARK Stephen —— he's similar. He's got/he's disabled, partly

ANDREW Ooh er, so what?

   (*Chorus of comments, untranscribable*)

JUDITH You did it.

MARK I didn't you liar.

ANDREW Ooh er.

JUDITH Somebody said you did it

MARK I couldn't have chopped all his fingers off.

JUDITH Somebody said you got a knife and just went like that.
   (*Makes a chopping motion*)

MARK Ooh er, I wouldn't have done that

ANDREW I'll read you this. (*Turns to a poem in his book*)

TEACHER So really, 'Timothy', (*turning to Andrew*) just a second dear, so really 'Timothy Winters' isn't all that an old-fashioned poem because you know people like Timothy Winters, don't you?

? Mm.

? Yes.

MARK Even if Michael —— is an orphan he's still horrible.

ANDREW You think he's horrible, but I don't.

JUDITH I don't.

MARK Well if you knew him you

TEACHER Well, is Timothy Winters horrible?

? No.

MARK He sounds it.

TEACHER Is that what/is that what the poem is saying?

JUDITH No.

MARK Yes. it's telling you ... er ... he's the same as Michael ——.
'When the teacher talks he won't hear a word
And shoots his head down like an arithmetic-bird.'

TEACHER No, 'Shoots down *dead* the arithmetic-bird'. Well does that make him horrible?

CHORUS No

MARK No, but he's like Michael ——, he doesn't listen.

ANDREW No he doesn't, you're right.

JULIE Neither do you, Mark. (*Chorus of comments, untranscribable*)

TEACHER Well is the poem saying anything about why Timothy Winters doesn't listen?

MARK No.

TEACHER I think you're quite right he doesn't, does he, because he shoots down dead the arithmetic-bird, he never pays any attention. Does the poem explain why he doesn't listen? (*Pause*)

MARK (*Tentatively*) No.

TEACHER Think about it. Read it again. Read through and see if you can think why it might be he doesn't listen. Well just read it through to yourselves this time. (*Pause while they each read through the poem*)

MARK He doesn't have a wash very often

TEACHER Mm.

MARK Says his neck is dark.

TEACHER Mm.

JUDITH Well?

MARK Well it means he doesn't have a wash. Bet you could plant potatoes in it. (*Pause, while Mark continues to read silently*) It says 'He *won't* hear a word'. It doesn't mean he's disabled, it says he *won't*.

TEACHER Mm. What's/what's the difference, Mark?

MARK Well if you *won't* hear it, you can hear it but

JUDITH (*Interrupts*) You just don't want to try

MARK You just don't want to try.

TEACHER You've shut your ears against it deliberately

MARK No you can't shut your ears.

TEACHER Well . . . em . . . (*Groping for words*)

JUDITH Refuse to listen.

TEACHER Refuse to listen. I was saying . . . er . . . are we given any reasons why he refuses to listen?

MARK No.

JUDITH He's just lazy.

MARK Bone idle.

TEACHER Would that be your opinion, Julie, lazy, bone idle?

JULIE Yes really, I think he is

MARK A time waster

TEACHER Andrew?

MARK Michael —— wastes time as well

TEACHER Andrew, is that your opinion, he doesn't listen because he's lazy and bone idle?

ANDREW Yes. (*The bell goes and Julie leaves to catch her bus*)

 19

TEACHER Can we just have one more look and try and find out, do you think, why it is he doesn't listen. Is there a reason? Is it just his laziness I'm wondering?

JUDITH No, it's just 'cos he's unhappy.

TEACHER Go on, Judith.

JUDITH He just thinks/he just feels 'Oh I can't be bothered'.

MARK Well, I feel like that but I still listen

JUDITH 'I don't have good things in life', you know, 'I just get thrown in.' They just don't bother about him.

TEACHER Mm. So really it's not his fault, necessarily, that he doesn't listen. We talked a bit about

MARK (*Interrupting*) It's his fault that he doesn't listen but it/it isn't his fault

JUDITH (*Interrupting*) That he's unhappy

MARK That he feels that way.

TEACHER Mm. That's a very good remark, actually, very

accurate. Em ... he doesn't get on very well at school, does he? Em ... how do they feel about him at school?

MARK They don't like him.

TEACHER Why don't you think they like him?

JUDITH He doesn't try. They don't understand that he's unhappy

TEACHER Mm.

MARK 'At the morning prayer the master *halves*
  (*still trouble with the pronunciation*)
  At children less fortunate than themselves
  And the loudest response in the room is when
  Timothy Winters roars "Amen" '
He feels sorry for himself.

TEACHER Mm, do you/is it that he feels sorry for himself or perhaps ... well is it anything else?

MARK He feels sorry for himself

JUDITH He wants to have a bit of life

MARK I usually say 'Amen' loud.

TEACHER Do you?

MARK And all the rest of the Lord's Prayer

TEACHER Perhaps it is

JUDITH You're always talking

MARK I'm not

TEACHER Perhaps it is that he doesn't realise he's unfortunate.

2 Introduction

This tape was made in a small rural primary school. The pupils – Andrew, Mark, Julie and Judith – were top juniors in their final term at primary school before they moved to secondary schools. Although they were all from the same class, they were not close friends, and unlikely to have worked as a small group on previous occasions. The teacher was an experienced English teacher who did not know these particular pupils. The aim of this tape was to explore the language of small group interaction outside the narrow context of 'classroom' and 'lesson'. The pupils and teacher were grouped round a small table in the school hall, with the tape recorder visible, and the microphone standing on the table. The group was given the poem 'Timothy Winters' by Charles Causley, and after reading it, they talked about their responses with the teacher.

3 The teacher's aims

The teacher's stated aim here was to look at small group interaction, and specifically the ways in which language was used in the processes of understanding. The teacher did not regard the poem as a hunting ground for similes and metaphors, and in fact very few technical terms are used in the discussion, though the pupils do reveal some interesting conceptions about poetry. Andrew seems, at times, to see the discussion of the poem as a closed task in which there are certain 'correct' answers – 'That's solved that bit'. (It may be that despite the teacher's stated aim, she too saw the activity as something of a closed task, with the 'pursuit' of the poem as the main aim, rather than the examination of language in understanding.)

The emphasis was on helping the pupils to realise in personal terms what it might be like to be Timothy Winters. Several poems were selected, but the discussion here focused on 'Timothy Winters', chosen because it appears in a number of school anthologies, and seemed to the teacher to present uses of language, particularly the figurative and ironical, which might be outside the range of the children's normal language, and which might not be found to the same extent in more factual subjects. For example, what picture of Timothy Winters does the reader gain from the cumulative effect of the imagery, 'Ears like bombs, teeth like splinters/A blitz of a boy is Timothy Winters'?

4 The role of the teacher

It is obvious that the children enjoy reading the poem from the way in which they fall in with Mark's eager allocation of the verses, and do in fact achieve a group reading with varying degrees of skill, without the presence of the teacher. While the word 'bloody' predictably causes some embarrassed laughter, this does not prevent the children completing the poem with a chorus as finale.

It is unfortunate that the teacher is not sensitive to this mood of enthusiasm when she returns and interrupts the activity of the group with the question 'What about talking about it?' While this is in question form, it is in fact a concealed command – 'Now, we're doing a poem and we're going to talk about it.' The teacher here is so intent on carrying out her aim of promoting discussion that she fails to realise that a discussion is already under way without her interference. Andrew's request to read the poem again is a sensible one, because coping with the unfamiliar language on the first reading had presented the group with problems, and in any case it was unrealistic of the teacher to expect an instant response to something unfamiliar. In the classroom, obsessed by the demands of the syllabus and the shortage of time, we often demand an instantaneous and possibly superficial response from children, which even as adults we should find difficult to make. The vagueness of the teacher's initial question is also a mistake. What are the children to 'talk' about? It serves to throw the emphasis on the poem, rather than on the children's responses to it, as is the case in 'Cider with Rosie'. Is there, in fact, any reason why the pupils should *want* to discuss the poem, which has no obvious relevance for them at this point?

This failure to 'read' the mood of the group is perpetuated in the way in which the teacher again takes the initiative by saying to Andrew immediately after the second reading has finished, 'You said you liked this poem. You said it's good . . . well let Andrew tell us why he likes this poem.' In its abruptness this produces a predictably embarrassed response from Andrew which Mark makes scornful fun of. Although the teacher's questions are couched in statement form, they are intended by the teacher to be questions requiring answers, and Andrew from past experience interprets them in this way. They are open-ended questions, but so open-ended that Andrew is bewildered. It is a good example of the way in which such a question at the wrong moment may be so lacking in focus that the pupil is given absolutely no sense of direction. In the same way Julie's comment on the 'arithmetic bird' prompts the teacher to ask vaguely 'Anybody got any ideas on that?' Fortunately Judith does reply, 'He doesn't like arithmetic', but it might have been more helpful to focus in specific terms on whether Timothy liked school, and whether the teachers enjoyed teaching him. In another instance the over-concentration on the imagery and its exact meaning proves too difficult for the group as the question is framed. ' "Eyes as wide as a football pool, em, Ears like bombs", What's/what's that mean?' It would have been far better if the teacher had approached this in a less abstract way, and had simply asked the pupils to describe what Timothy looked like.

A delicate point in the discussion is reached when the teacher asks the question, 'When the poem says "They *say* there aren't boys like him any more", well what are they saying about him? Like what?' Mark's repetition of the name 'Stephen' passes almost unnoticed but it is clear from a further reference that Mark is linking Stephen, another pupil at the school, with Timothy. A teacher familiar with the group and the school, and listening sensitively would have noted that the connection had been made, and allowed the reference to pass without further comment. This teacher, however, presses the group to make an explicit link

263

between Timothy and anybody they know in school in a similar situation. The question would not have been asked in a classroom, and it is doubtful whether, even in the intimacy of a small group, it should ever have been asked so explicitly. It is a mark of Andrew's tact that he tries to suppress the discussion. 'Oh, shut up 'cos Michael's an orphan'.

Some of the teacher's questions do promote useful discussion, particularly when they follow up an issue raised spontaneously by the group. The children refer to the phrase 'Welfare State' and the teacher then invites them to comment with: 'Nobody's heard of the Welfare State?' Tentatively they contribute from their own knowledge.

> MARK I know there's er/there's er fifty states, but I didn't know that was one of them.
>
> ANDREW It's er . . . they look after children . . . It's not a sort of . . . a drinking place . . .

(This is a reference to the local Miners' Welfare social clubs.) So far they are seeking to define the phrase as a physical entity, while the teacher's definition which follows brings out the abstract element. Then the group take up the teacher's comment and develop it further by discussing the different nature of the care offered in other countries.

Later in the discussion the teacher does begin to listen more carefully to what the pupils have to say, and encourages them to develop their comments in more detail. So Mark's statement, 'he doesn't listen', is followed by a specific question from the teacher, 'Well is the poem saying anything about why Timothy Winters doesn't listen?' Even though Mark's initial response to this is 'No', a further encouragement to the children to read the poem to themselves does show how perceptive Mark can be about the implications of a particular use of language. 'It says he *won't* hear a word. It doesn't mean he's disabled, it says he *won't*.' And then, with Judith's help he expands on why Timothy won't listen.

Of course, not all pupil comments in a swiftly flowing discussion can be taken up, particularly when the teacher is no longer seen as the only one to initiate and control discussion, to choose the topic and the speaker, as he is in the traditional class lesson. So Julie is not given the chance to develop her tentative response to the teacher's comment about Timothy being lazy and bone idle: 'Yes really I think he is', because Mark quickly endorses this comment with 'A time waster'. In a class lesson it is unlikely that Julie would have been given a chance to say much more, because the teacher would have responded to her original comment with a doubtful 'Yes' on a rising intonation which would have indicated to Julie that the answer was not entirely satisfactory, but was not being totally rejected. Other pupils would then have been encouraged to offer answers more in accord with the teacher's expectations.

This teacher shows all the uncertainty attendant on changing the method of approach from a class lesson to small group discussion. We are still often unable to free ourselves from the impression that a piece of writing, or a lesson structured on a question and answer basis, provides concrete evidence of aims being achieved, even though an analysis of such class lessons reveals the non-participation of the majority of pupils, and often positive evidence of a failure of understanding on the part of others. Because of our training as teachers, and our desire for results, we tend to transfer the same question and answer approach to small group discussion, taking it upon ourselves to initiate the discussion, to nominate speakers, and to structure the pupils' responses by the shape of our questions. Yet, as the next section shows, pupils are quite capable of asking their own questions and of co-operating to seek answers. There are occasions on which they achieve understanding, almost despite the teacher's interruptions and interference.

5 Methods of approach used by pupils

Suitable criteria for assessing the development of continuity and progress in spoken language, to be found in the Bullock Report 10.24, are also helpful as a focus for looking at the tape of 'Timothy Winters'.

Bullock's first criterion is a progression from simple anecdote to shaped narrative. In the transcript 'Cider with Rosie' the children show varying degrees of skill in relating anecdotes. Such a use of language is not evident in 'Timothy Winters', but this is to be expected because of the different nature of the discussion. In the 'Cider with Rosie' transcript, where the children are recounting their memories, the developed narrative is an essential means of acquainting the other members of the group with the key experiences in their lives. In the 'Timothy Winters' transcript, the poem, of which they all have copies, is the focal point of the discussion, and, as the reading is an experience they have all shared, there is no need for detailed references back to the poem. Often the quotation of a line is sufficient to draw the attention of the others to a salient point. The discussion flows rapidly from one speaker to another as points are stated, questioned by another speaker, elaborated upon or contradicted. One of the dangers in setting up criteria such as those listed in the Bullock Report is that it may then seem to be implied that they should all be relevant in every discussion. In fact, of course, we need to look at the purposes for which language is being used in a particular discussion before we can decide which features to expect.

Bullock's second criterion, 'the ability to range backwards and forwards over the discussion'[1] – taking up points made by the previous speaker – is very clearly exemplified in 'Timothy Winters'. Andrew's doubts about Timothy sleeping on a sack on the kitchen floor are corrected by Mark's response: 'Tramps do, and slummers, people who live in slums . . .'. Mark's questioning of the meaning of the line about the Welfare Worker is also echoed by Andrew. (Incidentally, it is noticeable on this tape how ready the children are to voice their doubts about the meaning of certain parts of the poem, in a way which would be very rare in a class discussion, where initiative springs mainly from the teacher.) Another good example of the spontaneity with which they contribute to a cumulative picture of Timothy occurs in response to the teacher's question about whether Timothy's family looks after him. Each of the pupils makes a point about the neglect suffered by Timothy, drawing on the examples given in the poem.

Bullock's third criterion, which is concerned principally with the complexity of the participants' dialogue and the ability to modify an individual viewpoint, is well illustrated in the discussion on the meaning of the phrase 'Welfare State'. At the teacher's prompting the children consider what it means to look after people, and Mark and Andrew refer to the TV programme they have seen, 'People from Other Lands', which was principally about China and Japan. This is an instance of something which might seem superficially to be a digression actually being pertinent to the discussion, because the children are concerned with the quality of care offered in each country. The ability to use previous knowledge, to restate it to illuminate another context, is an important element in learning, and Mark is able to do this, generalising in a very helpful way ('The families look after them better, but they haven't got many Welfares') to draw attention to Timothy's neglect by his family. Mark seems to have a particular skill in summing up a complex discussion and argument succinctly, as when he makes an accurate assessment of what Timothy can be held responsible for. 'It's his fault he doesn't listen, but it/it isn't his fault . . . That he feels that way.' In a class discussion it is usually the teacher who draws all the arguments together and formulates the concluding remarks which round off the discussion, but here Mark shows that he is quite capable of this task.

The group also reveals sensitivity to, and awareness of, fine shades of meaning, and the ability to convey subtle nuances by the use of intonation. In the discussion about what it means to be an orphan, Mark's initial comment, 'He's still got one of his parents', is modified by Andrew 'His mother's still *alive*', with the implication that she may be alive but uncaring of him, and this is then made quite explicit by Judith, 'Oh still *alive*. She doesn't look after him, does she?'

Personal references play their part in this discussion, as they do in 'Cider with Rosie', and the children make quite explicit comparisons between Timothy and Mark, whom they also characterise as 'rough', and a 'hooligan'. Judith's mother would, no doubt, be horrified to know that she had been included in the number of those with 'splintered teeth'. The reference to children they know in Timothy's situation, which has already been discussed, is another way in which they apply this poem to themselves. John Dixon (1975) in *Growth Through English* (chapter 9) makes reference to the different levels of abstraction on which discussion takes place in the classroom, from the personal and particular, where the speaker is fully involved with the dramatis personae, to general situations in which personal reference plays no part. This relates closely to one of the criteria suggested by Bullock: the move from the subjective to the objective viewpoint. It is important to note that the objective view of Timothy's plight, stated by Mark and Judith, has been reached through close reference to the particular and personal, an element which, Barnes notes, is lacking in schools, particularly at the secondary level. This movement between levels seems to be a necessary part of coming to terms with new ideas and knowledge, which we have somehow to integrate with what we already know.

The cooperation of the children on certain occasions has already been noted. Initially they were quick to organise a reading of the poem with the more able readers, Judith and Julie, offering both Andrew and Mark help with difficult words, such as 'exclamation' and 'blitz'. Some of their help is understandably ignored, and they never quite succeed in convincing Mark of the correct pronunciation of 'Suez'. Positive statements about the poem do emerge at the end of the discussion from Mark and Judith, partly because of the desire to go home as the bell has rung, but these are nevertheless comments showing considerable understanding of Timothy's plight.

MARK Well if you *won't* hear it, you can hear it but but

JUDITH You just don't want to try.

Judith also succeeds in translating the teacher's image, 'You've shut your ears against it deliberately', into a phrase understood by Mark, 'Refuse to listen'.

Mark's role in this discussion deserves consideration. He is clearly a leader, the one who organises the initial reading, who is sufficiently confident to be openly scornful of Andrew's efforts to explain his enjoyment, to question Andrew's use of the word 'presume', and to project the image of himself as a fighter, challenged at peril. Whenever the discussion reaches a difficult point, or he wishes to draw attention to himself, he refers to a poem he likes about rooks. The others are clearly resigned to his extrovert display, and the teacher here encourages him to say the poem, which would have been an unlikely move in a class discussion. Perhaps, too, he would not have raised this issue in class.

6 Group interaction in discussion

In a small group discussion the personalities of the children play a large part in the achievements of the group. This teacher, however, is often over-concerned with the content of the poem, and neglects the interactional features of the group, which in a tightly structured lesson may never have been given an opportunity to emerge. In the classroom the teacher sees language primarily as a tool for learning, with the result that other language uses, particularly the interactional, are neglected. The work of Flanders on classroom interaction is inadequate because it fails to take into account the different relationships of the speakers and the way in which these can affect the use of language. He assumes a common aim in discussion, a shared body of meanings, but from the 'Timothy Winters' discussion it is easy to see how the speakers, as well as joining in a common discussion, are also concerned with private preoccupations, which surface through language. In a more formal classroom situation these preoccupations may not be voiced, but they are always present, often unnoticed by the teacher over-concerned with lesson content. If small group interaction is to play an increasing part in classroom method, as suggested by Bullock, then teachers will need to be aware not only of subject matter, but also of social matters, the interactional features which affect them as well as their pupils.

The teacher who led this discussion was disappointed when the tape was played back: by her own obvious determination to control the discussion, by her inability to relax and follow up the children's concerns, and by doubts about the achievements of individuals. However, when comparisons are made with the apparently neat and ordered class discussion, one must remember that the picture of the classroom is generally an idealised one – the day when, for once, a lesson went superbly and everyone was fully involved. Bullock makes clear by diagram (p. 147) that only a few pupils are involved in class discussion, usually those nearest to the teacher. In the discussion of 'Timothy Winters' all four children were involved for most of the time. It is also unrealistic, in any case, to expect the same level of response from each pupil in the class, when levels of understanding differ so widely.

If teachers give up the urge to dominate discussion, to choose the topic, the speaker, and the style of discussion, then they can no longer say either explicitly or tacitly 'You'll discuss this poem because I say it's poetry this afternoon.' They will have to think clearly about the reasons for doing certain things rather than others. The word 'discussion' usually implies voluntary participation, and if this approach is genuinely adopted in the classroom, the implications of the pupils' choice of topic and mode of discussion will have to be considered. Wilkinson has said that 'oracy and democracy are closely related' and the acceptance or rejection of the need for democracy in a school community will influence all the interactions of adults and pupils within it.[2]

7 Suggestions for further work and discussion

a. Examine the roles of each of the children in 'Timothy Winters' and look at the ways in which they project these roles through language. Compare these with the roles they adopt in 'Cider With Rosie'.

b. Why did Andrew use the word 'presume' on this occasion, when, as the others said, he didn't normally use this word?

c. How does the teacher view her task in 'Timothy Winters'? How does her attitude affect the language she uses in her interaction with the group? Compare the teacher's attitude here with her attitude in 'Cider With Rosie'.

8 References

[1] *The Bullock Report* (1975) HMSO, 10.24

[2] Wilkinson A. (1965) *Spoken English* University of Birmingham Press, p. 59

19 Cider with Rosie

In this section there is no commentary. Readers are invited to use the experience gained from studying the earlier material to explore a transcript for themselves.

---

1 Introduction
The children on this tape are Judith, Julie, Mark and Andrew, the same group who took part in the discussion of 'Timothy Winters'. This is an earlier discussion, referred to in the 'Timothy Winters' discussion, arising out of a reading of the opening paragraph of *Cider With Rosie* in which Laurie Lee describes how he was set down in the long grass the day his family moved house. Forgotten by his family in the upheaval of the removal, he feared he was lost. The passage served as a stimulus for a discussion by the group of their own childhood memories.

2 Suggested lines of enquiry
a. Examine the structure of the discussion. What are the major themes?
b. What accounts for the changes in direction that occur?
c. In the case of particular children what do we learn about
   i.   their linguistic resources?
   ii. their skills in discussion?
   iii. their personalities?
d. Consider the role of the teacher with reference to
   i.   being a good listener
   ii. encouraging individuals to contribute
   iii. initiating changes of direction in the discussion
   iv. encouraging children to be explicit
   v. helping children to sum up their ideas
   vi. other functions.

e. Assess the children's skills in spoken English in the light of the criteria proposed in Bullock 10.24.

f. What is your attitude to such uses of language as Mark's 'it were when I were only five'?

g. How do you think your attitudes were acquired?

3 Transcript†

TEACHER Were you telling us about when you were lost? Was it to do with the same time or was it something

MARK No, it were when I were only five.

TEACHER Yes, oh go on, tell us about it.

MARK Er ... er ... me ... er ... and me cousin were walking wiv the dog and/and we got/went down this path. We took the wrong turning, there's a big path and a small one and we thought it might be a short cut, and went down and then ... er ... there were an arch sort of thing and went inside there and then we turned somewhere and we got lost and found this building and we were scared to go in.

TEACHER Mm.

MARK 'Cos there'd been a few things that had happened there ... there's a ghost and we were scared to death, and we waited until my Dad came.

TEACHER What's the earliest thing people can remember? You know, the boy in the story got lost in the grass.

MARK When I was about four, boy next door to us at Swanwick he ... er ... no, boy next door to that ... er ... named Kevin Marlborough broke into our house and nicked all my toys.

TEACHER Oh dear. I say. What/what can *you* remember?
    * (*Turning to Julie*)

JULIE When I was about three or four I was playing horses on the chair and my brother Peter came in and knocked me off, and I was unconscious ... and straight after that I fell down the stairs.

TEACHER It's a wonder you're here, isn't it?

JULIE Yes.

TEACHER (*To Judith*) And what can you remember?

JUDITH Well I/I was at a place called ?Dawden in ... near ... Nuneaton ... and ... em ... I was out playing in the field and a farmer came past with two great big horses ... can't remember whether they were shire ponies or ... em ... Welsh cobs, and ... em ... then he says, 'Would anybody like a ride?'

† For an explanation of transcription symbols, see p. 21.

because he was a very friendly farmer and we knew him well
... and you know of course I says, 'Oh please', and he/and he
let me have a ride and fell off on a/on a grass verge and
scraped all me knee and my dad/me dad says, 'Right, that's
the end, you're not riding any more,' but I've started doing it
again now.

TEACHER And can you/can you really remember this, although it
was quite/it was a long time ago?

JUDITH Yes, you know, I remember just coming off.

TEACHER Mm.

JUDITH It was a terri/I was terrified when I found my head touch
the ground.

TEACHER Mm.

JUDITH I thought, oh no, what happ/what's going to happen.

TEACHER Yes, you can remember the sensation of it banging on
the ground.

JUDITH Yes.

TEACHER And what's the earliest thing Andrew can remember?

ANDREW Well, I can't really ... say I can remember it but ... I
can really remember it, like. When ... er ... we got burgled in
Alfreton. We got £25 taken an ... some ... oh I don't know
what it was ... something else ... an it was *me* who found
them. So I

TEACHER You found them?

ANDREW I started to cry and my Dad went downstairs and they
found out he'd ramshacked the 'ouse, and they'd took all the
money like.

TEACHER Mm, and were you frightened?

ANDREW Well, I/I don't know really 'cos I was only a baby then.

TEACHER Yes ... who else can remember any

JULIE I can remember when I was about one or two when I first
had my first ride on a pony. It was one ... em ... just up the
road; it was a pit pony called Dick, a white one; my father
used to lead me on it, and it only got a halter on sort of, I used
to cling on to the mane and I can remember once when I
nearly fell off but I managed to stop on.

TEACHER Frightened?

JULIE Yes, really.

? Yes.

TEACHER I can/I can remember when I we/went riding ... em
... one day when I went, I didn't ride very well and I went on
a much bigger horse than I should have done, and some

friends, we galloped across a field and I can remember the feeling, am I going to be able to stay on, or am I going to fall off, you know, desperately like clinging on. Wh/wh/what's the earliest thing you can remember? (*Turning to Mark*)

MARK Er . . . I've forgot now. I was going to say but I've forgot. Er . . . oh er . . . when me and er . . . er Worth's likkle lad were having a fight once and I chased after him, and I fell an er . . . this rock sticking up and it 'it me in stomach an I . . . er . . . went out for a few minutes, and I got up an fell in a dyke.

TEACHER Mm.

MARK Just fell in a dyke after it.

TEACHER Mm.

MARK And then went home . . . crying.

TEACHER I see.

MARK Soaking wet.

TEACHER Yes, I can remember . . . erm . . . something from my school days really. When I was coming home one day, there was a dyke on the way home, and a friend and I said, 'Let's jump this dyke, let's see if we can jump it', so we started to jump and I fell in and I'd got woollen socks on and you can imagine how the water got in the wool, can't you? So I took my socks off and wrung them out and we were ever so late home, you know we only got one and three-quarter hours' lunch time; and I was just busy wringing my socks out when my mother came up the road to see where I was, and was so angry with me. There I was standing on the pavement with no socks on wringing the water out of them; and that evening my father had bought me a yo-yo – you know those wooden things that you bounce up and down on a string, well they're steel are they now? – Well, my father had bought me one of these and my mother said I couldn't have it because I'd got these socks wet. But they did let me have it eventually.

CHORUS Mm (*in a thoughtful and reflective way*).

ANDREW I can remember when I was at the Welfare once and me and Mark wasn't agreeing with each other.

TEACHER Yes. (*Laughter from some as this was a standing joke*)

ANDREW And . . . er . . . we was going to have this fight. I were coward an I run away and he threw this bottle at me head, an it hit me right there, and it were bleeding for about ten minutes.

MARK It wasn't bleeding, was it?

ANDREW Yes, an I had a great big bump right on me head.

JUDITH I can remember the first bonfire night that I ever went to and I daren't hold a sparkler, ever, and me Mum says, 'Go on it won't hurt you'. She says, 'Look I can even put me hand through the top of it'. I says, 'No it might hurt me', but at the end, you know, I thought, all right I think I've got enough courage to just hold one. Unluckily, it was the last one and I just/I was just starting to enjoy myself and it went out.

TEACHER Oh, an/and you weren't afraid?

JUDITH No, it was/I was all right after that, you know, I couldn't wait until the next bonfire, and I was only about three.

TEACHER Mm.

JULIE I can remember something yesterday that happened. Mark smashed a window. He kicked a ball at it and em . . . Andrew was in the porch and . . . em . . . and all the/he was facing/his back was to the window, and the glass went on his back and it cut his back a bit and it 'it Timothy, another boy just there, and that's about the third window he's broke.

TEACHER That Mark sounds a real demon, hitting people on the back of the 'ead with bottles, breaking windows.

ANDREW He's broke six at this school.

JULIE About.

MARK Three.

ANDREW Well you said six to me.

MARK I didn't! Three. Six of them broken, one by Nicholas ———, three by me, one by Nigel and one by Jane ———.

ANDREW Rosemary ———.

MARK Jane ———.

ANDREW Rosemary. (*Laughter by all*)

JUDITH I think they both did, they both did.

MARK Jane ———.

ANDREW Rosemary. (*Laughter*)

JULIE They both did.

ANDREW He put his arm through it, like that.

MARK So did Jane ——— but *

JULIE Rosemary!

MARK Jane! (*Noise from the gymnasium next door*)

TEACHER They're going to come through, bursting through, aren't they? Do/do you like this school? What

CHORUS Yes. No. I do

JULIE I'd sooner have it than

JUDITH If I get to a secondary school, at Swanwick, the grammar school, you know, I'd love to go there because me sister goes there and she says how nice it is, 'cos you know the teachers are all very nice, you can make fun of them, and on school trips you go to Egypt. Me sis

TEACHER Egypt!

JUDITH Yes me sister's going to Egypt in ... er ... November £65 – and she's going all round the ... em ... pyramids and

TEACHER Yes

JUDITH Touching them, and my Dad says you better bring some of the rock back.

TEACHER Mm ... You don't like it much, Andrew, school?

ANDREW Well, I don't, you know, I'd rather, not when I'm in trouble. (*Laughter by all*) I got hit on back of the head by Mr —— other day (*Laughter*) for fighting in class ... me and this other lad ... Mind you we're friends again now.

MARK I can remember/I can remember once when I'd just first come to this school an ... er ... went on Park's Avenue with Pete —— and Robert —— and we'd heard about these swords in a field near Timothy ——'s and we went to it and we found that we ... er ... we went across this river and we couldn't get back, and we were saying, 'Circle the river', and we tried/we hadn't looked at this part where there was a lane leading out and we tried to cross it to get to this other field where the swords were, so they said, and ... er ... there was this ... er ... log going across, and I went on the log and then Robert —— he went on, and Pete ——, and then ... er ... Peter went home, then Robert jolted on it and we both fell in. We had to swim for the shore. But we didn't find these swords.

TEACHER No ... what a disappointment.

JUDITH I'd sooner have this school than any other school, because ... em ... I shouldn't really like to leave this school, sooner have it than Marshmer or Swanny grammar.

ANDREW
MARK (*Chorus*) A good school, though. It is ... but
JUDITH I'd sooner have this one.

ANDREW When you go ... really ... when you're going to Alfreton school you think well ... you've finished all your primary stuff and you're starting/starting a new life, like.

TEACHER Mm ...

ANDREW You ... you really think ahead of you and not think of the past and that's it.

275

TEACHER Mm. How/how you/you say you think ahead, how are you feeling about, you know, going to your secondary school?

ANDREW Pleased.

TEACHER Are you? What are you looking forward to?

ANDREW Well, you've got better things there ... this is only a little school.

MARK They've got 110 cameras for putting in television sets ... 50 television sets.

ANDREW **

22 JUDITH You start feeling grown up when you get to a bigger school with all these bigger people, and you feel more reliable and people look at you better.

TEACHER Mm ... well you're the biggest here now, aren't you?

JUDITH No, I'm the youngest.

TEACHER Oh!

MARK I'm the oldest here.

TEACHER Yes, but, I mean you're some of the most grown-up people in this school.

CHORUS Yes.

JUDITH Well, I try to be grown up, and me Mum says, 'Well if you/if you act grown-up you'll be ... em treated as a grown-up, but,' she says, 'if you don't act grown-up so you're not going to be treated as it', so I think, right then, just see.

TEACHER So you're doing your best.

JUDITH Yes. I remember once, oh it was only a few weeks ago when Julie had just had Rebel (her pony) and she jumped about that high you know and it was her first jump and she looked ever so confident and

JULIE It wasn't my first, it was

JUDITH Well, you know that high and she felt ever so confident. And then her Aunty Lola came and she says, 'Julie, let Judith have a go', and I says, 'No thank you', 'cos I couldn't walk very well because of my ankle and kept watching Julie, you know she kept going higher and her Aunty Lola says, 'I'll have a go at that'.

TEACHER And did she?

JUDITH No she never did.

TEACHER No. Are you looking forward to going to your new/other school?

MARK Yes.

TEACHER Are you? What are you looking forward to?

MARK Going in team.

276

TEACHER In the?

MARK In the football team, I want to get my county colours.

TEACHER Oh do you?

MARK Mm . . . I doubt if I will though.

TEACHER Well you don't know. Are you in the football team here?

MARK Yes.

TEACHER Mm.

MARK I've been for two years.

TEACHER Have you, and what position do you play?

MARK Er . . . on wing or centre half.

TEACHER Yes, is that where George Best plays?

MARK I don't know.

ANDREW Inside left.

TEACHER Does he?

MARK I don't support Manchester United.

TEACHER I see.

JULIE We leave this school in em . . . July, and em (*whispered conversation*)

? We go/we leave *this* school July but we go to Marshmer or Swanwick in September and we

JULIE I really will like to go to Alfreton or Swanwick 'cos I like . . . em . . . gymnastics a bit

TEACHER Mm . . .

JULIE And all sports

TEACHER Mm . . .

JULIE * looking forward to going on the trampoline.

JUDITH Me sister says, at Swanwick, she says she had a go on the trampoline and it really is *easier* than it er . . . looks she says; you know you feel confident 'cos it's soft landing when you fall.

TEACHER Yes. I'd just be afraid of bouncing out of the side, I don't know.

JUDITH The only thing I don't trust's hockey because me sister keeps saying 'Oh that ankle when I did it in, you know it really hurt me'. And when she was playing rounders with one of those wooden balls it hit her thumb and nearly broke it, and I thought right, I'm not playing/*ever* playing rounders with a wooden ball but you've got no choice.

TEACHER No, no, you've got to play with wooden things, haven't you?

JUDITH Yes, the only thing I like about parties, is these grown-up parties they have all these dances. Once I went to Swanwick, well I've been twice – but last year at Christmas erm . . . I had to dance with the headmaster, and his name's Mr ──.

TEACHER Yes.

JUDITH I says, 'I don't know the steps to these', and he says, 'Well you soon learn them'. Oh it's dreadful, you know. Oh gosh I'm going to let him down.

TEACHER Yes, and what dances did you do?

JUDITH Em . . . the Dashing White Sergeant, the Waltz, two step

MARK Which waltz?

JUDITH Just plain * There's the Westminster Waltz, just the plain waltz, the preliminary waltz, I think. I go ice-skating you know, and er

MARK I go ice-skating

JUDITH I try to learn as many as I can. I've just learnt Silver Samba and that's rather a hard dance 'cos it goes very quickly.

TEACHER Mm . . . and you go too, do you? (*To Mark*)

MARK Yes, but I don't have lessons.

TEACHER Pardon?

MARK I don't have lessons.

TEACHER No, no, and when you were dancing with Mr ──, how long were you dancing with him?

JUDITH Oh about ten minutes.

TEACHER Oh, so it wasn't such an ordeal.

JUDITH No, but then they had the dance repeated because everybody was enjoying it, you know . . . and . . . it was the Dashing White Sergeant I did with him and with another person. And you know you really get puffed out and you have to go round eight times and then back. You get rather fed up when you've done it twice.

TEACHER Yes, who else likes parties?

JULIE Well I know a boy when we had the Christmas party here he had about, er . . . six . . . er . . . glasses of orange juice.

JUDITH Timothy ── that was.

JULIE Yes, Timothy and Ian he had about fourteen sandwiches.

TEACHER And what do you do at the party?

JULIE Eat. (*Laughter*)

? *

ANDREW You have to go to parties to enjoy yourself. (*Laughter*) When I go to parties I try to enjoy myself and that's all there is to do with it.

20 Epilogue:
Letting them talk

Helen, Matthew, Michael, Mark, Andrew, Julie, Judith — and Ralph in his way — have all had their say, and it would be in the spirit of the book to leave the last word with them. But a few things should be made clear about the children, the transcripts, and the course of language development in general.

These children are not being held up as models: it is their very normality and the ordinariness of the situations which justify our presentation of them. Both Helen and Matthew are probably 'good talkers', but it is essential not to see them as somehow representing a standard of proficiency, as though other children should be at the same stage of development at the same age. Common sense and the facts of our experience tell us that children differ in almost every other aspect of their development, so why not in language? The route to adult competence may be well-defined, but there is no fixed pace at which children should pass along it. Children will differ, too, in the degree of interest they show in things linguistic, and many a child has appeared to be slow to talk, yet has arrived at school as articulate as his fellows. We must remember that talking is in any case only one aspect of skill in using language, and the silent child is not necessarily failing to take things in. A small boy was pushed in his pram round Bolton Abbey and its environs, scarcely saying a word, but when at the end of almost two hours his Daddy made for the car park, saying 'Down we go!' there came the rejoinder 'Back to the car'. Thank goodness? At last? And about time too? Who can claim that the child capable of that pat reply was previously mute from inability to say anything?

At least he was being taken out and given novel experiences. Far more important to these children than expensive toys and equipment, or anxious glances over the shoulder at so-called norms and milestones, has been the willingness of parents and teachers to talk to them, to encourage them to talk, and above all, to listen to what they have to say. 'Let them talk' by all means, but let it be, in Joan Tough's phrase, 'talking to some purpose' — and to interested and skilful listeners. Listening to children on tape gives us the opportunity to do what in the pressure of a normal situation is difficult, and that is to concentrate not only on what is being said, but also on how well. It is not a question of proposing some new set of classroom procedures: teachers already use tape recorders and need no exhortations to use them more. All that is being suggested is that it is easy to underestimate both the diversity of the functions of language and the potential skill of children in exploiting them. Recording children's speech need have nothing to do with speech training or preparation for public performance. It would not necessarily be a case of playing back the tapes to children at all, but rather of teachers listening to them in a situation in which they could concentrate on the children's language, and remind themselves of what was there to be developed. We might learn about more than just the children. 'Do I really talk so much?' was one teacher's reaction. We should do well to remember the comment of a girl in a junior school after a visitor had departed: 'She didn't listen much, did she? She talked so much that I didn't have the chance to learn anything.'

Appendix: Using a tape recorder

In this section we shall not give specialist advice on the purchase of a tape recorder, or on the use of highly technical electronic equipment – both these topics would fill books themselves. Many good shops will be happy to give demonstrations and such advice; there are specialist magazines available for those interested in pursuing the matter further; and schools and colleges generally have a technician or member of staff available who is willing to help. The taped material from which the transcripts in this book were made was recorded by people familiar with using tape recorders, but by no means experts, and we have drawn on their experience here, aiming our remarks at the interested layman, and concentrating on creating the right circumstances for producing good recordings, rather than on technical detail.

1 It is important to know your own machine thoroughly before using it in a practical taping session. It is off-putting for you and for the group being recorded if you are not aware of how the controls of a particular machine work, and it is very frustrating to find that something valuable has been missed because the 'record' button was not depressed. The manuals accompanying most recorders describe the basic operating principles, but frequent practical use is the best method of getting to know a recorder. If your machine is battery-operated you should have a spare set of batteries handy in case they should be needed, and in the case of other machines, a set of adaptor plugs and a screwdriver, so that any necessary modifications can quickly be made.

2 Most recordings made in the school or home are not made in the ideal conditions of a sound-proofed studio, and, particularly when taping very young children, opportunities often have to be seized when they present themselves, as the child may be inhibited by a pause for careful preparations. As the tape of Matthew, made in the park, shows, surprisingly good sound quality can be achieved in conditions which are not apparently ideal. If there is time to choose a setting for taping, then it is best to avoid a large empty room, where sound can bounce back from walls and furniture. Even a small corner in a busy classroom can be turned into a recording

studio by using chairs or a clothes-horse with coats or blankets thrown over as a screen, which will cut out some of the classroom noise.

3 In difficult recording circumstances, do not turn up the recording volume to its maximum. This not only distorts the voices you are recording, but amplifies the background noise. In these circumstances, better results are obtained by keeping the recording level fairly low and turning up the playback volume. From experience, it is possible to decide how far the subjects need to be from the microphone, and from which directions the microphone picks up sound most successfully. If the recorder has a volume level indicator, this can be used as a guide to the recording level which will produce the best results.

4 With young children such as Helen, the recorder can prove a distraction, with its interesting knobs and the movement of the tape. Conceal the recorder under the crib, or behind the table, and stand the microphone on a low table at the level at which the child is playing. If toys or books are to be used, have these handy, so that the child does not wander off out of range of the microphone. Do not bewilder the child by presenting him with all the toys and books at once, but introduce a few things at a time, and remove those in which the child is obviously not interested, substituting others. Young children often respond best to adults who are familiar − in Helen's case her mother, who knew which were her favourite toys, the kind of games she enjoyed playing, and the language she was capable of using. There is something to be gained from introducing a new book or toy, or the novelty of a new adult, but young children do not 'perform' to order and the familiar does often produce the best results. There are times of the day when very young children are more alert and lively and the mother is likely to know the best times for taping.

It is often easier for two people to work with very young children − one concerned with interacting with the child and introducing new books and toys, while the other makes notes on what the child is handling at any time, as this may prove important in understanding the tape later on. With a young child like Ralph, where phonological development is still taking place, it is useful to know which picture the child is pointing at when he says a particular word, because his sound patterns may not be consistent, or he may have his own idiosyncratic words for certain things, which need to be noted. In these circumstances, an observer can be invaluable for noting details which make sense of the conversation.

282

With older children, concealing the tape does not usually produce good results. Elaine and Stuart, at 6+, were not initially aware of the fact that the tape recorder was picking up their speech, but even when this was pointed out by an older child they were only momentarily distracted, because they were so fascinated by the tank of snails. But they are unusual in their concentration on the task in hand. Michael, aged five, was thoroughly familiar with the recorder, which had been used in his classroom by the pupils for some time. Familiarising children with the recorder usually produces better results than concealing it. As Douglas Barnes points out in his SSRC report, some children are so disturbed by hearing their own voices for the first time, and by the nature of spoken as opposed to written language, that they are inhibited in their work with tape recorders. They need to be given time to become accustomed to having themselves on tape before, for instance, a tape on which they feature is played to a class. Before making the tape on *Cider with Rosie*, teacher and pupils were involved in changing a plug on the recorder, and this time gave them an opportunity to get to know each other, and for the teacher to explain what she was doing. Children do sometimes interpret the task as a 'test' and this can seriously affect the way in which they approach conversation when they know that they are being recorded and that the teacher may listen later to what they have said. Therefore a relaxed and friendly atmosphere, where children are shown how to operate the tape recorder and given a sense of responsibility, is likely to produce better results than an unfamiliar and potentially threatening situation.

Care should be taken to position the group round the microphone, which should not be handled, and to avoid intrusive sounds like the ticking of a clock. Three or four pupils seems to be an optimum number for picking up the sound and for identifying the voices for transcription. Until pupils are used to group work, it is perhaps better to choose friendship groups, and with younger adolescents single sex groups, where extraordinary demands are not made on pupils' social skills in interacting and in settling arguments to the exclusion of fruitful discussion. As Douglas Barnes notes, the way in which the children are introduced to the tape recorder and the task plays an important part in determining the quality of the results achieved.

5 It is all too easy once the recording session is over to forget important details about the occasion and participants. Before the taping starts, record on the tape the date, the place, the number and

names of the speakers, and the details of the task they are engaged in. Note toys and books used, if you know what they will be; these may not be referred to explicitly on the tape and yet may be the focus of the child's attention. If you are recording a group, ask them to state their names at the beginning, as this helps to identify voices for transcription. These details can be noted on the tape box, but boxes can be lost or tapes exchanged between boxes, and listening time can be wasted sorting out the muddle. After taping, note on the tape any special features which have arisen during the taping, such as a child's invented name for a toy, which could cause confusion later.

There is always an element of luck in taping children talking, and this has to be accepted philosophically. The tape which breaks in the cassette, a sudden loss of power on the circuit, a faulty connection can mean the loss of excellent material, but it happens to everyone from time to time. The tape of Elaine and Stuart, on the other hand, was a happy accident – the tape recorder was set up for another group when Elaine and Stuart can e in. A combination of careful preparation, knowledge of the mach e, and luck, should produce some material worth transcribing.

Further reading

The Tape Recorder in the Classroom, John Weston, published by the National Committee for Audio-Visual Aids in Education. First published in 1960. Fourth edition, revised, 1973. Some of the explanations are couched in rather technical terms, but there are good sections on the choice of microphone and tapes, and the care of tapes, with creative suggestions for use in the classroom by pupils and teachers.

Tape Recorders for Education, D. J. Chatterton, published by Print and Press Services Ltd, 1972. Don't be put off by the small print and poor photographs – the techniques of using a recorder are explained very clearly.

BBC booklet, *School radio and the tape recorder*, published by the British Broadcasting Corporation, 1968. Brief explanations of the working of tape recorders, cataloguing, care and storage of tapes; very helpful advice on taping radio broadcasts and using them in school; and a list of useful addresses from which further information on the use of the recorders can be obtained.

The New Media Challenge, Nelson Trowbridge, Macmillan, 1974. Deals principally with the use of the cassette recorder. Excellent suggestions for the use of tape and slides in stimulating

284

language work in the classroom.

SSRC Project on Communication and Learning in Small Groups: 'Monitoring Small Groups – A Manual for Teachers', by Douglas Barnes and Frankie Todd, Institute of Education, University of Leeds (1974 & 1975). Helpful on the technicalities of equipment, recording conditions, group composition, and the framing of tasks for groups. They also stress methods of relaxing a group and making them feel a personal interest in the job.

Glossary

The terms explained in this glossary are printed in **bold** type on their first occurrence in the text.

Accent

The way in which a language is pronounced because of the effect of particular phonological features.

See   Wilkinson (1965) pp. 22–3
        Abercrombie (1965) Ch. 2

Addressor/Addressee Register

See also **Style**

Those features of language in a communication which are governed by the relationship of the speaker and listener and factors such as age, social and professional status. Terms of address such as the use of titles, surnames, christian names, or nicknames are often very good indicators of the relationship of speakers, and are one aspect of the **Addressor/Addressee Register**.

See Wilkinson (1971) pp. 37–46

Addressee/Subject Register

See also **Register**

The kind of English suitable for a particular occasion and purpose. Features which may be concerned are partly lexical (e.g. the use of technical terms in an occupation like medicine, or in a sports commentary, such as 'flying tackle'), but they may also be syntactical (e.g. the language of instruction manuals where the article is omitted – 'Turn

screw to the right for 45 degrees'), and phonological (e.g. the special kind of delivery used in a running commentary on a horse-race as opposed to the pace of delivery of a later report of the same race).

See Wilkinson (1971) pp. 37–46

Adjunct

'An adjunct is the part of a sentence which answers questions other than "Who or what?" after the verb.' Berry (1975) p. 64

Thus in 'John did the errand on his way home', we ask, 'John did the errand when?' and the answer is 'On his way home'. The adjunct is therefore 'on his way home'. Other questions could be 'How?', 'Where?', 'Why?'

Allomorph

'A non-distinctive variant of a morpheme.' Hartmann and Stork (1972) p. 1

In the following plurals of nouns, the same morpheme is used (-s).

hats, lids, horses

but in each case the -s is pronounced differently. There are three allomorphs of -s.

Antonymy

See **Synonymy**

Aspect
See **Tense**

Babbling
A stage, often called vocal play, through which all children pass, in what many would term the pre-linguistic period. Children produce a wide range of sounds, not all of them to be found in the language they will acquire, and some of which will be the last to be acquired as phonemes. One characteristic is the production of repeated syllables like 'dada'.

Behavioural Theory of Meaning
'The behavioural theory of meaning focuses on the use of language in communication. It postulates that the meaning of an expression is the set of responses it produces in the hearer.' Dale (1972) p. 135

Bound Morpheme
See **Morpheme**

Clause
In traditional grammar a clause is defined as a group of words containing a subject and a verb.

Collocation
The tendency of certain words to co-occur frequently with other words. An item is said to 'collocate' with another item or items.
See Halliday, McIntosh and Strevens (1964) pp. 33–5
Wilkinson, Stratta and Dudley (1974) p. 32

Command
See **Contextual Types of Utterance**
Complex Sentence
See **Sentence Structure**
Compound Sentence
See **Sentence Structure**
Consonant
'A speech sound produced by obstructing or impeding the passage of air at some point in the vocal tract above the glottis.' Hartman and Stork (1972) p. 49
Consonants may be classified in various ways, including the following:
1 Voicing (whether or not there is vibration of the vocal cords)
/b/ in 'big' and /d/ in 'dig' are voiced
/p/ in 'pig' and /t/ in 'pit' are unvoiced
2 Stop or continuant
In the first case there is total closure in the vocal tract, in the second partial.
/b/ in 'big' is a stop consonant
/f/ in 'fig' is a continuant

Contextual Types of Utterance
Four types have been proposed:
1 statement – 'It's a lovely day.'
2 question – 'Are you going out?'
3 command – 'Get out of my way!'
4 response – 'Tomorrow, probably.' (In reply to a question such as 'When's he coming?')

Continuant
See **Consonant**

Declarative
See **Structure-Dependent**

Deep and Surface Structure
Transformational-generative grammar puts forward three hypotheses:
1 Every sentence has both a deep and a surface structure.
2 The deep structure tells us all that we need to know about the meaning of the sentence.
3 The surface structure of a sentence tells all that we need to know about what the sentence sounds like.
Deep structures are generated by what are called 'phrase structure

rules', and the resulting strings form the input to a different set of rules known as 'transformations', which map the deep into the surface structures.

'The lamb was too hot to eat' has one surface structure and two deep structures.

See Lyons (1970)

Dialect

A form of language associated with a particular geographical region which has its own grammar, lexis, and phonology.

See Halliday, McIntosh, and Strevens (1964) Ch. 4
Wilkinson (1965) pp. 22–3

Displaced Speech

The use of language to refer to things not physically present, for example 'When will your brother be arriving?' or 'I'd like to go to America.'

Echoing

A form of exchange between parent and child which occurs when part of what the child says is unintelligible. The parent then imitates all that can be understood of the child's utterance and replaces the rest with a 'Wh' word:

Child I'm making a wobby pie.
Parent You're making a what pie?

See Dale (1972)

Expansion

One of the most frequent forms of response to children's utterances. 'An expansion is an imitation in reverse. An adult, imitating a child's ~ntence, typically adds ~ sentence the parts he ~hild to have omitted.' ~9)

An example would be:
Child Sit wall
Adult You're sitting on the wall, are you?

Experimental

This refers to the method of studying children's language by eliciting language from children or testing their understanding of language in controlled situations, as opposed to the 'naturalistic' method in which children's language is observed in everyday situations.

Fillers
See **Stabilisers**

Free Morpheme
See **Morpheme**

Fricative

A speech sound made by forcing air through the partially obstructed vocal tract so as to produce audible friction. Can be voiced (/v/) or unvoiced (/f/).

Grammar

A word which is used in several different senses. If we speak of T.G. grammar or systemic grammar, we are thinking not of linguistic table manners, a set of prescriptions about how people should speak or write, or even of a description of a particular language, but of a theory of the nature of language itself.

With such theories there are various usages. Grammar can be seen as a subdivision of one of the three primary levels of language (substance, form, and situation). As a subdivision of form, it contrasts with lexis. In this view 'grammar is concerned with classes of linguistic items and the patterns in which classes of linguistic item occur.'
Berry (1975) p. 38

Traditionally, grammar has been divided into two elements: syntax, which is concerned with the ways in which words are combined with each other to form larger structures; and morphology, which deals with the forms of individual words. Thus one can study how children learn to combine words in their early sentences or how they learn to use the various morphemes.

Grammatical Relationships

A simplified version of a phrase marker in T.G. grammar might look something like this

N.P. (2), is derived from V.P. (verb phrase).

N.P. (1) is the subject of the verb; N.P. (2) is the object ('the rabbit' is the subject of 'ate' and 'the lettuce' is the object of 'ate'). This is a formal way of arriving at the answer to the question 'What is the subject of the verb?' without having to consider the meanings of any of the words concerned.

In the sentence 'The lettuce was eaten by the rabbit' the surface subject now looks like 'the lettuce', but the same diagram would be

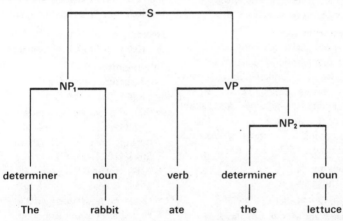

This diagram clarifies the structure of the sentence 'The rabbit ate the lettuce'. It identifies the subject of the verb and the object of the verb. If you look at the diagram, you will see that 'the rabbit' is derived from a symbol N.P. (noun phrase) and the same is true of 'the lettuce'. The difference lies in the relationships between the respective N.P.s and other parts of the diagram. The one we have labelled N.P. (1) is derived from the first symbol S, while the second, which we have labelled

used to represent the deep structure of the sentence and the logical subject would remain 'the rabbit'.

Hesitation Phenomena

The tendency for pauses and hesitations before certain words and phrases which do not seem to be related to linguistic structure or intonation patterns, but are concerned more with the efforts of the speaker to think and plan structures as he speaks and to choose his words as he goes along.

See Wilkinson, Stratta and Dudley (1974) p. 33

Heuristic Model
See **Relevant Models of Language**

Holophrase

A term used to describe the single word utterances of young children.

'The lexical item forms, by itself, an utterance that is functionally independent and complete.' Halliday (1975)

'A word which expresses on its own the meaning of an entire sentence.' Hartmann and Stork (1972) p. 104

There is less agreement now than formerly about the holophrase being a 'word-sentence'.

Holophrastic Speech

Speech consisting of holophrases.

Holophrastic speech 'means that children are limited phonologically to uttering single words at the beginning of language acquisition even though they are capable of conceiving of something like full sentences'. McNeill (1969)

Hyponymy
See **Synonymy**

Imaginative Model
See **Relevant Models of Language**

Inclusion
See **Hyponymy**

Infinitive

'A form of the verb which is not limited by person, number, or tense ...' In English it may stand alone, e.g. 'I must go', or it may be preceded by the particle 'to' e.g. 'I want to go'. Hartmann and Stork (1972) p. 111

Initial Markers

Lexical items such as 'Well', 'Right', 'Now' used by a speaker at the beginning of a contribution to the conversation, serving to indicate that the speaker now wishes to participate.

See Wilkinson (1965) appendix I

Innateness Hypothesis

Chomsky proposes that such is the speed of language acquisition, irrespective of the intelligence of the child, or the nature of the language that he hears from his parents, or the lack of systematic teaching by them, that the building up of his knowledge of a complex and abstract grammar must depend upon a highly specific innate predisposition.

Instrumental Model
See **Relevant Models of Language**

Interactional Model
See **Relevant Models of Language**

Interrogative
See **Structure-Dependent**

Intonation

'Melodic pattern produced by the variation in pitch of the voice during speech.' Hartmann and Stork (1972) p. 117

By means of some six basic tunes, speakers of English can signal both whether what they are saying is a statement, question or command, and also their own attitudes to the facts they are stating. (For a good simple introduction to this topic, look at the fourth chapter of Wallwork, 1969.)

Lexical Item

A unit (e.g. word, phrase) of the vocabulary of a language.

Lexis

'This usually comprises the vocabulary items of a language as well as their lexical or semantic meaning in specific contexts.' Hartmann and Stork (1972)

Linguistic Stage

There is less agreement than there was about the dividing line between the prelinguistic and the linguistic stage of language acquisition. According to some, the linguistic stage could not be said to have begun until the child started to understand the language of adults, according to others, until he could produce recognisable words with the intention to communicate. Others would argue that language acquisition begins much earlier: if a child of eight months, for example, is using English intonation patterns in his 'scribble talk' then, they would say, he has acquired part of the language system.

Listener Code Markers

These are indications from the listener which provide feedback for the speaker to indicate that he still has the listener's attention. These can take the form of words such as 'Yes', 'Mm', or gestures such as nods, renewed eye contact and looks of interest. Looks of boredom, yawning or shuffling can indicate, conversely, that the listener is no longer interested in what is being said.

See Wilkinson, Stratta and Dudley (1974) Ch. 2
Wilkinson (1965) p. 23

Meaning

This is much too elusive and controversial a word to be dealt with briefly in a glossary. Readers are advised to read the entry in Hartmann and Stork (1972), the treatment in chapter 6 of Dale (1972), and Pit Corder's article in Fraser and O'Donnell (1969). There

is also a good chapter in Bolinger (1975).

Modals

Verbs which form a part of verbal groups and indicate an attitude towards the verb they modify.

Examples: I can, I am to, I must, I may, indicating respectively ability, obligation, necessity and permission to perform the action of the verb dependent on them.

Morpheme

A morpheme is one of the units of English grammar, the others being: sentence, clause, group (or phrase) and word.

'A morpheme can be identified in one way only, by reference to the part it plays in the structure of a word. A morpheme has no grammatical structure of its own ... The morpheme is the smallest grammatical unit and therefore there are no smaller things from which it can be constructed.' Berry (1975)

The word 'house' consists of one morpheme.

The word 'houses' consists of two morphemes.

The word 'lighthouse' consists of two morphemes.

The word 'lighthouses' consists of three morphemes.

If a morpheme can stand alone, like 'house', 'light', 'elephant', it is said to be a *free morpheme*. If it can only occur in conjunction with others, like the *plural morpheme* '-s' in 'houses' and 'ladybirds'; or the *possessive morpheme* '-'s' in 'Cleopatra's wiles', it is called a *bound morpheme*.

Morphology
See **Grammar**

Narrowing

A stage through which children pass in acquiring word meanings. A word is used in a more restricted sense than it would be in the adult vocabulary. For example, a child might restrict the word 'white' to milk and reject its application to something else of that colour.

Naturalistic

See **Experimental**

Noun Phrase

'A word or group of words with a noun or pronoun as its head and functioning like a noun as the subject, object, or complement of a sentence.' Hartmann and Stork (1972) p. 155

Examples:

'*He* was going home.'

'*The man* was going home.'

'*The old man* was going home.'

'*The man with a beard* was going home.'

'*The old man with a beard* was going home.'

Number

See **System**

Object

See **Grammatical Relationships**

Open Class

See **Pivot and Open Classes**

Ostension

Pointing to and naming objects so that children may learn, or show their knowledge of, the appropriate words.

Overextension

A process in the development of word meaning for children, in which a word like 'Daddy' is used to refer to men in general rather than a particular referent. (Cf. **Narrowing**.)

Paralinguistic Features

Gestures, facial expression, tone of voice etc. which may give additional meanings to lexical items and grammatical structures.

See Wilkinson (1975) Ch. 13

Wilkinson, Stratta and Dudley (1974) Ch. 2

Participant and Spectator Language

Terms used by J. Britton to define language used for different purposes, briefly summed up in the following quotation from Britton (1970) chapter 3, p. 122.

'Informing people, instructing people, persuading people, arguing, explaining, planning, setting forth the pros and cons and coming to a conclusion – these are the participant uses of language, uses of language to get things done. Make believe play, day-dreaming aloud, chatting about our experiences, gossip, travellers' tales and other story-telling, fiction, the novel, drama, poetry – these are the uses of language in the spectator role.'

See Britton (1970)

Personal Model

See **Relevant Models of Language**

Phatic Communion

A term invented by the anthropologist, Malinowski, to describe language such as greetings or small talk (e.g. in English about the weather) where the intention is to establish or cement relationships rather than to convey information.

See Halliday, McIntosh and Strevens (1964) p. 91

D. Bolinger (1975) pp. 524–5

B. Malinowski (1935*b*)

Phone

See **Phoneme**

Phoneme

Phonemes can be classified as either segmental or supra-segmental.

Segmental.
The words 'car' and 'far' are differentiated by contrast in the first segment. The words form a 'minimal pair' and demonstrate that /k/ and /f/ are phonemes of English. Minimal pairs can be used to establish all the phonemes of a language. See the appendix in Quirk (1962) for a demonstration of this. English has forty-three phonemes. So far this explanation appears to suggest that 'phoneme' is another word for 'sound', but this is not the case. If we listen to

i. our own pronunciation of the words 'key' and 'car'

ii. the word 'tea' pronounced by a variety of different speakers,

we notice that in the first case the sounds made for the first segments of the words are not identical, although both would be classed as /k/; and in the second, both the /t/ and the /i:/ would be represented by a selection of sounds. These different members of the same family of sounds are called *phones* and the families of sounds themselves are the phonemes. You will find phones shown in books in square brackets like this [d] and phonemes in marks like these / /: /d/ /t/ etc.

Suprasegmental
Contrast in sounds is also made in the areas of stress and intonation. These are known as suprasegmental phonemes because they extend beyond the boundaries of single segments.

Phonology

A word used to describe the sound system of a language (its patterns of phonemes) and also the study of that system.

Phrase Structure

'The arrangement of syntactic elements to form larger units, e.g. noun phrase+verb phrase, to make a sentence.' Hartmann and Stork (1972)

Pivot and Open Classes

Terms used by Martin Braine to distinguish two classes of words in children's early utterances. According to this characterisation there is a small number of *pivot* words like 'allgone' and 'on' always used in fixed positions and a much larger class of *open* words with the pivots. For example,
'allgone shoe' (PIVOT+OPEN)
'allgone lettuce' (PIVOT+OPEN)

Plural Morpheme
See **Morpheme**
Polarity
See **System**
Possessive Morpheme
See **Morpheme**
Prelinguistic Stage
See **Linguistic Stage**
Present Continuous

The form of the verb normally used to describe ongoing action (sometimes called the *present progressive*): 'I am going out.' 'Present' refers to *tense*, 'continuous' to *aspect*.

Present Perfect

Verb forms such as 'have gone' in 'They have gone'. (See **Tense**)

Present Progressive
See **Present Continuous**

Privilege of Occurrence

The position in a sentence that a word may occupy. The words 'red', 'woollen', 'fashionable', 'stolen', 'provocative' can all fill the slot in 'She was wearing a ... dress.' and thus have the same privileges of occurrence.

Prompting

A way in which parents respond to their children's utterances. If a child fails to understand, say, a question in the usual adult form, the parent rephrases the question in such a way as to give the child a possibly simpler task in answering it. Thus, if 'What do you want?' elicits no reply, the parent can try 'You want what?', giving the child at least the word order of the reply.

Question

One of the *contextual types of utterance*. In English there are four kinds of question:

1 using intonation alone
'You're leaving already?'
2 yes/no question
'Is the heater on?'
3 'wh' question
'Who's that down by the gate?'
4 tag question
'The church is over there, isn't it?'

Questions like (2) can be answered with 'Yes' or 'No'; those like (3) start with words like 'Who' and 'Where' and cannot be answered with 'Yes' and 'No'. Tag questions usually seek confirmation of the statement with which they begin, and the tag at the end reverses the polarity of the statement, i.e. positive statements ('The church is over there') have negative tags ('isn't it?') and vice versa.

Received Pronunciation

An English accent which does not reflect the pronunciation of any particular geographical area; it is often associated with the public school.

See Wilkinson (1965) p. 23
    Abercrombie (1965) Ch. 2

Reduction

This is rather like expansion in reverse. The child hears an adult utterance and imitates it, or rather produces a version of it from which certain elements (inflexions and 'little words') are missing.

Adult He's going out.
Child He go out.

Redundancy

The indication of meaning by more than one signal, e.g. 'they are' signals the plural twice in the form of the pronoun and the particular form of the verb 'to be'. In spoken language redundancy relates specifically to the repetition of words and phrases for a number of reasons.

See Wilkinson, Stratta and Dudley
    (1974) p. 23

Referential Theory of Meaning

This states that *the meaning of a word is its referent*. In other words, words are symbols that stand for something other than themselves, something in the world, namely, their referents.

See Dale (1972) p. 132

Register

A variety of language appropriate to a particular situation, for example a sports commentary, or a church service, or associated with a particular occupation, for example the law or medicine. Here we are concerned with features which are partly syntactic, e.g. 'powers of attorney', and sometimes phonological, e.g. the particular intonation of sports commentaries. A. Wilkinson uses as an equivalent term, Addressor/Subject register, which is the term used in this book.

> See Halliday, McIntosh and Strevens (1964) pp. 87–98
> Wilkinson (1971) pp. 39–46
> Bolinger (1975) pp. 358–63

Regulatory Model
See **Relevant Models of Language**
Reinforcement
'... anything that increases the probability of behaviour that systematically precedes it.' Mednick (1964) p. 16

Relevant Models of Language
In his 1969 paper 'Relevant Models of Language' (published in the November 1969 issue of *Educational Review*), Halliday proposes that children have internalised a 'model' of language as a result of their experience.

'The child knows what language is because he knows what language does.'

The model is more complex than adults realise, and in fact it would be more useful to speak of the 'models' that the normal child has acquired by the age of five. Halliday suggests the following:

Instrumental Model ('I want')
'The child becomes aware that language is used as a means of getting things done.'
'Language is brought in to serve the function of "I want", the satisfaction of material needs.'

Regulatory Model ('Do as I tell you')
'This refers to the use of language to

regulate the behaviour of others.'
The child will learn this model from the adults' use of language to control him and will in turn use language in increasingly elaborate ways to control others.

Interactional Model ('Me and him')
'This refers to the use of language in the interaction between self and others.'
Language can help not only to maintain close personal relationships like those within the family but to facilitate other less permanent relationships like those of the peer group and neighbourhood.

Personal Model ('Here I come')
'This refers to his awareness of language as a form of his own individuality.'
'The child is enabled to offer that which is unique to himself, to make public his own individuality; and this in turn reinforces and creates this individuality.'

Heuristic Model ('Tell me why')
'The heuristic model refers to language as a means of investigating reality, a way of learning about things.'

Imaginative Model ('Let's pretend')
'Here, the child is using language to create his own environment; not to learn about how things are but to make them as he feels inclined.'

Representational Model ('I've got something to tell you')
'Language is, in addition to all its other guises, a means of communicating about something, of expressing propositions.'
'This is the only model of language that many adults have; and a very inadequate model it is, from the

point of view of the child.'

Response
See **Contextual Types of Utterance**

Semantics
The study of meaning. Like 'meaning' not a word to be dismissed in a brief glossary entry. See the entry in Hartmann and Stork (1972) and Chapter 9 in Wallwork (1969).

Sentence Structure
Sentences can be classified according to the number and relationship of their constituent clauses:

Simple sentences consist of a single main clause: 'All the nice girls love a sailor.'

Compound sentences consist of two or more main clauses connected by such conjunctions as 'and' or 'but': 'They went home and had their tea.'

Complex sentences consist of at least one main clause and one dependent clause linked by subordinating conjunctions like 'when', 'because', 'where': 'I'll go when I'm ready'; 'Because the weather was so bad the trip was cancelled.'

Simple Sentence
See **Sentence Structure**

Spectator Language
See **Participant Spectator**

Stabilisers
Sounds such as 'er' and 'mm' which fill the silences between words or utterances while a speaker is choosing the correct word or phrase, deciding what to say next, or simply alerting the listener to the fact that he has not finished speaking. Phrases such as 'you know', 'sort of', 'kind of' may fulfil the

same function or may also be appeals for audience response.
See Wilkinson (1965) p. 29

Standard English
A form of language shared by members of the English-speaking world.
See Doughty, Pearce and Thornton (1972) Ch. 10
Quirk, Greenbaum, Leech and Svartvik (1972) Ch. 1

Statement
See **Contextual Types of Utterance**
Stop Consonant
See **Consonant**
Stress
'Greater force exerted in the articulation of one part of an utterance compared with another, thus accentuating a certain part of the utterance, giving it more prominence.' Hartmann and Stork (1972)

Strong Verb
See **Verb**

Structure-dependent
According to Chomsky, language users need to 'know' the underlying structure of sentences. In the following sentences the (a) version is a statement or *declarative* and the (b) version a question or *interrogative*:

1 (a) The world's my oyster.

(b) Is the world my oyster?

2 (a) His ability to balance an eel on the end of his nose was the admiration of all who knew him.

2 (b) Was his ability to balance an eel on the end of his nose the admiration of all who knew him?

The groups of words transposed with 'is' in (1) and 'was' in (2), are 'the world' in (1), and 'his ability to balance an eel on the end of his nose' in (2). These two very different sets of words have one thing in common: they are the N.P.s (noun phrases) which are the subjects of their respective sentences. Ability to perform the operation of forming questions depends on 'knowing' the structure of the sentences. The operation is *structure-dependent*.

Style

This term is sometimes used in a non-technical sense, as in the phrase 'an author's style', meaning the sum of features which characterise his writing. However, in technical linguistic usage it refers to the features of speech which are appropriate to a particular occasion, listener, or addressee, and the way in which these features reflect the relationship of speaker and listener. Wilkinson uses the term 'addressor/addressee register', which is the one referred to in this book.

See Halliday, McIntosh and Strevens (1964)

Wilkinson (1965) pp. 25–8

Wilkinson (1971) pp. 37–46

Martin Joos (1962) in *The Five Clocks* suggests five ranks for the scale of Style, ranging through *frozen, formal, consultative, casual* to *intimate*.

Wilkinson gives the following examples of these.

1 *frozen*: 'I should be glad to be informed of the correct time.'

2 *formal*: 'I should like to know the time, please.'

3 *consultative*; 'Do you have the time on you please?'

4 *casual*: 'What's the time?'

5 *intimate*: 'Time?'

Subject

See **Grammatical Relationships**

Surface Structure

See **Deep and Surface Structure**

Synonymy

The relationship between synonyms (words with identical meaning). Other relationships between words include *antonymy*, the relationship between words of opposite meanings, and *hyponymy* (or inclusion). In the latter, one word is said to be *superordinate* to its hyponyms. Thus 'fruit' is superordinate to 'apple', 'orange', 'banana' and so on.

Syntax

The part of grammar that deals with the arrangement of words in sentences.

System

'Systems are lists of choices which are available in the grammar of a language.' Berry (1975)

Some examples of systems in English are:

number: singular
         plural
polarity: positive
        negative
person: first
       second
       third

Tag Question

See **Question**

Telegraphic Speech

A term first used by Roger Brown (but now considered by him to be inadequate) for describing the early sentences of children.

'The curious fact is that the sentences the child makes are like adult telegrams in that they are largely made up of nouns and verbs (with a few adjectives and adverbs) and in that they generally do not use prepositions, conjunctions, articles, or auxiliary verbs.' Brown (1973)

Tense

When we use verbs there is a difference expressed between the time of our utterance and the events we are describing, e.g. 'I went to the butcher's'. It is the tense of the verb that enables us to express this difference.

However, some of the 'tenses' of traditional grammar are now described in other ways. 'Aspect', for instance, marks the duration and the type of the action expressed by the verb. Thus, 'I have been there' would have been described as perfect tense but would now be described as perfect aspect. 'I went there' is past tense.

Terminal Markers

Phrases such as 'That's that', 'You know', at the end of a speaker's contribution indicate that the speaker has completed what he intended to say and is handing over to one of the other participants. See Wilkinson (1965) appendix 1

Transformational-Generative Grammar (T.G.)
See **Deep and Surface Structure**

Unvoiced
See **Consonant**

Utterance

'Stretch of speech between two periods of silence or potential silence.' Hartmann and Stork (1972) p. 242

Some linguists would not admit the use of 'sentence' to describe what is produced in speech.

Varieties of Language
See also **Dialect, Register** and **Style**

Although we recognise a single 'English language', there are, within this, recognisable varieties each with a slightly different linguistic organisation in terms of phonology, lexis and and syntax.

See Halliday, McIntosh, and Strevens (1964)

Quirk, Greenbaum, Leech and Svartvik (1972) chapter 1

Verb

'A part of speech which may function as predicate in a sentence. The traditional definition of verbs as "doing words" is inadequate, since many verbs do not imply any action, e.g. in *I am cold* or *She looks happy enough . . .*' Hartmann and Stork (1972) p. 248.

(Weak verbs are those which add an inflexion to the stem to form the past tense [kill/killed, step/stepped]; strong verbs change their root vowel [dig/dug, swim/swam].)

Verb Phrase

A group of words having the same syntactic function as a simple verb in a sentence. For example, in 'You might have been killed' the verb phrase is 'might have been killed'.

Virtuous Error

A form in child speech that is wrong in terms of the adult system but which demonstrates that the child has worked out a productive rule for himself that applies in many other cases. The example most often cited is of overgeneralising the '-ed' morpheme used to form the past tense of weak verbs and applying it to the strong verbs also 'swimmed', 'digged' etc.

Voiced
See **Consonant**

Vowel

A speech sound which is produced by vibration of the vocal cords but, unlike the consonant, without closure of the vocal tract above the glottis.

Weak Verb
See **Verb**

'Wh' Question
See **Question**

Yes/No Question
See **Question**

References

Abercrombie, D. (1965) *Studies in Phonetics and Linguistics* OUP

Berry, M. (1975) *Introduction to Systemic Linguistics* Batsford

Bolinger, D. (1975) *Aspects of Language* Harcourt, Brace & Jovanovich, 2nd edition

Britton, J. (1970) *Language and Learning* Allen Lane

Britton, J. (1975) 'What's the Use' in A. Wilkinson *Language and Education* OUP

Brown, R. (1973) *A First Language* George Allen & Unwin

Dale, P. S. (1972) *Language Development: Structure and Function* Dryden Press

Doughty, P., Pearce, J. and Thornton, G. (1972) *Exploring Language* Edward Arnold

Fraser, H. and O'Donnell, W. R. (eds.) (1969) *Applied Linguistics and the Teaching of English* Longman

Halliday, M. A. K., McIntosh, A. and Strevens, P. (1964) *The Linguistic Sciences and Language Teaching* Longman

Halliday, M. A. K. 'Relevant Models of Language' *Educational Review* 22, no. 1, November 1969

Halliday, M. A. K. (1975) *Learning How to Mean: Explorations in the Development of Language* Edward Arnold

Hartmann, R. R. K. and Stork, F. C. (eds.) (1972) *Dictionary of Language and Linguistics* Applied Science Publishers

Joos, M. (1962) *The Five Clocks* Mouton

Lyons, J. (1970) *Chomsky* Fontana

McNeill, D. (1969) 'The Development of Language' in P. N. Maussen, (ed.) *Carmichael's Manual of Child Psychology* Wiley

Mednick, S. A. (1964) *Learning* Prentice-Hall Inc.

Quirk, R., Greenbaum, S., Leech, G. and Svartvik, J. (1972) *A Grammar of Contemporary English* Longman

Wallwork, J. F. (1969) *Language and Linguistics* Heinemann

Wilkinson, A. (1975) *Language and Education* OUP

Wilkinson, A. (1971) *The Foundations of Language* OUP

Wilkinson, A. (1965) *Spoken English* University of Birmingham Press

Wilkinson, A., Stratta, L. and Dudley, P. (1974) *The Quality of Listening* Macmillan

Bibliography

Abercrombie, D. (1965) *Studies in Phonetics and Linguistics,* OUP

Aitchinson, J. (1976) *The Articulate Mammal,* Hutchinson

Ashworth, E. (1973) *Language in the Junior School,* Arnold

Barber, C. L. (1964) *The Study of Language,* Pan

Barnes, D. (1969) *Language, the Learner and the School,* Penguin

Barnes, D. (1976) *From Communication to Curriculum,* Penguin

Barnes, D. and Todd, F. (1974 & 1975) *Communication and Learning in Small Groups,* SSRC Project, Leeds University Institute of Education

Bellack, A. A., Kliebard, H. M., Hyman, R. T. and Smith, F. I. (1967) *The Language of the Classroom,* Teachers College Press

Berko, J. (1958) 'The Child's Learning of English Morphology', *Word,* **14,** 150-77

Berry, M. (1975) *Introduction to Systemic Linguistics,* Batsford

Bloom, B. (1964) *Taxonomy of Educational Objectives,* Book 2: *The Affective Domain,* Longman

Bloom, L. (1970) *Language Development: Form and Function in Emerging Grammars,* MIT Press

Bloom, L. (1973) *One Word at a Time: The Use of Single Word Utterances Before Syntax,* Mouton

Bloom, L. (1975) 'Language Development Review' in Horowitz *et al.* (eds) *Review of Child Development Research,* vol IV, University of Chicago Press

Bloomfield, L. (1933) *Language,* Arnold

Bolinger, D. (1975) *Aspects of English,* Harcourt, Brace & World (second edition)

Bowerman, M. (1973) *Early Syntactic Development: A Cross-linguistic Study with Special Reference to Finnish,* CUP

Braine, M. D. S. (1963) 'The Ontogeny of English Phrase Structure: The First Phase', *Language,* **39**

Braine, M. D. S. (1971) 'The Acquisition of Language in Infant and Child' in C. Reed (ed.) *The Learning of Language,* Appleton

301

British Broadcasting Corporation (1968) *School Radio and the Tape Recorder*, BBC Publications

Britton, J. (1965) 'Speech in the School' *NATE* **2**, no. 2, Summer

Britton, J. (1970) *Language and Learning*, Allen Lane

Britton, J. (1973) in N. Bagnall (ed.) *New Movements in the Study and Teaching of English*, Temple Smith

Britton, J. (1975) 'What's the Use' in Wilkinson (1975)

Brown, R. (1970) 'The First Sentences of Child and Chimpanzee', *Psycholinguistics: Selected Papers*, Free Press

Brown, R. (1973) *A First Language*, Allen & Unwin

Brown, R. and Bellugi, U. (1964) 'Three Processes in the Acquisition of Syntax', *Harvard Educational Review*, **34**, 133-51

Brown, R. and Fraser, C. (1963) 'The Acquisition of Syntax' in C. N. Cofer and B. Musgrave (eds) *Verbal Behaviour and Learning Problems and Processes*, McGraw Hill

Brown, R. and Hanlon, C. (1970) 'Deprivational Complexity and Order of Acquisition in Child Speech' in Hayes (1970)

Bullock, A. (1975) *A Language for Life*. Report of the Committee of Inquiry appointed by the Secretary of State for Education and Science, HMSO

Campbell, R. and Wales, R. (1970) 'The Study of Language Acquisition' in Lyons (1970 *b*)

Carroll, J. B. (1953) *The Study of Language*, Harvard University Press

Cazden, C. B. (1966) 'Subcultural Differences in Child Language: an Inter-Disciplinary Review', *Merrill-Palmer Quarterly of Behaviour and Development*, **12**, 185-219

Chatterton, D. J. (1972) *Tape Recorders for Education*, Print and Press Services Ltd

Chomsky, C. (1969) *The Acquisition of Syntax in Children from Five to Ten*, MIT Press

Chomsky, N. (1959) 'Review of Skinner's *Verbal Behaviour*', *Language*, **35**

Chomsky, N. (1965) *Aspects of the Theory of Syntax*, MIT Press

Chomsky, N. (1968) *Language and Mind*, Harcourt, Brace & Jovanovich

Chukovsky, K. (1963) *From Two to Five*, University of California Press

Clark, E. (1974) 'Some Aspects of the Conceptual Basis for First Language Acquisition' in R. L. Schiefelbusch and L. L. Lloyd (eds) *Language Perspectives – Acquisition, Retardation, and Intervention*, Macmillan

Coulthard, M. (1974) 'Approaches to the Analysis of Classroom Interaction' in *Functions of Language*, University of Birmingham Press vol. 26, no. 3, June

Cromer, R. F. (1974) 'The Development of Language and Cognition' in B. Foss (ed.) *New Perspectives in Child Development*, Penguin

Crystal, D. and Davy, D. (1969) *Investigating English Style*, Longman

Dale, P. S. (1972) *Language Development: Structure and Function*, Dryden Press

Dixon, J. (1975) *Growth Through English* OUP (third edition)

Donaldson, M. C. and Wales, R. J. (1970) 'On the Acquisition of Some Relational Terms' in Hayes (1970)

Doughty, P., Pearce, J. and Thornton, G. (1972) *Exploring Language*, Arnold

Edwards, A. D. (1976) *Language in Culture and Class*, Heinemann

Ervin-Tripp, S. M. (1966) 'Language Development' in M. Hoffman and L. Hoffman (eds) *Review of Child Development Research*, University of Michigan Press, vol. 2

Ervin-Tripp, S. M. (1971) 'An Overview of Theories of Grammatical Development' in Slobin (1971)

Ferguson, C. A. and Slobin, D. I. (eds) (1973) *Studies in Child Language Development*, Holt, Rinehart & Winston

Fillmore, C. J. (1966) 'The Case for Case' in Emmon Bach and R. T. Harms (eds) *Universals in Linguistic Theory*, Holt, Rinehart & Winston

Flanders, N. (1970) *Analysing Teaching Behaviour*, Addison Wesley

Fraser, H. and O'Donnell, W. R. (eds) (1969) *Applied Linguistics and the Teaching of English*, Longman

Golding, W. (1955) *The Inheritors*, Faber

Greene, J. (1972) *Psycholinguistics*, Penguin

Halliday, M. A. K. (1969) 'Relevant Models of Language' in A. Wilkinson *The State of Language*, University of Birmingham School of Education

Halliday, M. A. K. (1975) *Learning How to Mean: Explorations in the Development of Language*, Edward Arnold

Halliday, M. A. K., McIntosh, A. and Strevens, P. (1964) *The Linguistic Sciences and Language Teaching*, Longman

Hartmann, R. K. and Stork, F. C. (eds) (1972) *Dictionary of Language and Linguistics*, Applied Science Publishers

303

Hayes, J. R. (ed.) (1970) *Cognition and the Development of Language*, Wiley

Herriot, P. (1970) *An Introduction to the Psychology of Language*, Methuen

Joos, M. (1962) *The Five Clocks*, Mouton

Klima, E. S. and Bellugi, U. (1966) 'Syntactic Regularities in the Speech of Children' in J. Lyons and R. J. Wales (eds) *Psycholinguistic Papers*, Edinburgh University Press

Leech, G. (1966) *English in Advertising*, Longman

Lenneberg, E. H. (1967) *Biological Foundations of Language*, Wiley

Leopold, W. F. (1939-49) *Speech Development of a Bilingual Child: A Linguist's Record*, vols I-IV, North Western Universities Studies in the Humanities

Lewin, R. (ed.) (1975) *Child Alive*, Temple Smith

Lewis, M. M. (1936) *Infant Speech*, Routledge & Kegan Paul

Lyons, J. (1970a) *Chomsky*, Fontana

Lyons, J. (ed.) (1970b) *New Horizons in Linguistics*, Penguin

McCarthy, D. (1954) 'Language Development in Children' in L. Carmichael (ed.) *Manual of Psychology*, Wiley

McNeill, D. (1969) 'The Development of Language' in P. N. Mussen (ed.) *Carmichael's Manual of Child Psychology*, Wiley

Malinowski, B. (1935a) *Coral Gardens and their Magic*, Allen & Unwin

Malinowski, B. (1935b) 'The Problem of Meaning in Private Languages' in C. K. Ogden and I. A. Richards *The Meaning of Meaning*, Routledge & Kegan Paul

Miller, W. and Ervin, S. M. (1964) 'The Development of Grammar in Child Language' in U. Bellugi and R. Brown (eds) *The Acquisition of Language: Monographs of the Society for Research in Child Development*, **29**, 9-34

Norwich Feasibility Study. Coordinated by NATE for Norwich Education Committee. Coordinator Mrs Ethel Seaman.

Orton, H. and Dieth, E. (1962) *Survey of English Dialects*, Arnold

Phillips, J. R. (1970) 'Formal Characteristics of Speech which Mothers Address to Young Children', unpublished doctoral dissertation, Johns Hopkins University

Potter, S. (1960) *Language in the Modern World*, Penguin

Preyer, W. (1882) *Die Seele des Kindes*, Leipzig. (English translation by H. W. Brown (1888-9) *The Mind of the Child*, 2 vols, Appleton

Quirk, R. (1962) *The Use of English*, Longman (first edition)

Quirk, R. (1966) *The Use of English*, Longman (second edition)

Quirk, R., Greenbaum, S., Leech, G. and Svartvik, J. (1972) *A Grammar of Contemporary English*, Longman

Rogers, S. (ed.) (1976) *Children and Language: Readings on Early Language and Socialisation*, OUP

Sapir, E. (1921) *Language*, Harcourt, Brace & World

Schlesinger, I. M. (1971) 'Production of Utterances and Language Acquisition' in D. I. Slobin (ed.) *The Ontogenesis of Grammar*, Academic Press

Sinclair, J. McH., and Coulthard, R. M. (1975) *Towards an Analysis of Discourse: The English Used by Teachers and Pupils*, OUP

Sinclair, J. McH., Forsyth, I. J., Coulthard, R. M. and Ashby, M. C. (1972) *The English Used by Teachers and Pupils*, SSRC project, University of Birmingham

Slobin, D. I. (ed.) (1971) *The Ontogenesis of Grammar*, Academic Press

Slobin, D. I. (1972) *Leopold's Bibliography of Child Language*, revised and augmented by D. I. Slobin, Indiana University Press

Slobin, D. I. (1973) 'Cognitive Prerequisites for the Development of Grammar' in C. A. Ferguson and D. I. Slobin (eds) *Studies of Child Language Development*, Holt, Rinehart & Winston

Staats, A. W. (1971) 'Linguistic-Mentalistic Theory Versus an Explanatory S. R. Learning Theory of Language Development' in Slobin (1971)

Staats, A. W. (1974) 'Behaviourism and Cognitive Theory in the Study of Language: Neopsycholinguistics' in R. L. Scheifelbusch and L. L. Lloyd (eds) *Language Perspectives – Acquisition, Retardation and Intervention*, Macmillan

Stern, C. and Stern, W. (1928) *Die Kindersprache*, Leipzig (fourth edition)

Stern, W. (1924) *Psychology of Early Childhood* (translated by A. Barwell), Allen & Unwin

Templin, M. (1957) *Certain Language Skills in Children*, University of Minnesota Press

Thornton, G. (1974) *Language, Experience and School*, Edward Arnold

Tough, J. (1973) *Focus on Meaning: Talking to Some Purpose with Young Children*, Allen & Unwin

Trowbridge, N. (1974) *The New Media Challenge*, Macmillan

Trudgill, P. (1974) *Sociolinguistics*, Penguin

Velten, H. V. (1943) 'The Growth of Phonemic and Lexical Patterns in Infant Language', *Language*, **19**, 281-92

Wallwork, J. F. (1969) *Language and Linguistics*, Heinemann

Weir, R. (1962) *Language in the Crib*, Mouton

Weston, J. (1973) *The Tape Recorder in the Classroom*, National Committee for Audio-Visual Aids in Education (fourth edition)

Wilkinson, A. (1965) *Spoken English*, University of Birmingham Press

Wilkinson, A. (1971) *The Foundations of Language*, OUP

Wilkinson, A. (1972) 'Total Communication', *NATE*, **6**, no. 3, Winter

Wilkinson, A. (1975) *Language in Education*, OUP

Wilkinson, A., Stratta, L. and Dudley, P. (1974) *The Quality of Listening*, Macmillan

Index

Where an entry is printed in **bold** type, there is a corresponding entry in the Glossary, page 286.